Patriotic Culture
in Russia
during
World War I

PATRIOTIC CULTURE IN RUSSIA DURING WORLD WAR I

Hubertus F. Jahn

Cornell University Press

ITHACA AND LONDON

First published 1995 by Cornell University Press
First printing, Cornell Paperbacks, 1998

Printed in the United States of America

Library of Congress Cataloging-in-Publication Data

Jahn, Hubertus.
    Patriotic culture in Russia during World War I / Hubertus F. Jahn.
        p.   cm.
    Includes bibliographical references and index.
    ISBN 0-8014-3131-X (cloth : alk. paper)
    ISBN 0-8014-8571-1 (pbk. : alk. paper)
    1. World War, 1914–1918—Russia. 2. World War, 1914–1918—Propaganda. 3. World War, 1914–1918—Theater and the war. 4. World War, 1914–1918—Art and the war. 5. World War, 1914–1918—Motion pictures and the war. 6. Popular culture—Russia. I. Title.
D639.P7R85   1996
940.3'47—dc20   95-8512

Cornell University Press strives to use environmentally responsible suppliers and materials to the fullest extent possible in the publishing of its books. Such materials include vegetable-based, low-VOC inks and acid-free papers that are recycled, totally chlorine-free, or partly composed of nonwood fibers.

Cloth printing   10 9 8 7 6 5 4 3 2 1

Paperback printing   10 9 8 7 6 5 4 3 2 1

Я думаю, любовь к берёзам торжествует за счёт любви к человеку. И развивается как суррогат патриотизма. . . .

I think that love of birch trees triumphs at the cost of love for humanity. And develops as a surrogate of patriotism. . . .

—Sergei Dovlatov, *Zapovednik*

Ni mansuétude ni rectitude dans le nationalisme.

There is neither clemency nor rectitude in nationalism.

—Julien Teppe, *L'Idole patrie . . .*

Contents

Illustrations

Acknowledgments

T his book is the result of crossing many new frontiers. It required me to live in several cultures and work in many cities. Everywhere I have found good friends and helpful colleagues. Without the encouragement and support of my friends and teachers Richard Stites and David Goldfrank, this book would never have gotten started. They helped me move from Munich to Washington and made me feel at home in the United States. To David and Richard I extend all my gratitude.

Financial support for my research was provided by the German Fulbright Commission, Georgetown University, the Deutscher Akademischer Austauschdienst (DAAD), and the Verband der Osteuropahistoriker Deutschlands. I also thank the staffs of the institutions where I conducted my research: in Washington, the Library of Congress and in particular its Prints and Photographs Division; in Finland, the Slavonic Library of the University of Helsinki; in St. Petersburg, the Gosudarstvennyi muzei istorii Sankt-Peterburga (and especially Elena Korzhevskaia), the Gosudarstvennyi muzei tsirkovogo iskusstva, the Gosudarstvennyi muzei politicheskoi istorii Rossii, the Russian National Library, and the Tsentral'nyi gosudarstvennyi istoricheskii arkhiv Sankt-Peterburga; in Moscow, the Gosudarstvennyi tsentral'nyi teatral'nyi muzei imeni A. A. Bakhrushina and the Gosudarstvennyi muzei V. V. Maiakovskogo.

At Georgetown University, I benefited from many candid discussions with James Shedel, Mat Oja, David Rich, and Thomas Barrett. Beyond the Beltway, Stephen Frank, Mark Steinberg, and James von Geldern generously shared their interest and knowledge of Russian popular culture. Without the friendship of Thomas Newlin, life in the Leningrad dormitory would not have been the same. I also thank friends and colleagues in Germany, especially Renate Döring-Smirnov, Igor Smirnov, Gabriel Superfin, and Helmut Altrichter. I owe a special debt of gratitude to Graciela Wiegand. Julia, Horst, and Anni Werdermann of the *kleine typografie* have always been generous with their hospitality; their friends at the Hamburg Hochschule für Bildende Künste valiantly transformed color negatives into black-and-white photographs. Finally, Bele and Wolfgang Jüngling have provided nourishment for heart and soul over many years.

In Russia, numerous friends have extended personal, intellectual, and (not to forget) culinary support. Valentin Gerasimenko not only made St. Petersburg my second home but also introduced me to such diverse worlds as (then) underground art and (more recently) Karelian dachas. With wit, persistence, and hospitality, Konstantin and Svetlana Azadovskii showed that one must never give in (except to friendship). Al'bin Konechnyi and Ksana Kumpan revealed the diversity of popular entertainment in old St. Petersburg and the pleasures of sitting around a true Russian table. Each of these friends has taught me more about Russia than I could possibly have learned on my own.

Roger Haydon and Barbara Salazar of Cornell University Press have been patient and encouraging editors through the vicissitudes of transatlantic publishing. The not-so-anonymous readers of my manuscript, Peter Kenez and Hans Rogger, were especially helpful, and for Rogger's close and candid readings I am particularly grateful.

During the last stages of this work, Susan Morrissey has read both my manuscript and my heart. In both endeavors, she has shown unique perceptiveness and understanding. For her love and companionship I am more than thankful. Finally, to my parents and my sister, Heidi, who have nothing to do with Russian history but have supported my work wholeheartedly for many years, I owe a special debt of gratitude. It is to my family that I dedicate this book.

Unless I indicate otherwise, all translations are my own.

HUBERTUS F. JAHN

Erlangen

Note on Transliteration and Spelling

In transliterating Russian words and names I have used the Library of Congress system—except for names (such as Tchaikovsky) that have become familiar in other spellings—and have partially changed old-style orthography to conform to modern usage.

ABBREVIATIONS

d.	*delo* (file)
f.	*fond* (collection)
GMB	Gosudarstvennyi tsentral'nyi teatral'nyi muzei imeni A. A. Bakhrushina, Moscow
GMISP	Gosudarstvennyi muzei istorii Sankt-Peterburga, St. Petersburg
GMPIR	Gosudarstvennyi muzei politicheskoi istorii Rossii, St. Petersburg
l., ll.	*list, listy* (folio, folios)
MTsI	Gosudarstvennyi muzei tsirkovogo iskusstva, St. Petersburg
op.	*opis* (inventory)
PPDLC	Prints and Photographs Division, Library of Congress, Washington, D.C.
TsGIA SPb	Tsentral'nyi gosudarstvennyi istoricheskii arkhiv Sankt-Peterburga, St. Petersburg

Patriotic Culture

in Russia

during

World War I

Introduction: Patriotism and Its Metaphors

Russians, like people elsewhere in Europe, greeted the declaration of war in 1914 with a great outburst of patriotic enthusiasm. Large crowds gathered in the streets to sing the national anthem, waving banners with patriotic slogans and pictures of the tsar. But the war they cheered soon turned into a military, economic, and social debacle for the Russian Empire. It contributed to the fall of the Romanov dynasty and helped trigger a revolution that profoundly shaped the history of the twentieth century.[1]

Historians investigating World War I have traditionally written about strategies and battles, victories and defeats. They have counted the human and economic losses, discussed technological innovations, and analyzed the decisions of politicians. More recently, social and cultural issues have risen to prominence in studies focused primarily on Great Britain, France, and Germany. Unfortunately, the failure of these works to address patriotic culture specifically makes it difficult to compare the Russian situation with that of other countries. Soviet researchers largely neglected World War I, which for ideological reasons they did not see as a direct contributor to the October Revolution. Since the fall of the Soviet regime, however, this disregard in official historiography has given way to widespread curiosity and an intense search for sources on the immediate prerevolutionary period.[2]

This interest in a hitherto largely taboo and distorted period in Russian history is reflected not only in the revival of prerevolutionary symbols and names but also in exhibitions on World War I in Moscow and St. Petersburg. To create a modern kind of nationalism, moreover, Russian nationalist groups have appropriated much of the war's nationalistic imagery for propaganda purposes. Indeed, questions about national identity are behind much of the resurgent interest in the Russian fin de siècle. In an attempt to construct historical links with the prerevolutionary period in a time of ideological breakdown, these questions address the role of patriotism and nationalism both before the revolution and since the collapse of the Soviet regime. Russian patriotism during World War I has thus become a popular and rather nebulous point of reference.[3]

Patriotism and nationalism in general have received considerable scholarly attention in the years since World War I. Most studies have a rather theoretical character. Some aspire to explain patriotism and nationalism from a sociological or psychological point of view while others trace the history of nationalism in political philosophy and the rise of nation-states. These works also provide basic definitions of patriotism—"love of country or native land" (Carlton Hayes) or the "more or less conscious convictions of a person that his own welfare and that of the significant groups to which he belongs are dependent upon the preservation or expansion (or both) of the power and culture of his society" (Leonard Doob)—which itself, they suggest, may take an active form as nationalism. In an effort to provide more nuanced definitions, Earl Hunter has argued convincingly that patriotism can also entail criticism of state and authority, and Eric Hobsbawm has pointed out that since 1789 patriotism has also been the ideology of revolution, providing the basis for opposition to the existing state and for the conscious decision to form a nation based on mutual consent. Both arguments have particular relevance to the Russian case.[4]

In the immediate prewar years, Russian urban society, following the classic formula of Leopold Haimson, had become increasingly destabilized as deep rifts opened up between the working class, the educated and privileged sectors of society, and state authority.[5] In the wake of Haimson's thesis, this destabilization was extensively studied as a phenomenon of social and labor history. One has to wonder, however, whether it was only social fragmentation, more or less exacerbated by the ruptures of the war, that helped to bring about the events of 1917, or whether the disintegration of national identity also contributed to the end of the old regime. Revolutions, after all, do not only change governments and class relations; they also redefine loyalties, including those to state and nation. Yet at the same time, the patriotic wave that temporarily quelled massive labor unrest at the beginning of the war suggests that strong patriotic convictions can indeed subdue revolutionary tendencies. In the case of Russia, therefore, either a decline in or redefinition of patriotism appears to have been a prerequisite for a successful revolution.

I have no wish to develop a new theory of patriotism or to write a new history of the World War. Rather, I attempt to pin down the understandings and concrete results of patriotism in a specific society over a specific stretch of time. Wars usually heighten self-awareness— they often sort out loyalties, harden convictions and polarizations. On such occasions, patriotism also comes to life because people have to decide where to locate the home where their hearts are. On the first day of World War I, this was obviously not a problem for the crowds in the streets of St. Petersburg. By February 1917, however, loyalties had shifted, and the meaning of patriotism had changed for many people. But what was this patriotism? What was its content and form? In which social groups did it appear and how intensely? And finally, how did it change? Answers to these questions provide a clue to the events of 1917. They certainly contribute to a clearer picture of the spiritual condition of Russian society at war—a war, after all, that affected almost everyone in the country.

An investigation of a society's patriotism raises serious methodological problems. How is it possible to discern and measure the patriotic attitudes of people who lived many years ago? Nationalist philosophy and official propaganda constitute one important source, indeed the primary one in most investigations of nationalism. Despite their clear relevance, however, they provide little more than abstract concepts and hardly reflect the patriotic beliefs of most members of society. Pan-Slavism as a philosophical idea was the business of only a small segment of the Russian intelligentsia, and official propaganda was little developed and rather weak. Neither can be regarded as a genuine expression of popular patriotism, for both were directed at the population rather than developing within it.[6]

No opinion polls, of course, were conducted in World War I Russia. But one way to get into the minds of people is to look at their cultural life and the entertainments that provided some of what Victor Turner called the "metaphors and paradigms in their . . . heads." After all, a common culture is both an important component of national consciousness and one of the constituent parts and regular reference points of patriotism. An investigation of cultural life during World War I should help us to recreate patriotic "image worlds," in David Nye's phrase, and thus to draw conclusions about patriotic attitudes in Russian society in those years.[7]

The term I employ in this book, "patriotic culture," refers to the patriotic activities of artists, entertainers, and cultural entrepreneurs as well as to the reactions of audiences and society in general. I argue that a situation of give-and-take—indeed, of mutual conditioning—exists between artists and audiences. The artist and the audience merge particularly in mass culture, where artists sometimes even remain anonymous (as in cheap popular prints or folk songs) and where audiences are susceptible to identification with stars and fashions. Art and entertainment thus reflect both the individual standpoints of artists and the spiritual diversity of society. Culture, accordingly, is both active and passive. By expressing and shaping values and the changes in them within specific social groups, culture is both the conveyor and the creator of weltanschauung. In this context, patriotic culture represents the expression of and the search for national identity through artistic means. It reflects the "system of ideas and signs and associations and ways of behaving and communicating" that Ernest Gellner has identified as a component part of a nation.[8]

Like other forms of collective self-identification, patriotism is a complex and ambiguous phenomenon that exists along multiple axes. It can be a deeply rooted personal conviction or a passing fashion. Its meanings can be modified over time or remain unchanged. A person or social group, for example, can move from a conservative to a revolutionary understanding of patriotism, not necessarily in a linear or transparent manner. Similarly, patriotism can exist in different forms in different contexts and in combination with other attitudes. A painter who critiques the horrors of war in his art can at the same time parody the enemy in biting cartoons aimed at a mass audience. That very audience would be free to purchase a postcard satirizing Wilhelm II, one featuring a movie star, or both cards together. In addition, patriotic culture as a whole was shaped by the demands of its media. Postcards and opera and movies have their own conventions of style, form, and content, unrelated to the demands of war. In other words, patriotism and patriotic culture cannot be neatly categorized but must be examined within the intersection of time, place, and genre.

An investigation of Russian patriotic culture faces some basic difficulties with sources and interpretation, which ultimately apply to all historical writing. Very little is known about patriotic convictions in the Russian countryside, for example, and to convey patriotic or any other emotions so that readers may feel their force is a daunting task. In addition, there is the problem of cultural translation from Russian into English (via German, I might add), which raises the question of equivalencies in meanings and messages. Atmospheric descriptions are thus biased by the describer's perceptions and ambiguity is sometimes inevitable.[9]

An attempt to explore all forms of cultural production in a single volume would be foolhardy; I have therefore chosen to exclude literature and the fine arts from consideration and to focus instead on the many forms of popular entertainment and mass culture. Some of the sources I have used—posters, postcards, cartoons, memoirs, contemporary journals, archival materials—are abundant; relatively few recordings and motion pictures have been preserved. The materials I have investigated, however, are so diverse that they convey the richness of Russian cultural life early in this century, and the convergence of the conclusions they point to compels us to take those conclusions seriously.

Russian culture during World War I was, of course, embedded in traditions and itself gave birth to new developments. The major social changes that arose from Sergei Witte's industrialization campaign at the end of the nineteenth century had led to changes in cultural life as well. The customary distinctions of high and low, urban and rural culture began to blur as a new, predominantly urban mass culture developed. Reflecting the social and demographic changes of the era and the growing diversity of cities, this mass culture was in constant flux, producing subcultures and blending older urban traditions with the rich variety of Russian village culture. The opera houses and concert halls certainly continued to flourish, but their patrons might also go to the movies or to variety shows and mix with people they would never meet privately. Village culture in the meantime was becoming increasingly commercialized as mass-produced *lubki* (broadsides) and other artifacts flooded the countryside. The many migrant workers who returned to their villages for the harvest brought with them tales and objects from the city. All of these changes were accompanied and supported by massive borrowings from Western countries and by the appearance of such new media as the cinema.

Patriotic culture was certainly not peculiar to World War I, either. It drew on longstanding native and foreign traditions in both form and content. The Napoleonic Wars gave rise to patriotic plays and satirical lubki about the French army and its leader. After the founding of the German Empire in 1871 and the war with Turkey of 1877–78 with its outpouring of Pan-Slavism, national stereotypes of the Turks and particularly of the Germans appeared in tableaux vivants and circus pantomimes and began to acquire meanings that were still valid in World War I. In 1878 the taking of Constantinople as the ultimate symbol of Russia's superiority over the Ottoman Empire became ever more relevant, and the dramatic rise of Germany's economic and military power changed the long-held perception of that country as a land of culture and philosophy; "German culture" now became "Prussian civilization." This development in particular had a crucial impact on the centuries-long love-hate relationship between the two countries that Walter Laqueur has described. It transformed clichés of the petty bourgeois into those of the ugly German, and it fueled Pan-Slavic sentiments against an alleged *Drang nach Osten*. These sentiments culminated in the famous speech by the notorious and popular general and self-declared nationalist Mikhail Skobelev, who in 1882 prophesied a final showdown between Germandom and Slavdom.[10]

Patriotic culture of World War I also built upon countless self-stereotypes promoted in the late nineteenth century and before. Russians' ideas about their own national identity and their traditions of patriotic symbolism and iconography had created a continuity of heroes who were particularly cherished among political conservatives but were also, of course, available to everyone else. Images of the tsar, icons of St. George, and references to such historical figures as Aleksandr Nevskii, the legendary victor over the Teutonic Knights in 1242, and Generals Aleksandr Suvorov and Mikhail Kutuzov, both heroes of wars against the French, reflected the traditional loci of power, spiritual order, and national might: the monarch, the church, and the military. Over the course of the war these customary rallying points became the crumbling pillars of patriotic imagery around which stories about contemporary heroes and the successes of Russian arms were draped.[11]

At the beginning of the war, the Russian military was indeed successful. It drove the Germans out of East Prussia and the Austrians out of most of Galicia and Bukovina. The success in East Prussia in early August, however, was reversed by the end of the month, when the Second Russian Army under General Aleksandr Samsonov was encircled near Tannenberg—where the Teutonic Knights had been defeated in 1410—and routed by German forces commanded by General Paul von Hindenburg (soon eulogized by German nationalists as the "Victor of Tannenberg"). The Germans recaptured East Prussia a little later in a battle at the Masurian Lakes. During much of the next winter the Russian troops on the northwestern front endured the miseries of trench warfare; those in the southwest managed to take the fortress of Przemysl from the Austrians after a long siege in March 1915.

That spring the "Russian steamroller" was rolled back by a broad Austro-German offensive under General August von Mackensen. Between April and September the Russians had to retreat to a line from Riga to Tarnopol, losing all their previous gains in the southwest as well as large parts of their own territory, including Poland, with its important industrial centers. With about one million dead Russian soldiers and a similar number taken prisoner, the 1915 retreat was more than a military disaster; it amounted to a national catastrophe too grave to be offset by later successes. The taking of Erzurum in March 1916 and other victories in the Caucasus secured the southern front against the Turks, who had declared war against Russia in October 1914, and the offensive under General Aleksei Brusilov in the summer of 1916 led to impressive gains in Volynia and Galicia, but these victories were achieved at the cost of heavy losses by an increasingly demoralized army. Altogether, 1.8 million Russian soldiers were killed between 1914 and 1917, 2.8 million wounded, and 2.4 million taken prisoner. In four years of warfare the German army lost a comparable number of men killed but far fewer taken prisoner.[12]

Had courage been the decisive factor, the Russian figures would have looked quite different. But wars are fought not only by brave men. World War I was also a battle of technologies, economies, and societies. In all of these spheres, Russia failed to adjust adequately, in large part because of the incompetence of the tsar and his government. In a country ill prepared for war from the start, the 1915 disaster seriously aggravated the existing problems of transportation, fuel supply, and matériel. At times recruits were thrown into battle without rifles or leather boots. Not until the end of 1916 was the economy sufficiently restructured to be able to supply the army with enough weapons and ammunition. But this late "success" was achieved largely at the expense of consumer industries and the agricultural sector. With basic consumer goods in increasingly short supply and the inflation rate higher than in any of the other warring countries, speculation became rampant in the cities. Peasants had no incentive to sell their grain and had to be forced to do so through the introduction of quotas in late 1916. This measure, however, did nothing to resolve the food crisis, which was felt both in the army and in the booming industrial centers, and which eventually led to the demonstrations in Petrograd of February 1917 that brought down the tsarist regime.

The incompetence of the tsarist government was evident as soon as hostilities began. Large segments of society joined together in patriotic efforts, but the regime feared any organized activity it did not control; the police tried to suppress patriotic demonstrations, and military and civilian officials often obstructed the independent efforts of the newly created Unions of Towns and Zemstvos to organize war relief. Instead of enlisting the popular support he was offered, the tsar rebuffed it, and he compounded the problem by appointing several clearly incompetent ministers and retaining the disreputable Rasputin at court. The estrangement of state and society was also reflected in the Duma. It had strongly supported the government in 1914, but by the summer of 1915 the Progressive Bloc emerged as a broad opposition coalition and became the strongest parliamentary force. In November 1916 the liberal Pavel Miliukov drew the inevitable conclusion: in a speech to the Duma he listed the government's blunders and asked after each one, "Is this stupidity or is this treason?"

He might as well have asked about the status of Russian patriotism. For him and for most other educated Russians, the tsar—the traditional focus of patriotic loyalty, especially among the peasantry—had become unpatriotic, and the country's real interests were actually being served by an emergent civil society. The outburst of patriotism at the beginning of the war is therefore difficult to assess. In St. Petersburg and Moscow thousands of people joined in tumultuous celebration of all major Russian victories up through the taking of Przemysl in March

1915; then the demonstrations tapered off. Many of the celebrants were students, but workers and others were well represented too. Whether the loyalties of these people lay with the tsar (a few pictures of him usually appeared on these occasions), the Slavic peoples whose victories they celebrated, or their fellow Russians can hardly be determined. There was no ambiguity, however, about the huge wave of charitable activities that gathered momentum throughout the war—patriotism as social action. Even in 1914, then, Russian patriotism had more than one meaning: it was both conservative in the traditional sense and revolutionary in Hobsbawm's sense.[13]

Cultural life reflected both understandings of patriotism. All artistic genres reacted to the war in various ways and with varying intensity. An investigation of these patriotic responses and messages should yield a sufficiently representative picture of Russian culture at war and of Russian society redefining its identity in a period of painful flux.

1

Picturing Patriotism:
The War for the Eye

A rt historians and art critics have examined visual materials from the perspective of stylistic and aesthetic problems, pictorial motifs and messages, but these materials can also serve as sources for historians: we can interpret the texts of images, their political and cultural meanings, and the ideologies encoded in their style, format, and content. Visual materials thus allow us both to gather complex information and, by putting ourselves in the viewer's position, to approach the "image worlds" of people distant in place and time. Both functions are of particular importance when the period under observation produced massive amounts of visual material that reached almost all levels of society.[1]

At the beginning of World War I a well-developed network of publishing houses and distributors served a growing readership all over Russia.[2] But it was not only the word that was spread in the many cheap novels, serials, and periodicals. Many publishers also produced broadsides, postcards, calendars, and posters. When war broke out, these media became important carriers and promoters of patriotism.

The War and the *Lubok:* The Last Battle of an Art Form

The *lubok,* the Russian version of the popular broadside, was in many ways the ancestor of all the visual media discussed in this chapter. Originating in the seventeenth century as simple woodcuts with religious subjects or satirical scenes from fairy tales and everyday life, lubki soon developed into more sophisticated copper engravings, which also depicted both current and historical events. Their distribution was handled by peddlers who traveled from village to village, and they were for sale at fairs and at rural and urban marketplaces. Even a poor peasant far from any city could spare a few kopecks for a lubok. Aside from icons in the local church, lubki were the only pictorial materials available for the mass of Russians, so they held an important place in both urban and rural popular culture. By the second half of the nineteenth century, they could be found in almost every peasant hut and in most dwellings of the urban lower classes.[3]

Traditionally the most frequently depicted foreigners in lubki were Germans. Germans lived among the Russians as rural colonists, urban artisans and merchants, and state officials. They were both admired for their skills and ridiculed for their pedantry, and at least until the mid–eighteenth century, they were seen as the prototypical (Western) foreigner. During the Seven Years' War this perception became more differentiated when the Prussians were clearly identified as the enemy. In 1759 the first *voennyi* (war) lubok appeared—a picture of a Cossack beating a Prussian dragoon, in honor of the Russians' victory over the Prussians at Kunersdorf. Such stereotypes of German and Russian soldiers were still seen in lubki produced during World War I: Germans were usually better armed and stronger, but the Russians were faster, braver, and in the end always victorious.[4]

After 1759, lubki regularly adopted the war theme, and during times of war voennye lubki were always in high demand. The typical portraits of heroic generals on horseback in glittering uniforms, pointing their sabers toward the enemy, were joined later by highly imaginative and increasingly colorful scenes of battles and the storming of fortresses. Particularly famous were the lubki produced during the war of 1812 by Aleksei Venetsianov and Ivan Terebenev. Taking up the style of engravings and caricatures brought to Russia by the French, these were the first satirical war lubki, with such scenes as Napoleon's frantic escape from Russia and a Cossack poking a French soldier with his lance.[5]

Realism and satire employed to document the heroic deeds of one's own military and to ridicule the enemy survived as the main characteristics of war lubki up to World War I. When the Wanderers school promoted realism in the fine arts in the second half of the nineteenth century, however, lubki also began to put so much emphasis on "realistic" details that they came to be called *protokol'nye* (reporting) lubki. This emulation of fine art was encouraged by the introduction of new printing techniques, especially chromolithography, which allowed for high-quality reproductions in large quantities. It now was possible to print battle scenes containing hundreds of soldiers, explosions, smoke, and light beams with almost photographic accuracy and in a host of colors. The Russo-Japanese War of 1904–5 saw the first boom of this kind of war lubki; more than three hundred of them were produced, most of them devoted to the defense of Port Arthur.[6]

The high quality of the prints produced by the new techniques did not necessarily stimulate interest in lubki as such. At the turn of the twentieth century, a large part of the traditional audience for broadsides, the urban lower class, was turning to other entertainments, especially the movies and, with a rise in literacy, cheap novels and serials. At the same time, serious artists began to cultivate folklore and even organized an exhibition of lubki in Moscow in 1913. While lubki seemed to be dead as a genuine genre of folk art, relegated to mass-produced kitsch in the villages, they were elevated to objects of study and inspiration by intellectuals and artists in the cities.[7]

With the outbreak of World War I, however, the situation changed dramatically. With the encouragement of the state, thousands of war lubki were designed and produced in millions of copies. Publishers all over the country joined the boom, often putting out runs of a couple of titles a day, and new publishing houses were established to meet the demand. For the many urban and peasant families whose sons were serving in the army, these pictures were, as in earlier wars, the only means to document the heroism of their children, the cruelty of the enemy, and particularly the technical innovations of modern warfare.[8]

The styles of war lubki expanded together with production. Models dating from the eighteenth century and from 1812 were revived and integrated into the new context. The two Petrograd printing houses of

Bussel and Shmigel'skii, for example, published a joint collection of one hundred lubki in the traditional style, black and white with only sketchy coloring. A famous eighteenth-century lubok of the fool Farnos riding on a pig was reprinted with Farnos as an Austrian bugler announcing Austrian "victories." The chicken thief of another eighteenth-century lubok became a German marauder; the seven-headed monster that was beaten by the mythical hero Eruslan Lazarevich in old lubki now symbolized German states and the hydra of Prussian militarism.[9] Ironically enough, some of the revived models were older German engravings that had come to Russia in the eighteenth century. An Augsburg copper engraving showing a poor fellow who loses the eggs he is taking to market while he dreams of the money he will get for them was adapted for a woodcut in which Wilhelm II dreamed of Belgium, France, and Russia (Fig. 1).

Bussel and Shmigel'skii copied old models quite literally, changing only small details and the captions, but other publishers' output only evoked the style of earlier prints. In 1914 artists associated with the avant-garde art journal *Mir iskusstva* produced war lubki that stylized those of 1812 and thus aestheticized the war. Osip Sharleman' designed lubki that looked like old copper engravings with the sparse coloring of the 1812 pictures. The graphic artist and book illustrator Georgii Narbut worked in a similar manner. His "Cossack and the Germans" was the most famous example of the 1812 style, though research has shown that it was inspired less by the earlier lubki than by the French engravings and caricatures on which they were modeled. Contemporaries recognized the works of Narbut and Sharleman' as well composed and beautifully done, but very distant from folk art. They were rightly seen as works made for the people and not by them—but so were most other lubki of the period.[10]

Other elite artists sought new styles in lubok art as well. Supported by the publisher of *Gazeta kopeika*, Mikhail B. Gorodetskii, they founded their own publishing house in Moscow under the name Segodniashnii Lubok. Though they were called "futurists," the circle included not only Futurists but a wide range of avant-garde artists: the leader of the Suprematist art movement Kazimir Malevich; the poet Vladimir Maiakovskii; the Cubo-Futurist David Burliuk; and Il'ia Mashkov (working under the pseudonym I. Gorskin) and Aristarkh Lentulov, both affiliated with the Moscow School of Art and famous for their still lifes and landscapes.[11]

МЫСЛИ-ВѢТРЕНЫЯ:

ВИЛЬГЕЛЬМЪ: Завоюю слѣдующія государства: Бельгію, Францію и Россію, а Сербію Австріи отдамъ.

1. "Windy Thoughts" (Mysli vetrenyia); no. 35 in the series *Kartinki—Voina russkikh s nemtsami* (Petrograd: Bussel, Shmigel'skii [1916]), 21 × 32 cm.

The main characteristics of this group's lubki were their common style (so that attribution is difficult), biting wit (the captions were written in rhyming couplets by Maiakovskii), and a certain crudeness that many people found more appealing than the stylizations of the *Mir iskusstva* artists. Printed as broadsides (56 × 38 cm) and postcards (14 × 9 cm), they typically depicted such scenes as a Russian peasant thrashing German soldiers or picking up an Austrian with a pitchfork (Fig. 2). Others show a brave Cossack attacking a German zeppelin, which his wife later makes into a pair of trousers (Fig. 3), and the Russian army taking Berlin while the Germans try to seize Paris. The reaction of contemporary art historians ranged from enthusiasm about this "curious crudeness," which "was reminiscent of folktales," to rejection of the pictures as the overly intellectual fruits of the "exotic

Шелъ австріецъ въ Радзивилы,
Да попалъ на бабьи вилы.

2. Kazimir Malevich, "The Austrian Went to Radziwillow . . . " (Shël avstriets v Radzivily . . .) (Moscow: Segodniashnii Lubok, 1914), 58 × 40 cm. Helsinki University Slavonic Library.

3. Vladimir Maiakovskii, "The Coarse Red-Haired German . . . " (Nemets ryzhii i shershavyi . . .) (Moscow: Segodniashnii Lubok, 1914), 56 × 38 cm. Helsinki University Slavonic Library.

moods of Futurists." Despite the controversy, these lubki were the stars of an exhibition in Petrograd in late November 1914.[12]

The exact role played by Maiakovskii in the production of lubki issued by Segodniashnii Lubok remains unclear. His authorship of several lubki (including Fig. 3) is undisputed, but stylistic analysis suggests that he was responsible for several unsigned pictures as well. It thus appears that he was more active in drawing than he was once thought to be. He turned to drawing again during the Civil War, when he produced the famous propaganda lubki for the windows of ROSTA, the Russian telegraph agency.[13]

The lubki of *Mir iskusstva* artists and Segodniashnii Lubok have received some attention by art historians, largely because of their famous creators, but the mass editions of war lubki have usually been considered too lacking in artistic quality to merit serious study. Contemporary art critics looked down on them as stereotypical and "simply bad illustrations," and later Soviet observers dismissed them as unartistic Great Russian chauvinism.[14] It was those lubki, however, that had the widest circulation and the largest editions and hence the greatest impact on people's attitudes toward the war. Most of the lubki issued by the large publishing houses were produced by anonymous drudges, and in composition and motifs they were almost interchangeable. Not artistic individuality, therefore, but the creation and confirmation of a common and traditional aesthetic were their raison d'être—and their recipe for commercial success.

The foremost publisher of mass editions was Sytin & Co. of Moscow, which as early as 1914 accounted for more than 25 percent of all printed material published in Russia and produced lubki editions of a million or more copies. Other publishers participated in the war boom as well, but Sytin's output was so prominent that realistic and protokol'nye lubki came to be known as *sytinskie*. Like their predecessors during the war with Japan, they depicted the famous battles, great generals, military technology, and vileness of the enemy with almost pedagogical attention to detail. Many were printed in long series, such as Korkin, Beideman & Co.'s *Great European War,* which included more than 190 lubki, and Strel'tsov's *European War* (Fig. 4); most of them had an explanatory text at the bottom consisting of the official report of a battle.[15]

The iconography of the battle scenes was simple: as little background and countryside as necessary and as many explosions, flashes, fighting soldiers, and dying enemies as possible. Yet in all of these pictures small side scenes allow the viewer's eye to relate to something human: two men in hand-to-hand combat in one corner, a wounded enemy holding his head or trying to escape in the other. Some artists tried to encourage viewers' involvement in the scene by giving their soldiers elaborate facial expressions: a resolute-looking Russian cavalryman striking out against a German infantryman, a laughing Russian jumping over a cannon to impale an Austrian on his bayonet, an Austrian officer with his eyes (and his horse's too!) opened wide in terror.[16]

Lubki devoted to the atrocities committed by the enemy reflected a theme common in all countries that took part in World War I. Like the battle scenes, they tended to draw the eye to the peripheral details. In the lower right corner of a scene showing an execution by a German firing squad, a German soldier lifts a woman's head by the hair (Fig.

РАЗГРОМЪ НѢМЦЕВЪ ПОДЪ ВАРШАВОЙ.

4. "The Rout of the Germans at Warsaw" (Razgrom nemtsev pod Varshavoi), no. 10 in the series *Evropeiskaia voina* (Moscow: Strel'tsov, n.d.), 55 × 41 cm. Helsinki University Slavonic Library.

5). Several small bloody scenes can be found in another lubok depicting Turkish and Kurdish cruelties: a lusty-faced Kurd lifts a woman's severed head while next to him a grim-looking Turk stabs a heroic woman holding dynamite in her hand; another Turk smiles as he dangles a baby he has just snatched from the mother; and a family sits on the ground as the father lies apparently dying from a head wound. These vignettes of terror often have a stronger attraction for the viewer than the ostensible subject of the picture. Some contemporaries saw lubki of this kind as unfit for the walls of one's home, where children could see them.[17]

Technology also occupied a central place in many lubki. Sea battles with as many armored ships, submarines, and torpedoes as the artist could fit in the picture's space gave a colorful impression of the latest

5. "Russia's War with the Germans: German Atrocities" (Voina Rossii s nemtsami: Zverstva nemtsev) (Moscow: Krylov, n.d.), 54 × 40 cm. Helsinki University Slavonic Library.

maritime technology (Fig. 6). Air battles, preferably between planes and zeppelins, were an entirely new motif, which Sytin featured in a special series (Fig. 7). To highlight the personal style of warfare in the air, however, most of these lubki focused on some heroic pilot as he courageously attacked the enemy. Particularly noteworthy was one P. N. Nesterov, who saved Russian ground troops by his kamikaze-like attack on a German plane at the beginning of the war. Here a familiar and old motif, the brave and clever Cossack, was combined with technology and taken into the air.[18]

Heroes could of course be found on the ground as well. A whole range of lubki were devoted to the heroic deeds of courageous generals, nurses, and Cossacks. The most boring of these heroes were certainly the generals. Unlike those of earlier wars, they usually did

6. "Victory of the English Fleet in the Sea Battle Near the Island of Helgo-
land" (Pobeda Angliiskago flota v morskom boiu u ostrova Gel'golanda)
(Moscow: Sytin, 1914), no. 14, 86 × 64 cm. Gosudarstvennyi muzei istorii
Sankt-Peterburga.

not sit astride a horse but stood in authoritative poses among their
officers and an array of the latest technical gear. Order, cleanliness, and
the absence of blood were the norm for such pictures (Fig. 8).

Similarly bloodless, strangely enough, were scenes of nurses on the
battlefield and in hospitals. These lubki transformed these dedicated
women into Red Cross beauties who piously held the hands of
wounded soldiers or read newspapers to them in the garden of a clean
and homey hospital. Sunlight drenches these pictures. The logic is
clear: since not one Russian soldier is shown bleeding in battle, how
could any be bleeding here? As in war lubki of the nineteenth century,
blood and suffering were reserved for the enemy and his civilian
victims.[19]

7. "The War in the Air" (Voina v vozdukhe) (Moscow: Sytin, 1914), no. 45, 40 × 59 cm. Gosudarstvennyi muzei istorii Sankt-Peterburga.

Генералъ-адъютантъ **Н. В. РУЗСКІЙ,** герой Львова.

8. "Adjutant General N. V. Ruzskii, the Hero of L'vov" (General-ad"iutant N. V. Ruzskii, geroi L'vova) (Moscow: Sytin, 1915), no. 75, 64 × 42 cm. Helsinki University Slavonic Library.

Since the first voennyi lubok, Cossacks had been the standard heroes of Russian war imagery. They were shown as brave and dauntless, smart and witty, invincible supermen with peasant instincts and horseback acrobats. With warfare becoming less and less personal, however, Cossacks disappeared from realistic lubki and became the main positive heroes of satirical pictures, where they were shown beating up Kaiser Wilhelm or slyly fooling German soldiers.[20]

To allow easier identification and familiarity with this symbol of Russian wit and bravery, some Cossack heroes were identified by name. Cossack Lavin, for example, became famous for capturing nineteen Austrian soldiers, including three officers. When he saw the Austrians in a field, he made so much noise in his forest hideout that they expected an encounter with an overwhelming force and threw down their weapons. He then took them prisoner and led them off. In a lubok that captures their surrender, the Austrian soldiers embody the worst Austro-Hungarian clichés: an officer with cigar and monocle, a soldier taking snuff, another who reminds one of Josef Lada's illustrations of the Good Soldier Schweik, and finally an apparently feeble-minded drummer boy. Next to them the trim and smart Lavin sits laughing on his horse. Even the trees differentiate the two sides: around the Austrians are some pine trees; next to Lavin is a single "Russian" birch.[21] The ultimate hero among the Cossacks was Koz'ma Kriuchkov, who was said to have killed eleven Germans with his lance in one encounter at the beginning of the war. He came to be celebrated in circus and variety shows, in the movies, and particularly on postcards and lubki. Almost all publishers had at least one version of Kriuchkov in their assortment, usually showing him astride his horse with the German soldiers like kebab on his lance.[22]

With the elevation of Kriuchkov to a national hero, sytinskie lubki went beyond recording events and poking fun at the kaiser: they entered a world of allegories and national symbols with a quasi-religious touch. In these pictures, mythical and historical heroes came together with angels, zeppelins, and dragons. Russia appeared in the person of a woman to her soldiers and enemies, and Wilhelm II became the devil in person as "Enemy of the Human Race" in a famous lubok in the style of a medieval miniature.[23] Suvorov, the great Russian military commander, meets Slava, the angel of fame, in heaven and asks him about what is happening on earth (Fig. 9). Slava tells him about the German generals and the kaiser. They agree that these characters will pose no problem for the Russian Cossacks. And who would not believe these two guardian angels, representing heavenly powers and historically proven military expertise?

Russia depicted as a woman played several important roles in patriotic allegory. In one lubok she stands as Vera (Faith) between Liubov' (Love), a French woman, and Nadezhda (Hope), an English woman. The three beauties symbolize the Trinity-like alliance of Russia, France, and Britain against an obviously male barbarism raging in the background in the form of a (phallic) zeppelin, planes, explosions, and fighting men (Fig. 10). In another picture a soldier stands at attention before the throne of Mother Russia, now as a young red-haired woman in peasant dress. She calls on his personal bravery and evokes

СУВОРОВЪ и СЛАВА.

9. "Suvorov and Glory" (Suvorov i Slava) (Moscow: Chelnokov, n.d.), 74 × 55.5 cm. Helsinki University Slavonic Library.

his spiritual superiority in face of the German war machine. After all, she points out, the Germans excel only at drinking beer, and now these drunkards have come to molest her. The soldier vows to fulfill his duty for the holy motherland and to "serve" the Germans properly. The picture clearly refers to the old epic of Il'ia Muromets, a strong knight in the service of Mother Russia who derives his powers from absolute loyalty to her and loses them only through excessive pride (a message wisely omitted from the lubok).[24] Finally, Russia herself goes to the battlefield in "Russia for Justice" (Fig. 11). The caption, interestingly enough, refers not only to Russian military power but also to the help Russia gave to Prussia against Napoleon. Associations of a deceived bride mix with the image of an amazon; male sexual fears in

10. "Accord" (Soglasie) (Moscow: Mukharskii, n.d.), 53 × 71 cm. Helsinki University Slavonic Library.

the face of an all-powerful "feminine principle" (Faust's *Ewig-Weibliches*) are translated into the world of national competition.

Allegorical lubki also recalled St. George, the famous dragon-slaying patron saint of Muscovy, and a host of other strong knights.

11. "Russia for Justice" (Rossiia za pravdu) (Moscow: Mashistov, 1914), 57 × 83 cm. Helsinki University Slavonic Library.

Realistic scenes of clashing armies, planes, and exploding shells are penetrated by the supernatural, either from above (as in Suvorov's case) or more often at the very center of the picture. The captions are often at odds with the pictures. There are no German generals in Suvorov's lubok, no machine guns or beer mugs in the red-haired Mother Russia's. But, as Iurii Lotman has shown, a lubok's text functioned more to trigger thoughts and fantasies in the observer than to explain the picture. The allegorical lubki were more successful at this task than the more realistic battle scenes, which came closer to being mere illustrations of the captions.[25]

But even aside from the texts of the allegorical lubki, the iconography alone must have stimulated the imaginations of contemporary observers. Though few evoked God and almost none the Orthodox Church, all of these lubki had elements of religious icons. The angel in Suvorov's lubok is obvious. He reminds one of an Annunciation scene, this time heralding a Russian victory. The three women symbolizing France, Russia, and England can be seen as a Trinity; Russia and the soldier before her throne can be seen as Mother and Child. St. Michael adorns the heroine's shield in "Russia for Justice." All these associations added authority to the pictures and elevated the war to a holy cause. Most important, perhaps, they made the allegorical lubki appropriate neighbors for the holy pictures in the icon corner of the peasant house.[26]

As a popular art form, however, lubki largely disappeared after World War I. Their attraction had been declining for some time, and the boom during the war was a temporary aberration. What caused the renaissance? One factor was certainly curiosity about the war, the sensational (in the original meaning of the word) aspect of it: many people were somehow touched by or involved in the war. In the villages, where movies and other forms of visual information were hardly available, the lubok in its traditional form still satisfied people's interest in current events, the incomprehensible, and the unbelievable, as it had done since the nineteenth century. The provincial intelligentsia promoted war lubki for rural patriotic education, and they were often pinned up as attractions on rural fairground booths.[27]

The patriotic function of lubki was another important reason for their large output during World War I. The vast majority of prints appeared in the first few months of the war, at a time when public interest in Russian victories—in what it meant to be Russian as opposed to, say, German—was very high. The emphasis on a familiar aesthetic and a traditional, typically Russian art form, as in the case of the sytinskie lubki, reinforced an important aspect of patriotism; that is, the affirmation of a common culture through commonly recognized symbols, heroes, saints, or enemies. The attempts of the folklorists among the elite artists to revive lubki in a new style for patriotic purposes only confirm this nostalgic element.

When the war became more burdensome, the demand for war lubki decreased. Their output dropped sharply after the disastrous Russian defeats of May 1915; Segodniashnii Lubok had already closed in November 1914.[28] Among the more than two hundred lubki I inspected, not one appeared after 1915. Obviously, the last battle of the lubok was over even before the war ended. Like the strong knights, whose world was suddenly invaded by zeppelins and modern artillery, lubki finally had to give way to postcards, posters, and films. They still lived on for a while in the heads of avant-garde artists, influencing such projects as Maiakovskii's ROSTA windows during the Civil War, but as a phenomenon of mass culture they disappeared with World War I.

Fairground Interlude: *Raëk,* or Willi in the Box

A classical entertainment of the nineteenth-century Russian fairground, the *raëk* (peepshow, panorama), appeared for the last time during World War I. The *raëk* brought lubki to life through the explanations of a *raëshnik* (storyteller or barker). Lubki were placed in a box for the customer to view through magnifying glasses, and the raëshnik provided an often biting commentary on the display. Thus lubki were no longer merely pictures that told stories; now they formed part of a theatrical show that was a popular staple of carnivals (*narodnye gulian'ia*) in the nineteenth century.[29]

Like the lubki, raëk catered to the audience's curiosity. Functioning as an oral newspaper, it typically showed panoramas of cities and faraway places, or pictures of strange events. Not surprisingly, wars figured prominently in raëk, particularly after 1812. Many raëshniki were former soldiers, who had become literate in the army and "seen the world." Relying on both their military experiences and their peasant backgrounds, they usually made the voennye lubki come alive in the spirit of *kvasnyi patriotizm*, something like "beerhall patriotism," particularly prevalent around Moscow's Nikol'skii market, a main trading center for lubki and lubok literature. In these shows foreign enemies were attacked in the rude language of the village, and Russian folk heroes and their deeds were praised.[30]

Carnivals all but disappeared from Russia around the turn of the century. Either they were prohibited by authorities who feared their revolutionary potential, as in St. Petersburg, or they became the victims of new forms of popular entertainment, particularly the circus and people's theaters. With the carnivals went the raëk. According to Al'bin Konechnyi, many former raëshniki wandered about the country in search of work. At the same time, members of the intelligentsia awoke to the folkloric value of raëk and planned the revival of a typical Russian carnival on St. Petersburg's Field of Mars, where fairs had been held for many years.[31]

The outbreak of World War I put an end to the project, but some lubki in the patriotic tradition were produced for the raëk. Raëshniki—or people playing at being raëshniki—appeared at charity affairs organized in Petrograd in 1916, and in the provinces some functioning peepshows seem to have survived into the war. The famous circus clown Vitalii Lazarenko, for example, saw a raëk in Saratov at that time, showing scenes of the Boer War. In one provincial town a panopticon set up in an old house is said to have included raëk in the form of two panoramas and a stereoscope. It also featured a bust of Wilhelm II, introduced as *Imperator Germanskii Vil'gen ftoroi* [sic], right next to the popular detective Nat Pinkerton and the "American Baboon Grunia."[32]

In the tradition of the anti-German pictures that ridiculed Bismarck after 1871, many lubki made for the raëk during World War I attacked the kaiser. One of a different sort showed a map of Europe formed of faces, modeled on a lubok of 1883 and a standard motif of European graphic art in the nineteenth century. The text personified the various countries and their positions in the war, Germany being an "old troublemaker" and Russia a "strong young fellow."[33] A raëk created by Dmitrii Moor (pseudonym of Dmitrii Orlov), later famous as a poster artist and caricaturist, showed a potato metamorphosed into Franz Joseph of Austria, an onion into Wilhelm II, and a group of fly agarics into Wilhelm's sons. All these delicacies, it was claimed, had been planted by the devil himself, and when they were ripe, he let them loose on the world, thereby causing the world war.[34]

These two raiki were especially close to the patriotic originals in form and intent. Other raiki, however, reveal the commercialization of folklore. In its depiction of Wilhelm II with a raëshnik and a laughing audience, "Raëk" (Fig. 12) demonstrates the museum-like character of this art form as well as its continuing attraction. It is the work of A. Lebedev, a caricaturist who regularly worked for the Petrograd weekly *Voina* and produced patriotic postcards for the publishing house Sovremennoe Iskusstvo. The text was contributed by P. N. Ianov, who signed his works N. N. Ianov-Vitiaz' (Ianov-Hero) and wrote lubok texts with such titles as "Down with the Germans." In the raëk text Ianov attacks Germans as self-important, showing off their wealth abroad though at home they are nothing. When they started the war, moreover, they exposed their utter baseness. He extends his attack to the Germans living in Russia, depicting them as plundering the population through what they call "trade." Indeed, as colonists in Russia they were in reality Wilhelm's artillerymen. They called the Russians dirty, but they turned out to be the real pigs: a German pastry shop serves chocolate that a dog has fouled.[35]

Crude anecdotes and biting caricatures, however, were only one aspect of the raëk. The roots that nourished it and could have brought it to life as a multimedia spectacle had died with the carnival. Its brief revival during World War I was only an attempt by urban artists to capture old Russian forms of patriotic display. Thus the appearance of raëk during the war had the same touch of nostalgia as the flood of mass-produced lubki. Both highlighted the erosion of older popular traditions that had largely lost their constituencies by 1914.

Graphic Arts at War: Patriotic Cartoons and Illustrations in the Press

Both illustrations and cartoons in journals played important roles in visual patriotic culture. Periodicals had proliferated by the end of the nineteenth century to cater to a growing readership and a variety of tastes and intellectual levels. Although their main medium was the printed word, many journals included illustrations or cartoons to

12. A. Lebedev, "Raёk. The Devil Wilhelm and the German War" (Raёk. Vil'gel'm satana i nemetskaia voina) (Moscow: Strel'tsov, n.d.), 44 × 60 cm. Helsinki University Slavonic Library.

catch the eye and mind of the reader. Around the turn of the century even the fine arts were to some extent influenced by and reflected in the graphic art of such modernist journals as *Mir iskusstva* and *Apollon*.

In 1914 most journals turned to the graphic arts to comment on the war, relying on forms similar to those of patriotic lubki. Satirical cartoons and caricatures, realistic black-and-white drawings, allegories, and the aesthetic innovations of elite artists caught Russian readers' eyes as they perused the news, caught up on the latest installment of a serial novel, or read the aperçu of an avant-garde writer.

Patriotic illustrations of the lowest artistic quality appeared in journals targeted at men in the military. Weeklies with such telling names as *Voin i pakhar'* (The Soldier and the Plowman) and *Il'ia Muromets* offered instructive articles on agriculture, the lives of Russian heroes, "News from the Village," religious and moral admonitions, the latest flash from the front, and official announcements. Designed to provide informative readings in simple language for an often semiliterate readership, these journals preferred simple pictures and retouched photos.[36]

These illustrations are noteworthy for their symbolism of Russian might, their sentimentality, and their emphasis on military technology. The front page of *Voin i pakhar'* of 1 March 1915 shows an allegorical etching of the union between the Russian soldier and the Russian peasant: both are bearded as in pre-Petrine Russia, and both wear crosses on their chests. The soldier wears the coat of mail of the medieval knight; the peasant stands behind a plow in his typical tuniclike shirt. An assortment of flags, laurels, sabers, an anchor, a rifle, and a scythe can be seen, as well as a silhouette of the Kremlin in Moscow and a vignette of St. George. The picture emphasizes the old Russian values of devoutness and bravery in the service of Moscow and the tsar.

Similar but more realistic exaltations of the Russian soldier can be found in countless black-and-white sketches about life at the front. In comparison with the multicolored lubki that stimulated the observer's imagination, these little grayish scenes printed on bad paper make a rather sad impression. Special holiday editions, however, carried colored lubok-style pictures, and in 1916 *Il'ia Muromets* offered new subscribers a calendar featuring a colored reproduction of a picture purporting to show life in the trenches by the fairly well known patriotic artist V. V. Mazurovskii.[37]

It is hardly surprising that in this most "modern" war, these patriotic journals focused on the technology of warfare. Articles about the role of the navy, the capabilities of submarines, and the war in the air were accompanied by drawings of an eerie dripstone cave that served as a harbor for German subs and of German zeppelins hovering over London's Tower Bridge. The Petrograd weekly *Voina*, which was sold "at all kiosks and train stations" and catered to a somewhat wider readership than the purely military journals, devoted some of its issues exclusively to technological wonders. An issue on the air war featured a poem by Sergei Gorodetskii about the hero Nesterov and a science fiction story about a lone pilot coming from nowhere to save a French POW by shooting Prussians with a noiseless electric gun that emitted blue sparks. Black-and-white drawings showed duels in the air, a spy being thrown out of a zeppelin, and so forth, but these were mere quotations of lubok motifs and their quality was so bad that one has to assume the reader's familiarity with the colored originals.[38]

More impressive was the multicolored cover of *Voina*, which usually featured a drawing related to the theme of the issue. One issue depicted a submarine, underwater mines, and a "hydroscope" to locate them; one devoted to the "steel wonders" of the war showed a Krupp cannon with spider legs hovering over dead soldiers. An issue dealing with the "friends of man in the war" appealed to readers with touching portraits of faithful dogs and horses; a carrier pigeon flew over three dogs pulling an ambulance cart, the whole enhanced by laurel leaves and a flag. The front page of an issue about the "secret and unexplainable in the war" bore a drawing of the "White General," an apparition of the popular nineteenth-century general Mikhail Skobelev on a white horse in a snowy winter forest, who was said to bring fortune to the soldier he looked at and death to the one he ignored.[39]

Though the covers of *Voina* provide a fairly representative overview of the motifs of the patriotic press (there were other issues on the kaiser, the Turks, the sultan's harem, the Entente, heroic children, women, priests, and medical personnel), the journal itself was not representative of popular periodicals. Like *Voin i pakhar'* and *Il'ia Muromets*, it was an outgrowth of the war and dealt with nothing else. But well-established and widely distributed magazines also devoted most of their space to war themes and used visual material much more professionally than the patriotic publications.

Niva, which catered to the rural and urban lower and middle classes and was one of the most influential mass periodicals of the time, filled its pages with high-quality photographs, black-and-white drawings, and color pictures by well-known artists. The fifty-two issues of *Niva* in 1915 alone contained 1,048 illustrations related to the war, most of them photographs, and some 115 graphic contributions. As a "family magazine," *Niva* eschewed scenes of blood and horror in favor of idylls of life at the front, sentimental pictures of refugees, and informative depictions of places hit by the war. Though a fascination with technology was surprisingly absent from these graphics, it appeared in some of the many photographs. Despite the stylistic variety of the contributing artists, most of the pictures expressed an academic conservatism in their attempts at realistic depictions of landscapes and people. Particularly prominent were the works of Ivan Alekseevich Vladimirov, a painter of battle scenes. His favorite subject, Cossacks on horseback somewhere in the great outdoors, was so well polished that it acquired the static character of a perfect idyll. Next to the hard evidence of documentary photographs, these sentimental pictures may have fueled the dreams and illusions of *Niva*'s readers.[40]

Dreams of a different sort were stimulated by *Stolitsa i usad'ba*, a high-society journal, whose appearance coincided with the war years. Unlike the patriotic and popular press, this publication largely ignored the war to focus on horse racing, yachting, tourism, hunting dogs—all the trappings of the luxurious lifestyle that accorded with its motto, "Journal of the Beautiful Life." A couple of feuilletons did discuss the war as a splendid chance for the even greater development of Russian culture. As for depictions of the war, the most realistic were paintings and sculptures in reports of exhibitions and a photo of an ice statue of St. George in the park of Count Sheremetev (which unfortunately melted away in an untimely thaw in February 1915). Otherwise, the war appeared only in photographs of upper-class ladies dressed up as nurses to do volunteer work. Erotic drawings by Sergei Petrovich Lodygin, however, with such titles as "Orgy" and "World of Fantasies," in the style of Aubrey Beardsley, permitted the society reader to forget about hospitals and volunteer work. Apparently patriotism held little appeal for the very rich.[41]

Journals for the educated and artistic elite discussed the war's effects on artists and the arts. Some of these journals, including the two leading theater weeklies, *Rampa i zhizn'* and *Teatr i iskusstvo*, changed little in appearance, adding perhaps some photographs of actors drafted into the army. Others printed a host of allegorical illustrations and reproductions of war-related fine art. Artists close to *Mir iskusstva*, for example, contributed graphics to the reactionary literary-satirical journal *Lukomor'e*. Georgii Narbut was particularly productive and developed his own "war style" on the pages of that journal. Typical of this style were colorful allegories featuring heraldic animals such as eagles, lions, and cockerels. On the cover of one issue of *Lukomor'e*, a yellow lion with a sword, representing Belgium, faced a black German eagle holding a torch and the barrel of a (Krupp) cannon in his talons. From a burning city in the background billowed brown smoke above the words "The Bravery of Heroic Belgium Is Beyond Compare." Perfectly executed, the picture exhibited a certain aesthetic coolness. Beautiful form and composition obviously mattered as much as the patriotic message. The same could be said about the appearance of *Lukomor'e* as a whole. The war may have changed some of the contents, but the aesthetic precepts of the journal were in no way altered.[42]

Literary and satirical journals that catered to an educated audience were full of cartoons and caricatures attacking the enemy. The best of them found their way into volumes of war caricatures, along with reproductions from foreign journals.[43]

Russian caricature can be traced back to another moment of crisis, the war of 1812. Over the nineteenth century, censorship caused political caricatures to develop what John E. Bowlt has called an "element of inversion," a subtle and cautious approach to problems in Russian society. The hundreds of satirical journals that appeared after the Revolution of 1905, many of them modeled on Western publications, such as the German *Simplicissimus* and the French *Le Rire*, knew no such caution. Journals that published social criticism and political attacks tended to be confiscated, however, and by 1907 many of the new publications had been suppressed.[44]

The war that began in 1914 called forth a flood of caricatures. Skilled cartoonists and enthusiastic amateurs alike attacked and ridiculed the enemy. *Novyi Satirikon*, the leading satirical journal of the time, edited by the humorist Arkadii Averchenko, brought together a host of famous artists and young talents, many of whom went on to become celebrities in the Soviet years. Members of *Mir iskusstva* also worked for *Novyi Satirikon* from time to time. Ivan Bilibin, well known as an illustrator of old Russian tales, contributed one of the few war cartoons produced by that group: Wilhelm II as king of spades on a playing card, wearing a crown and a decoration on a ribbon around his neck, wielding a sword; when the card is turned upside down, Wilhelm appears wearing a fool's cap, a necklace of sausages, and a decoration in the form of a stein; instead of a sword, he bears a fork. (An unknown artist used the same motif on a satirical postcard of Nikolai II after February 1917.)[45]

Many of *Novyi Satirikon's* covers were the work of Re-mi (Nikolai Remizov), who usually drew large-format caricatures in clear, forceful lines without much detail. In one of his cartoons a fat pig with the face of Wilhelm II hovers over Paris like a zeppelin and drops "bombs" from its rear end.[46] Other patriotic caricatures in *Novyi Satirikon* came from the pen of Aleksei Radakov, who later made a career as a poster artist under the Soviets. His drawings usually were smaller and more elaborately detailed than Re-mi's, and therefore were not quite so hard-hitting. One showed what would happen if the Germans took Paris: the *Mona Lisa* would be retouched to have a beard like Wilhelm's and behind her would hover a zeppelin and the Eiffel Tower crowned by a German flag. The Venus de Milo would get new arms made by Krupp—the better to hold a beer mug and a chain of sausages. The gothic towers of Notre Dame would be replaced by German spiked helmets, its rose window replaced by a portrait of the kaiser.[47]

Vladimir Lebedev, a master of small decorative illustrations, also contributed a substantial number of war cartoons to *Novyi Satirikon*. Like Radakov, he was to become famous as a poster artist in the Soviet era and was still active during World War II, when his work appeared in the windows of the newly established Tass news agency in Moscow. His World War I work for *Novyi Satirikon* ranged from little sketches at the ends of columns to pairs of drawings of the "before and after" type and funny sketches to illustrate German press releases, all of them obviously produced rather hastily. A good deal of hatching replaces the condensed line of the decorative illustrations, and many details are only suggested. This kind of sketchy work can also be seen in a cartoon produced for *Novyi Satirikon* by the renowned artist Natan Al'tman. In patriotic cartoons, apparently, the message outweighed artistic merit.[48]

Like patriotic lubki, war cartoons sharply declined in number in 1915, replaced in *Novyi Satirikon* by social criticism and attacks on profiteers and black marketeers. The New Year's issue contained Lebedev's drawing showing how the rich, the middle class, and the poor greeted 1915. When the fat rich people in the first floor apartment open a bottle of champagne, the cork goes through the ceiling and the table of the middle-class family on the second floor, penetrates their ceiling and the empty table of the poor fellow on the third floor, and hits him right in the face. A comparison of the two covers that Remi drew for the *Maslenitsa* (Carnival, or "Butter Week") issues of 1915 and 1916 is also telling: in 1915, a voluminous woman, representing Maslenitsa, holds a well-buttered pan containing Wilhelm II. In 1916, a starving woman with her children stand within a circle of dancing society couples. When, the caption asks, will Maslenitsa for some and eternal Lent for others be over?[49]

The boom in patriotic caricatures and cartoons at the beginning of the war soon ended. For a short while the target of Russian cartoons shifted from internal social problems to an external foe. Like Napoleon in 1812, the kaiser became the primary focus of the satirists. He was the single subject of at least a third of all patriotic cartoons and appeared in many others as well, often together with Franz Joseph of Austria or the Turkish sultan. The latter two, by the way, ranked equally in the roughly 12 percent of all cartoons devoted to them.[50]

A set of standard features, indeed a satirical iconography, developed for the three main characters. Wilhelm, of course, was always identified by his oversized whiskers, and slightly less often by a spiked helmet or some other military outfit. Franz Joseph was always the senile fool with a big white beard and sometimes a walking stick or crutches. The sultan was usually characterized by a hooked nose, dark hair, and a fez, and was often shown as a dwarf or gnome. Clichés of strength, weakness, and racial characteristics dominated this imagery, together with traditional cultural attributes of dress, food, and behavior.

Patriotic cartoons were particularly prominent in satirical magazines catering to an educated readership. Apparently their irony and allusions were considered beyond the grasp of a semiliterate audience, and their ridicule of royalty would be seen as inappropriate for the lower classes. Hence the absence of cartoons in such journals as *Voin i pakhar'*. The positive patriotism of sentimental and heroic illustrations was certainly more appealing to the readers of these journals, who were, after all, all too well aware of the war's hardships. As an aesthetic challenge for intellectuals, however, the war lost its interest in the first half of 1915; after that it largely disappeared from their journals. Major Russian defeats at the front and increasing social problems at home became more important for cartoonists than yet another funny picture of Wilhelm or the sultan. What remained were the mass publications with their gray pictures on bad paper, their occasional color supplements, and their photographs of life in the trenches, all of which sent a message of despair rather than patriotic inspiration.

Patriotic Postcards: Nationalism in the Mail

As a relatively new medium of communication, the postcard experienced a boom during World War I in all the warring countries. Despite thousands of patriotic motifs and war-related photographs, the value of postcards as clues to Russian patriotism has long been neglected. Postcards allowed personal statements of patriotic feelings in a time of growing individualism. By signing on the back, one could identify oneself with the message on the front of a card. Because of this confessional character, postcards have rightly been called the campaign buttons or bumper stickers of World War I.[51]

The mode of distribution and the large-scale fragmented production pose some difficulties to anyone setting out to investigate postcards. It is virtually impossible to know how many were sent, by and to whom, or how many were actually produced. Even professional collectors do not have complete sets from that time, and the number of small publishing houses and samizdat activities is not recorded. The roughly four hundred photocopies and photographs of patriotic postcards in my collection come from about seventy-five publishers, and many of them were parts of series. A major publisher's series could comprise as many as six hundred cards, each issued in 10,000 to 15,000 copies. Several million patriotic postcards, then, must have circulated during World War I.[52]

A form of communication that came to Russia from Austria and Prussia, postcards first appeared in Russia in 1872 and the first picture postcard, a view of Moscow, in 1895. As most of the early postcards were produced and marketed by foreigners, they followed Western stylistic conventions. Urban, sentimental, and humorous scenes were the main subjects of prewar Russian postcards, with political cartoons joining in only after 1905.[53]

Wartime Russian postcards followed Western models only to a limited extent. Satirical postcards attacked the enemy, but documentary photographs and what have been called "patriotic fantasy" cards attempted to evoke patriotism by appealing to sentiment. With the exception of the photographic cards, Russian patriotic postcards drew much of their inspiration from traditional Russian visual arts, particularly the lubok and satirical illustrations, which were themselves influenced by satirical lubki.[54]

Patriotic postcards thus stood in the tradition of lubki. Not only were many of them pocket-size copies of lubki and other visual materials, such as posters and works of fine art, but, like the broadsides, many were pinned up on the walls of urban and rural lower-class homes. Thus a patriotic postcard was more than just a message in the mail, for it provided information and served as an amusing or inspirational wall decoration. It satisfied curiosity about the war in the same way as lubki.[55]

Photographs of generals, politicians, and Cossacks and posed shots of "life" at the front (church services for soldiers, a nurse soothing a fevered brow) supplied the most prosaic information about the war. Sherer, Nabgol'ts & Co. of Moscow put out a series of fifty photos of brave Cossack fighters, some of them engaged in horseback acrobatics. Innumerable photographic postcards were also published and sold for charity by the Skobelev Committee, a semiofficial propaganda organization that had been founded during the Russo-Japanese War by General Skobelev's sister and now enjoyed the august protection of the tsar. It produced newsreels and patriotic films as well as postcards. All of its postcards had the static quality of posed photographs, and the message always stressed humility and submissiveness to church and tsar. Prayers in the trenches, religious services, and award ceremonies at the front were favored scenes.

Quite different were postcards published by the Ladies' Circle of the Petrograd School of Army Medics to raise money for charity. These cards appeared in late 1915, just in time to be exhibited at a charity bazaar held by the organization. They showed refugees arriving in a town, Cossacks riding through a Carpathian forest, and soldiers crossing a river. With their accent on people and horses acting naturally in natural settings, these cards expressed movement and action. Of all photographic postcards, these were by far the most realistic and interesting. They proved that photographic postcards need not be boring and revealed private initiative to be much more inventive and creative than the official efforts of the Skobelev Committee.[56]

The sentimental or patriotic fantasy cards produced in Russia during World War I were not quite so well developed as their Western counterparts. Cards on the order of the German *Fürstenpostkarten*—cards depicting Kaiser Wilhelm in all sorts of environments, distributed among front-line soldiers to boost morale—hardly existed; few displayed photomontage or sophisticated printing techniques, either. Gone were the lubki's stout knights; the bulk of the patriotic fantasy cards bore sentimental drawings of lonesome soldiers, nurses caring for the wounded, and groups of Cossacks.[57]

One Riga publishing house, Gempel', produced high-quality photomontages that exude patriotic reverence. On one card photographs of the tsar, the tsarina, and the tsarevich are embraced by the wings of the double-headed eagle. Between the eagle's heads the tsar's crown rests in the center of a sun emitting yellow rays, beneath the first line of the anthem "God Save the Tsar." Russian flags and naval ensigns surround the royal figures; beneath them the Kazan' Cathedral in St. Petersburg and the Moscow Kremlin are framed in tricolor ribbons. Almost lost amid the patriotic display is a small St. George.

Aesthetically and technically more conservative postcards bore reproductions of fine art. Publishers that specialized in such reproductions before the war had only to select new subjects after 1914. I. A. Vladimirov's postcards, for example, showed stereotyped front-line scenes—a group of soldiers finding the tracks of "Teutons" in the snow, an artillery detachment waiting for an attack on the bank of the Vistula. The colors were somber, with no striking accents or deviations from a soft-focus style.[58]

Series of pen-and-ink sketches of life at the front were less academic. These were not the panoramas of the lubki but vignettes of military action: a soldier cutting through barbed wire, two Cossacks crossing a river, a medic carrying a wounded man. Landscape was often only hinted at; hatching and silhouette were the predominant techniques. Thus the war was reduced to a few lines and scribbles, colorless and prosaic. Sketches of this kind were among the postcards produced by the Latvian Aleksandrs Apsitis, later famous as Apsit, the Soviet poster artist. His topics, though not his style, sometimes went beyond the idyll to include German atrocities, the good understanding between Russian and allied soldiers, and the care given to wounded Germans by Russian nurses.[59]

Silhouettes were also employed by such elite artists as Georgii Narbut, and some publishers specialized in them. Usually focusing on a few figures, such as soldiers sitting around a fire or Kriuchkov fighting some Germans, these cards were characterized by forceful lines and sharp contrasts, as in a New Year's card by the Kiev publishing house Iskusstvo (Fig. 13). The absence of extraneous detail and the reduction of the content to black-and-white contrast enhanced the clarity of the messages of these pictures and gave them an almost iconic symbolism.[60]

Patriotic fantasy cards published by the Skobelev Committee were sold at "all the better paper and tobacco stores as well as at flower stands and in the foyers of theaters and cinemas in Petrograd and throughout the country." A prominent participant in this endeavor was the fashionable poster artist Elena Samokish- Sudkovskaia, a regular contributor to *Niva*. Although she had lived in Paris and was influenced by French art nouveau, her patriotic postcards for the Skobelev Committee were rather conservative and unimaginative. As a card bearing the Russian national anthem (Fig. 14) shows, the official and authoritative style that characterized the committee's photographic postcards found its way onto its fantasy cards as well.[61]

Much more sentimental were scenes focused on that symbol of patriotic virtue, the nurse. Fantasy postcards depicted these heroines as caring mothers, hand-holding lovers, and untouchable beauties. They were shown at work in a hospital, at the front, even in portraits, as on a card by the Kiev publishing house Nov' (Fig. 15). Not quite so idealized were the nurses in pictures by A. Lavrov, published by the Red Cross, which showed them reading the popular liberal newspaper *Russkoe slovo* to an attentive soldier with a head wound or bandaging the chest of an unconscious soldier at the front (Fig. 16). Although Lavrov's nurses conveyed a comparatively realistic picture of the profession and exhibited an understanding of the social (and political) motivation of these women, each scene was as neat and bloodless as that of a nineteenth-century lubok.[62]

Few women other than nurses appeared on patriotic postcards. The pronatalism so prominent in France, where pictures of loving couples encouraged women to increase the birth rate, was absent from Russia.

13. "Happy New Year! A Successful Blow" (S novym godom! Udachnyi udar) (Kiev: Iskusstvo, n.d.), no. 203, 9 × 14 cm. Helsinki University Slavonic Library.

14. E. P. Samokish-Sudkovskaia, "God Save the Tsar" (Bozhe tsaria khrani) (Petrograd: Skobelev Committee, n.d.), 9 × 14 cm. Helsinki University Slavonic Library.

Руеская сеетра милоеердія.

15. "Russian Nurse" (Russkaia sestra miloserdiia) (Kiev: Nov', n.d.), 9 × 14 cm. Helsinki University Slavonic Library.

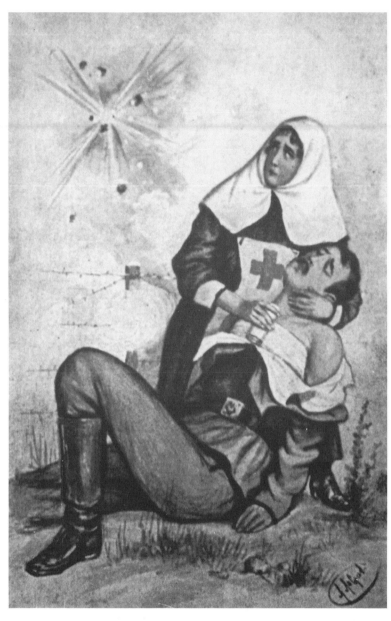

16. A. Lavrov, untitled (Moscow: Nikol'skaia Obshchina R. O. Krasnago Kresta, n.d.), 9 × 14 cm. Helsinki University Slavonic Library.

The card that came closest to that genre was one of Lavrov's showing a sailor kissing his girl good-by. The caption simply noted that when one parts from one's beloved, the two heartily kiss each other. Any suggestion that the hearty leave-taking might encompass more than a kiss was hard to read into the naively sentimental picture. Another of Lavrov's cards shows a young woman at a sewing machine making a shirt for a soldier, and a card issued by the Petrograd publisher Leont'ev bears a photo of a woman filling in for her drafted husband as a trolley conductor. Such pictures of women on the home front, however, were rare among Russian patriotic postcards.

The most touching and melodramatic postcards were those devoted to the lonesome soldier. Lavrov appealed to his audience's protective instincts with pictures of a young boy standing guard and a soldier on a snowy night looking at a distant apparition of wife, children, and home village. Christmas at the front marked the epitome of sentimentality. On one card, a lonely soldier on a body-strewn battlefield joins the only other person left alive, a wounded German, to gaze at the Christmas star (Fig. 17). Other cards showed soldiers standing around a Christmas tree in a trench or decorating it with candles. Patriotism and longings for peace became intertwined in a yearning for warmth and home.

Russian patriotic fantasy cards were thus quite conservative. They did not go far beyond the horizon of a simple observer in either their stylistic audacity or their thematic variety. Most were sentimental depictions of typical wartime situations, designed to reflect everyday reality without regard for such abstractions as Russian nationalism. Indeed, their message was sober and compassionate rather than aggressively patriotic. The heroes of these cards were the individual soldier and the caring nurse, people with whom the vast majority of Russians could identify. Those fantasy cards that explicitly promoted Russian nationalism did so rather unimaginatively, hauling out the usual symbols (flags, laurel) and only infrequently venturing into new aesthetic forms and techniques, such as photomontage.

Both the aesthetic conservatism and the thematic limitation suggest that Russian patriotic fantasy cards had a largely lower-class clientele. Readers of *Niva* and the patriotic journals were familiar with this kind of visual material; and the same type of pictures appeared on patriotic form letters that were made available to soldiers (Fig. 18). All that the illiterate or semiliterate soldier had to do was sign his name or make

17. "Christmas Eve" (Rozhdestvenskaia noch') (Moscow: Chelnokov, n.d.), 14 × 9 cm. Helsinki University Slavonic Library.

an X beneath the printed text, and shortly his family would receive an uplifting message: all the Russians were brave, they were fighting heroically to defend the motherland though they longed for home, God was on their side, and so forth. As a service both to the illiterate and to the cause of morale on the home front, patriotic letters thus reflected the same sentimental world as the patriotic fantasy postcards. They simply lacked the personal touch of the handwritten cards.[63]

The vast majority of patriotic postcards, however, had humorous or satirical themes. Postcards joined cartoons in the press in making fun of the enemy; and many artists worked in both media simultaneously. Satirical postcards varied widely in artistic quality, from cheap pen-and-ink sketches to highly professional color prints and even avant-garde pictures, appealing to the most refined taste as well as the most uncultivated.

Kaiser Wilhelm was the main target of satirical postcards; about a

п. 1.

Дорогіе мои уважаемые родители!

Въ первыхъ строкахъ моего письма увѣдомляю я Васъ, мои родные, что я, слава Богу, здоровъ, чего и Вамъ желаю отъ Господа Бога нашего.

Находился мы теперь на позиціяхъ и

Живемъ мы да поживаемъ

И родныхъ не забываемъ.

Бьемъ мы нѣмцевъ—а онъ, мизгура, все

„Ерапланомъ" льетъ,—

А нашъ братъ

Его штыкомъ доставаетъ.

Не кручинься, родители мои дорогіе!

Съ нами Богъ!

Прогремитъ скоро повсюдъ Русская!

Одолѣли мы врага нашего

Неприятеля прускаго!

И свяжимся мы `тогда съ Вами, родные, и радостна будетъ наша встрѣча. Уповайте на Господа Бога нашего и молитесь Вы Ему за Матушку—Русь нашу святую, за Батюшку— Царя и еиновъ Его.

Плохо приходится нѣмцу отъ насъ; раньше писала онъ: „гохъ" да „гохъ", а теперь только и слышишь: „охъ" да „охъ!" Да и подѣломъ ему!

Пусть Вильгельмъ въ не хоронится, пусть знаетъ, что не такъ легко одолѣть нашего брата-солдата.

Хоть и скучновато жить безъ родной маменьки и отца дорогого,

Но все-таки обо инъ не безпокоитесь.

Я, слава Богу, живъ и здоровъ,

Лучшъ нѣмцевъ съ пера и боковъ.

Дома родной и вспоминаю

И съ Вами свидѣнья желаю.

Прошу Васъ, дорогіе мои, передайте низкій поклонъ всѣмъ роднымъ и знакомымъ, и еще прошу Васъ—пришлите весточку о Вашемъ здоровьи и благополучіи.

Засимъ—до-свиданія!

Очень не скучайте

И меня съ Георгіемъ дожидайте`

Остаюсь любящій Васъ

Вашъ любезный сынъ

18. A patriotic letter. Gosudarstvennyi muzei politicheskoi istorii Rossii, St. Petersburg, f. IX, no. 9032.

third of all cards were devoted to him alone, and he showed up on numerous other cards as well. His popularity as a figure of fun and infamy was not restricted to Russia; most satirical postcards produced in the Allied nations focused on Wilhelm II as the main villain of the war. Next in line were the Turkish sultan and the Austrian emperor; they accounted for about 16 percent each as single subjects and, like the kaiser, appeared with other figures as well.[64]

Some publishers produced satirical postcards of great originality and high typographical quality. Segodniashnii Lubok put out cards in the same style as its lubki, showing defeated Germans and zeppelins turned into trousers (Figs. 3 and 19); Sovremennoe Iskusstvo in Petrograd published a large number of cards that were at least as crude and witty (Fig. 20). Iskusstvo in Kiev issued a series of over two hundred cards signed Nevskii, which were notable for their high quality. A cartoon of Wilhelm II blowing soap bubbles representing the German air force (Fig. 21) is typical of his work. A similar aerial motif appears on two cards by the Riga publisher Varvara Veis, which depict Germany as a balloon blown up by the kaiser and burst by a Cossack (Fig. 22). Indeed, German "inflatedness" was a persistent theme, with soap bubbles, zeppelins, and balloons functioning as allegories of overblown German imperial aspirations. And they continued to be associated with Germans in the popular Russian imagination well into the Soviet period: the villain of the 1936 comedy film *Circus* was a German circus performer who enhanced his chest measurement by an inflatable device that he deflated only in private.[65]

Not all cartoon cards were so obvious; some were highly sophisticated. An unsigned and untitled card from Ekaterinoslav, for example, combines several motifs in a most original manner (Fig. 23). Here we see the futile attempts of Russia's enemies to make an impact on the motherland, each in his own way: Wilhelm with his zeppelin-sausage, Franz Joseph as a backward-walking crab, and the sultan sitting in a galosh in the Black Sea. "To sit in a galosh," in the Russian idiom, is to be in a hopeless and disastrous situation. Such sayings, proverbs, and even fairy tales were common points of reference for satirical postcards. They conveyed the message quickly in a way that evoked a common cultural heritage. Thus the meaning of a card by the artist who signed himself Iunak (Fig. 24) was conveyed not only by its picture but by a caption that evoked Pëtr Ershov's nineteenth-century fairy tale "The Humpback Horse," a popular and widely known story.[66]

Казаку жена Полина,
Шьетъ штаны изъ цепелина.

19. "The Cossack's Wife Polina . . . " (Kazaku zhena Polina . . .) (Moscow: Segodniashnii Lubok, 1914), 9 × 14 cm. Helsinki University Slavonic Library.

20. "Happy New Year!" (S novym godom!) (Petrograd: Sovremennoe Is-kusstvo, n.d.), 9.5 × 14.5 cm. Helsinki University Slavonic Library.

21. Nevskii, "The German Air Force" (Vozdushnyi flot Germanii) (Kiev: Iskusstvo, 1914), no. 221, 9.5 × 14.5 cm. Helsinki University Slavonic Library.

22. Evgenii Orlovskii, "Dream" (Mechta) and "Reality" (Deistvitel'nost') (Riga: Veis, 1914), nos. 3 and 4, 14 × 9 cm. Helsinki University Slavonic Library.

23. Untitled (Ekaterinoslav: Kudriavitskii, n.d.), 14 × 9 cm. Helsinki University Slavonic Library.

24. Iunak, "From 'The Humpback Horse'" (Iz "Kon'ka-gorbunka") (Moscow: Genegar, n.d.), no. 30-6, 14 × 9 cm. Helsinki University Slavonic Library.

25. Miss (A. V. Remizova), untitled, no. 20 in the series *Sovremennaia russkaia i inostrannaia karikatura i voina* (Kiev: Nov', n.d.), 14 × 9 cm. Helsinki University Slavonic Library.

Recipients of satirical postcards were not only exposed to their own cultural tradition; they could also savor the comic products of foreign artists. The publishing house Nov' issued a series of postcards bearing cartoons from English and French as well as Russian journals. Outstanding among the Russian artists represented in this series were A. V. Remizova, who signed herself "Miss," and another known only as Pem. Miss was a regular contributor to *Novyi Satirikon*, where her picture of the sultan tearing himself away from his harem to fight in the war (Fig. 25) was originally published. Pem's cartoon of Wilhelm choking on a bone in the restaurant Belgium (Fig. 26)—an allusion to the kaiser's overoptimistic plan to sweep through Belgium and "have lunch in Paris"—first appeared in the newspaper *Vechernee Vremia*.

26. Pem, untitled, no. 18 in the series *Sovremennaia russkaia i inostrannaia karikatura i voina* (Kiev: Nov', n.d.), 9 × 14 cm. Helsinki University Slavonic Library.

Васька Берлинскій.

Васька сумрачно глядитъ,
   Рваный, волосатый...
На спинѣ несетъ, бандитъ,
   Узелъ полосатый.
Обобрать честной народъ
   Для него сподручно,
Понакралъ и продаетъ —
   „Оптомъ и поштучно"!

27. P. N. Troianskii, "Berlin Willi" (Vas'ka Berlinskii) (Petrograd: Bussel, n.d.),
9 × 14 cm. Helsinki University Slavonic Library.

Wilhelm II appeared not only as himself but as the "ugly German" in general. Thus Pëtr Troianskii pictured him as a ragged marauding soldier (Fig. 27), and the Petrograd poster artist Luka Zlotnikov caricatured him as a beer-drinking king of diamonds (Fig. 28). Diamonds, incidentally, were the signs for convicts in Russia, and both pictures intimated greed and brutality. They prepared viewers for cruder caricatures—Germans as a wild boar in a spiked helmet (Fig. 29) and as cockroaches. (Cockroaches are called *prussaki* [Prussians] in colloquial Russian; in Germany, of course, they are *Russen* [Russians].) Cockroaches, pigs, and mad dogs were the usual menagerie reserved for the Germans and their ruler, and Cossacks often appeared as their trainers or exterminators—surely a unique form of pest control.[67]

These themes appeared in countless black-and-white series issued by a variety of publishers. Such postcards were often produced hastily and with little attention to artistic quality; a quick laugh was their raison d'être. Razsvet in Kiev, for example, had a series of over 370 such drawings by the artist V. Gulak, who signed himself Mukhomor (Fly Agaric). Crudeness of technique was often matched by crudeness of subject matter. The Moscow publisher Gramakov showed Wilhelm, Franz Joseph, and the sultan in a cage at the Moscow zoo (Fig. 30), and the Moscow artist P.R. gave the finger to the two enemy leaders (Fig. 31).[68]

Like the cartoons published in journals, many satirical postcards appealed to educated people who could grasp ironic allusions and metaphors, but as successors to lubki, postcards also became part of an emerging mass culture. The iconography developed to represent the three enemy leaders in newspaper cartoons—Wilhelm as beast, as new Napoleon, as would-be luncher in Paris; Franz Joseph as a sick old man; the sultan as a cowardly and lecherous dwarf; Germans as *kolbasniki* (sausage eaters) and beer-drinking fools—was carried over to patriotic postcards. A common enemy obviously produced common concepts of the enemy, regardless of social background or taste. As a medium serving a broad spectrum of society, satirical postcards reflected this communal patriotic spirit.

At the same time, the few available publication dates of patriotic postcards reveal an interesting difference between satirical postcards on the one hand and fantasy and photographic cards on the other. Most of the satirical cards were published in 1914 or early 1915, whereas more fantasy and photographic cards came out in 1915 and

28. L. T. Zlotnikov, "King of Diamonds" (Bubnovyi korol') (Petrograd: Zlotnikov, n.d.), 9 × 14 cm. Helsinki University Slavonic Library.

Вотъ боровъ прётъ нѣмецкій	Онъ въ самый „пятачокъ".	Да, видно, тутъ, прохвостъ,
Съ отвагой молодецкой,	Тѣмъ временемъ за хвостъ—	Тебѣ не сладко станетъ.
Но получилъ щелчокъ	Иной его врагъ тянетъ,—	

29. Untitled (Kiev: Razsvet, 1915), 14 × 9 cm. Helsinki University Slavonic Library.

ЗООЛОГИЧЕСКИЙ САДЪ

Воевали, воевали.... наконецъ въ Москву попали.

30. "Zoo" (Zoologicheskii sad) (Moscow: Gramakov, n.d.), 14 × 9 cm. Helsinki University Slavonic Library.

||| „Тройственный союзъ" |||

31. "Triple Alliance" (Troistvennyi soiuz) (Moscow: P. R., n.d.), no. 155, 14 × 9 cm. Helsinki University Slavonic Library.

1916. The forces that united the Russians against the common enemy had obviously weakened by 1915, a development paralleled in the publication of lubki. As jingoism lost its effectiveness, publishers turned increasingly to sentimental scenes (for the lower classes) and to photographic and fantasy cards (for public service organizations to sell to the educated). The patriotic spirit evident on satirical postcards issued during the first months of the war turned into appeals to hold out, addressed to the men in the armed forces and those willing to contribute to their effort. In other words, patriotic postcards reflected a development from an initial patriotic unity to a division between Russians voluntarily or involuntarily involved in the war and those not interested in it. By sending a postcard, one could identify with the group of one's choice and express one's own attitude toward the war.

Advertising Patriotism: Posters in the War

During World War I posters bloomed on the walls of buildings in Russian cities on an unprecedented scale. In the beginning, they called for donations to charities, invited people to benefit exhibitions and concerts, and drew attention to new films featuring the war's horrors and atrocities. Later the government issued posters asking for subscriptions to war loans. A relatively new medium in Russia, posters experienced their first boom during World War I.[69]

Russian and particularly Soviet posters have been subjected to intensive investigation, and all researchers agree that World War I was a catalyst for Russian poster art.[70] The historical value of the wartime posters' messages has been less widely recognized.

In the years before the war, posters were used mostly to advertise goods, services, and events. The style of these commercial posters was influenced both by the works of Western artists, such as Alphonse Mucha, a Czech who lived in France and produced some of the best art nouveau posters, and by Russian book illustrations and paintings. Film posters, relying on still photographs to convey the comedy or drama of the film being advertised, developed as a unique genre.

The war gave birth to a new kind of poster that became the direct precursor of the Soviet poster. The need to mobilize the home front and to integrate all of Russia's resources in the war effort gave rise to posters with sociopolitical and economic themes and with appeals to patriotism and charity.[71]

The first patriotic posters in Russia were the result of private initiatives by such organizations as the Red Cross and the Zemstvo Union, and by groups of artists who had joined together to raise funds for the soldiers. These posters advertised street collections of money and warm clothing, lotteries, and benefit exhibitions and concerts. Stylistically, they stood in the tradition of realistic painting and the Wanderers, but lubok traditions and national symbols were present as well.

In accordance with Frank Kämpfer's general model, patriotic posters fall into three categories: those containing only a written message, those containing writing and a graphic symbol, and those that bear a picture and a related text. Posters of all three types were produced in Russia during the war. Those in the first category, however, were used only indirectly for patriotic purposes. Benefit concerts, theater performances, ballet evenings, and the like were usually advertised on posters that contained only the words necessary to announce the event. Like prewar concert notices, they were printed on

32. "Patriotic Concerts by M. I. Dolina" (Patrioticheskie kontserty M. I. Dolinoi) (Petrograd: Tipografiia Imperatorskikh Teatrov, 1916), 54 × 63 cm. Gosudarstvennyi muzei istorii Sankt-Peterburga.

РОССІЯ = РАЗОРЁННЫМЪ ОКРАИНАМЪ
29,30,31 МАЯ 1915 ГОДА.

33. "Russia for the Destroyed Borderlands" (Rossiia razorennym okrainam) (Petrograd: Vefers, 1915), 55 × 36 cm. Gosudarstvennyi muzei istorii Sankt-Peterburga.

thin white paper with little visual imagination. There was no direct patriotic appeal, only an invitation to patriotic activities, such as concerts by the famous soprano Mariia Dolina (Fig. 32).[72]

Posters that used clear symbols to express patriotism were more sophisticated. Although a text communicated the main message, the observer's eye was first attracted by a pictorial element, such as a double-headed eagle or a red cross. Both of these symbols signaled national importance and social commitment but gave no information about the advertised event. Thus the double-headed eagle promoted an aid project for the borderlands and a Serbia Day (Figs. 33 and 34), and the red cross was used for an exhibition by Moscow artists in support of war victims.[73]

Aside from these obvious signs, pictures functioned as symbols in themselves. The often lengthy texts that accompanied them were unrelated to the pictures and were set apart from them. This technique derived from the allegorical lubki, and it is hardly surprising that

34. "Serbia Day" (Serbskii den') (Petrograd, 1915), 57 × 94 cm. Gosudarstven-nyi muzei istorii Sankt-Peterburga.

35. "XXXI Grand Patriotic Concert by M. I. Dolina" (XXXI-i grandioznyi patrioticheskii kontsert M. I. Dolinoi) (Petrograd: Golike i Vil'borg, [1914]), 68 × 50 cm. Gosudarstvennyi muzei istorii Sankt-Peterburga.

much of the imagery was taken from old broadsides. On a poster announcing a charity bazaar in Moscow, for example, the text stood next to a painting by Viktor M. Vasnetsov showing a medieval knight fighting a dragon. This picture expressed Russia's heroic past; it had nothing to do with the bazaar.[74]

More confusing were posters that sent several messages simultaneously. Sentimentality and bravery were combined on a poster announcing one of Dolina's patriotic concerts (Fig. 35). Superimposed on a panoramic battle scene is a picture of a mother clutching her children. The text adds to the confusion by highlighting the Circus Ciniselli and Dolina's name instead of "Patriotic Concert," which viewers might have related to one or the other of the pictures. In his determination to omit no conceivable appeal, the anonymous artist has garbled the message.[75]

Posters whose texts paralleled their pictures sent clearer messages. They promoted aid to war victims, donations of food for the poor, and collections by the Red Cross. Among the most notable was Leonid Pasternak's "Wounded Soldier" (Fig. 36). The tsar disliked this poster because it showed a "weak" soldier, but its impact was tremendous. When it first appeared, crowds gathered around it and women wept; the Bolsheviks used it to support their campaign for Russia's withdrawal from the war. Nina Baburina rightly attributes this overwhelming response to the humaneness of its theme and the naturalism of the lithograph. She might have included the composition of the work among its most effective elements. By showing nothing but a bleeding soldier next to four words asking for help for war victims, Pasternak stripped his poster of everything that could have cluttered its message.[76]

Despite differences in artistic quality, style, and clarity, the patriotic posters of 1914 and 1915 have several characteristics in common. Because their emphasis was on charity, they tended to use sentimental themes and idyllic scenes that could move observers to contribute to the advertised cause. These posters drew upon the traditional styles of lubok art, realistic painting, and national heraldry; abstract art and Western art nouveau had little influence. At the stylistic level, then, war relief posters were quite conservative, in keeping with the wide and artistically unsophisticated public they aimed to reach. The appeals to a great common past that were intended to close the social ranks behind the needy and war victims were less effective than such naturalistic posters as Pasternak's "Wounded Soldier." After all, it was the wounded soldiers and their families, not a medieval knight or a mythical eagle, that the fund-raising activities were meant to support. Most such posters made no attempt to glorify the war.

The Russian government, like those of the other belligerents, sold bonds to finance the war. In the spring of 1916 and again that fall the government launched war loan drives with full-page ads in the newspapers and a variety of posters. The war loan posters were a novel means of communicating with the people. With their appeals to civic duty and economic sacrifice, they were the first official propaganda posters produced in Russia.[77]

The use of posters to promote subscriptions to war loans was copied from Western countries, and Western posters influenced the style of their Russian versions. A lively exchange of poster exhibitions

36. Leonid Pasternak, "Aid to War Victims" (Na pomoshch' zhertvam voiny) ("The Wounded Soldier") (Moscow: Levenson, 1914), several sizes. From *Russische Graphik, 1880–1917* (Munich 1991), with kind permission of Bangert Verlag.

brought English recruiting posters to Petrograd in May 1916 and Russian war loan posters to London and to New York's Plaza Hotel in 1917. In addition, a long article in *Niva* in the fall of 1915, accompanied by several reproductions, introduced English war posters to the Russian public, just in time for the first war loan posters in early 1916.[78]

Russian war loan posters differed greatly from the war relief posters. Here the homespun lubok atmosphere gave way to perfectly executed large-format chromolithographs in often striking colors. Most of the pictures emphasized movement and activity. National symbols and historic heroes were far outnumbered by advancing soldiers, war machinery, and even the process of arms production. The words *Voennyi zaëm* (War loan) were always set in bold and striking type.

Thematically, Russian artists were in the mainstream of European war poster art. Their motifs could be found on posters in most other countries—a soldier with his hand lifted to his head, for example, looking straight at the observer as he points with the other hand to a pile of ammunition next to a cannon. This poster by Efim Cheptsov is one of many in which a military man makes eye contact with the observer, a motif first introduced by the famous British recruiting poster showing Lord Kitchener and later popularized in J. Montgomery Flagg's image of Uncle Sam saying "I Want You for U.S. Army."[79]

Two posters are noteworthy for their unusual scenes of armament production. In the first, by the Petrograd artist Rikhard Zarrin, the person at the workbench is a good-looking young man; in the other, which is not signed, the worker is a pretty young woman. Frank Kämpfer, who believes this depiction of a woman in industrial work to be unique, sees the attractive young workers as embodiments of an upper-class ideal of beauty. It seems likely, however, that their prototypes are two figures in a poster by R. S. S. Baden-Powell. Published in 1915 under the words "Are you in this?" it showed soldiers, a boy scout (of course), a nurse, a man in a civilian suit (a banker?), a steelworker, and a female worker checking cartridges. The steelworker and the woman are as attractive as their Russian counterparts and the two men have similar features.[80]

Aside from these few instances of Western inspiration, Russian war loan posters may be grouped around three motifs. The first revived traditional heroes and displayed national symbols and thus was the most loosely connected to the loan drive. One poster depicts the statue of the seventeenth-century heroes Minin and Pozharskii in Moscow's Red Square. On another, the Russian double-headed eagle fights with his German (one-headed) counterpart. The second motif, soldiers at work, was closer to the purpose of the posters. These posters typically display some sort of weaponry (to be purchased, perhaps, with the money raised by the subscription drive), some soldiers standing ready in the trenches with machine guns or advancing with their rifles in firing position, or some mounted Cossacks on the offensive. Posters of this sort produced by I. A. Vladimirov are not quite so detailed as his battle scenes. Reduced to the soldier and his weapon, they largely neglect the surrounding countryside.[81]

The needed war matériel was the third motif. These posters are reminiscent of commercial art. A poster by V. G. Eberling shows a warplane in action amidst imposing and decorative clouds. Vladimirov contributed a picture of a convoy of trucks loaded with ammunition. The huge missile in front of a factory on one poster can be found on an Austrian poster as well.[82]

The majority of Russian war loan posters, then, must be seen as a mixture of traditional battle scenes and professional commercial art, though the loan posters fell short of commercial posters in their use of color and in the originality of their composition. Despite the similarities, they are more conservative than Western war posters, less successful in engaging the observer's immediate attention. One reason is certainly the fact that with a few exceptions, the movement in the pictures is directed away from the observer: the truck convoy, the Cossacks, the warplane, the cannon are seen from behind, receding into a vague distance.[83]

The words on the posters are not very imaginative. Around the large "Voennyi zaëm" one usually sees some short slogans: "All for victory!" "Patriotic and profitable!" Sometimes one sees longer admonitions: "Participation in the loan is a patriotic duty for everyone"; "All must help our heroic soldiers, and those who can must subscribe to the loan." These texts were simply not very inspiring. Exceptions prove the rule, of course. Cheptsov's soldier points at the cannon, for example, next to the caption "The more money, the more ammunition," and the text on the missile poster reads "Abundance of ammunition—the guarantee of victory."

The Russian war loan drive met with little success. Whether its failure may be attributed to the communicative quality of the posters is questionable. Contemporary observers noted the rising prices, the increasing impoverishment of most strata of society, and the tendency of the rich to grow richer through speculation as the main reasons for the low number of subscriptions. More than posters were needed to counteract the widening gap between rich and poor, distrust of the government, and lack of faith in the war effort.[84]

Russian war loan posters were aimed at an audience only recently exposed to poster art, so it would be inappropriate to judge them by Western standards. Like other visual material, they belonged to a system of aesthetic conventions that had its own rules and traditions. If they lacked the originality of composition and lively style of Western posters, the familiar style of realistic paintings may have attracted some observers, even if they could not afford to subscribe to the loan.[85]

The success of war relief posters such as Pasternak's, however, suggests that war loan posters were expressing a kind of patriotism that many people found too self-confident. Though not so naively heroic as allegorical lubki, they still showed heroes in the form of advancing soldiers or patriotic and handsome workers. With the military defeats, the food crisis, and the growth of labor unrest in 1916, such images hardly reflected Russian reality. As the sharp decline in aggressively patriotic lubki, postcards, and cartoons in 1915 demonstrates, the atmosphere of patriotism had changed even before the first war loans were floated. The credibility of war loan posters was certainly not strengthened by the fact that they were swimming against the emotional tide.

Film posters reflected a completely different mood. As we shall see, the Russian film industry boomed during World War I. A large number of patriotic and war-related films were produced, and the posters that advertised them added two new elements to poster art: sensation and horror.[86]

War film posters vary widely in appearance and artistic quality. Because the products they advertise will be available only a short while, film posters must make an immediate impact at low cost, for they too are fated to disappear quickly. Many Russian war film posters were therefore printed on cheap paper, and often the only color is the red that calls attention to the title of the movie and its stars. The rest of the poster might show photographs from the film, sometimes with captions and a plot summary. At a time when the film industry was expanding rapidly, these simple posters were the easiest and fastest way to announce films to a very large audience.

Producers who emphasized the artistry of their work or who wanted to reach a more sophisticated public used more elaborate posters to advertise their films. In addition to still photos, colorful graphics purported to illustrate the film's action. Stylistically, these pictures ranged from lubok art and patriotic cartoons to almost photographic renderings of scenes. In general, they concentrated on one scene or motif, which they usually overemphasized to arouse the observer's curiosity.

Russian war films covered a wide range of themes. Newsreels and films glorifying Russian victories were allegedly based on reality. Many sentimental films told stories about refugees, heroic self-sacrifice for the motherland, weeping mothers, idyllic village life, and German atrocities. Some films were devoted exclusively to German bloodthirstiness and the secrets and mysteries of the enemy countries; others had a little bit of everything, a veritable patriotic potpourri. Finally, some films elevated the war to a giant "battle of the nations," complete with all the technological innovations of this first "modern" war.

The quality of a poster that announced a film was usually not related to its subject or to the company that was releasing it. A company would issue cheap posters for one film and lavish ones for a similar film. Films that featured military action, however, tended to be announced on shoddy posters; those that dealt with mystery and the sensational were usually advertised more elaborately. Thus the least imaginative posters were the standard fare of the Skobelev Committee, which put out a large number of newsreels and patriotic films and used nothing but national symbolism or photos on its posters (Figs. 37 and 38).[87] A big "battle of the nations" film, usually a Western import made with a vast budget and the much-vaunted "cast of thousands," was heralded by appropriately glossy renderings of dreadful futuristic weapons that foreshadowed the *Star Wars* epics (Fig. 39).

Whereas the purely military movies concentrated on front-line actions, films about the enemy dealt in atrocities and mysteries that captured the imagination of an audience. The posters for these films were consequently more original. Thus a film about the secrets of the harem (a very popular theme of the time), which featured a white slave, a journalist-detective, and people lost in the desert, was adver-

СКОБЕЛЕВСКІЙ
КОМИТЕТЪ

ЧТО СКАЗАЛЪ
ГЕНЕРАЛЪ-АДЪЮТАНТЪ
БРУСИЛОВЪ ?

37. M. Kal'manson's poster for *What Did Adjutant General Brusilov Say?* (*Chto skazal general-ad"iutant Brusilov?*) (Moscow: Skobelev Committee, n.d.), 71 × 103 cm. Gosudarstvennyi muzei istorii Sankt-Peterburga.

38. *The Poor Chap Died in an Army Hospital* (*Umer bedniaga v bol'nitse voennoi*)
(Moscow: Skobelev Committee, [1916]), 70 × 105 cm. Gosudarstvennyi
muzei istorii Sankt-Peterburga.

39. *Battle for the Freedom of Nations (Steel Wonders)* (*Bor'ba za svobodu narodov [Stal'nyia chudovishcha]*) (Moscow: Kozlovskii, Iur'ev, n.d.), 105 × 75 cm. Gosudarstvennyi muzei istorii Sankt-Peterburga.

tised on a rather spooky poster (Fig. 40). Austrian moral decay was the subject of a film based on the so-called Mayerling affair—the mysterious deaths of the Austrian archduke Rudolf and his mistress, Marie Vetsera, in 1889. The poster for this picture (Fig. 41) nicely conveys the expressiveness of film actors' faces in these silent films. "Bloody Wilhelm" actually showed up in a spy movie, advertised by himself in what appears to be the first Russian poster showing a crowned head of state as an animal or insect (Fig. 42).

Thus the style of a Russian war film poster depended on the subject of the film it was advertising. In comparison with posters that promoted relief efforts and war loans, they appear unconventional indeed. Nowhere else was it possible to see so much blood and so many corpses, so much suffering humanity and such fantastic weaponry. Interestingly, these were the only posters that depicted the enemy,

40. *The Secrets of the Harem* (*Tainy garema*) (Moscow: Kal'manson, n.d.), 70 × 105 cm. Gosudarstvennyi muzei istorii Sankt-Peterburga.

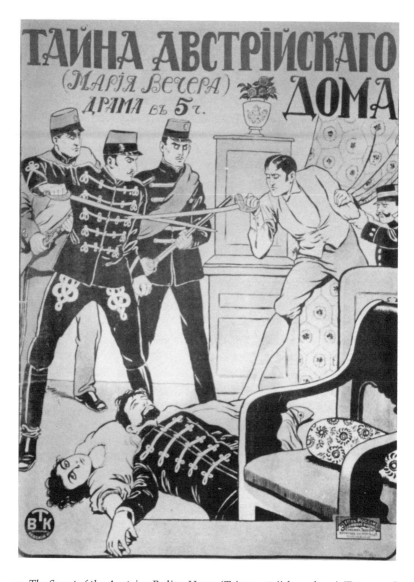

41. *The Secret of the Austrian Ruling House* (*Taina avstriiskago doma*) (Petrograd: Ekonomich. Tipolit., [1916]), 66 × 96 cm. Gosudarstvennyi muzei istorii Sankt-Peterburga.

42. *Bloody Espionage* (*Krovavyi shpionazh*) (Petrograd: Ekonomich. Tipolit., n.d.), 68 × 97 cm. Gosudarstvennyi muzei istorii Sankt-Peterburga.

though other types of wartime posters in the West frequently did so. Russian war relief and loan posters never showed so much as a German soldier, let alone Wilhelm. Film posters obviously borrowed from a greater variety of visual arts. Aside from lubki and commercial posters, they drew particularly on cartoons, postcards, and, of course, the films themselves.[88]

Film posters were closest to commercial posters in their function. They had to sell a product, so they had to fulfill the demands of the market, in this case the market for fantasy. Like the films they advertised, these posters represented a world far removed from the social consciousness, moralistic exhortations, and professional heroism of war relief and loan posters. They instead offered a feeling of patriotism for the belly—an inexpensive morsel to be enjoyed in the safety and comfort of a movie house.

Posters offering horrors, secrets and mysteries, sentimental stories, technological wonders, but also Russian heroism at the front attracted increasing numbers of people to the movie houses during the war. Thematically, they reflected what many people may have found most interesting about the war: its gruesome side, juicy clichés, some feeling of superiority, a clear-cut division between good and bad. As a subgroup of Russian war posters, they contributed the most original and daring motifs to that genre, despite the black-and-white prints on cheap paper and the often low artistic quality.

Russian war posters were so varied in their aims, messages, and stylistic forms that no overall critique is possible. Though Nina Baburina is certainly correct when she argues that Russian patriotic posters were not so straightforward as their Western counterparts, she considers only war relief and loan posters, which she subsumes under the emergent genre of "social poster" (*sotsial'nyi plakat*). Film posters, as we have seen, were less restrained. They openly attacked the enemy and played on patriotic feelings that were rooted more in the sensational than in social consciousness.[89]

As a phenomenon of mass culture and aesthetic conventions, Russian war posters thus reveal a variety of patriotisms. They reflect a social consciousness that was manifested in widespread charity and couched in patriotic imagery. Suffering soldiers and other realistic depictions had an edge on national symbolism and invocations of a great tradition: they were closer to the humaneness of charity and had a clearer message and a direct emotional appeal. War loan posters were certainly no lower in artistic quality. Some of them were highly professional, comparable to anything produced in the West. Yet by their very nature, they had to transmit some sort of official patriotism, and here their efforts were too timid to stimulate the emotions they aimed to arouse. By 1916 their clean and restrained heroism was no longer convincing.

War film posters asked for no financial sacrifice—enthusiastic audiences found the films well worth a few kopeks at the box office—and they were free of social or state-patriotic obligations. Like the films they were advertising, they covered a wide field of patriotic fantasies—the fears, horrors, feelings of national superiority, and sentimentality released by the war. These mostly low-budget productions reveal a totally different type of patriotism: patriotism not as social responsibility but as a consumer good, a cultural stimulus, and an exciting by-product of the war.

Russian war posters, consequently, reflected all aspects of patriotism, from popular civic attitudes to official propaganda and the commercial exploitation of patriotic feelings. They also displayed a wide range of styles, motifs, and artistic quality. Their target group, therefore, was obviously a diverse society with diverse understandings of patriotism, which the posters on the walls tried to tap and mobilize.

Russian patriotism manifested itself visually in a wide variety of forms. Coins bearing the heads of the allied rulers and the double-headed eagle were minted; tear-off calendars presented pictures of famous generals and included curious facts about the war among their daily "wisdoms" (Fig. 43); stamps were printed in honor of military units, usually showing soldiers in action or national symbols.[90] The widespread display of the national flag, especially at the beginning of the war, was the most common and conventional visual way of expressing patriotism. The tricolored badges worn by people who had contributed to street collections can be seen as a less sophisticated and individualistic means of expressing patriotism than postcards. Finally, there was the first propaganda train in Russia, long before the Bolsheviks introduced agitprop: French journalists on their way home after war was declared found their railroad car turned into a patriotic newspaper, covered with cartoons about Wilhelm II and the latest news and funny stories from the front. This spontaneous show of patriotic enthusiasm was not unique to Russia; German soldiers deco-

43. Tear-off calendar for 1915 (Moscow: Sytin, 1914). Gosudarstvennyi muzei istorii Sankt-Peterburga.

rated their trains with jokes and cartoons showing "Serbian terrorists" and "French weaklings."[91]

What connected such diverse genres as lubki, cartoons, postcards, posters, and calendars? Aside from their stylistic similarities and borrowings, they all drew on a set of traditional and historical themes, clichés, and symbols. Such "visual keywords," as Kämpfer calls them, transcend sociocultural borders. Wilhelm and the spiked helmet stood for the villain both in elitist cartoons and on cheap postcards; Cossacks, St. George, and the double-headed eagle represented Russian might both on the pages of peasant-soldier magazines and in the park of Count Sheremetev.

To be sure, there were qualitative and chronological differentiations within visual patriotic culture. Caricatures catered to an educated audience, lubki to the masses. For various reasons, both ceased to exist as purveyors of patriotism or as art forms early in the war. By offering a wide variety of styles appropriate for all occasions, the new postcards and posters encouraged the convergence of cultural levels beyond the sharing of patriotic imagery. This phenomenon of cultural convergence under the influence of a unifying patriotic stimulus, by the way, could also be noticed in England during the war.[92]

Russian patriotism, as reflected in the visual arts, took on a new quality in the first half of 1915. The sudden decline of exaggeratedly heroic pictures and satirical attacks on the enemy in favor of sentimental scenes and fantasy themes were obvious reactions to Russia's disastrous military situation. That charity replaced heroism on posters and postcards reflected a war-weary nation's longing for peace. Caricatures, too, dropped the patriotic theme and returned to social criticism. Only official propaganda—war loan posters, the various pictorial materials put out by the Skobelev Committee—tried to hold up heroic ideals. The split was not between high and popular culture but between the state and a society that had lost all interest in the war, relegated it to the realm of fantasy and sensation, or tried to minimize its repercussions in acts of social responsibility.

2

Performing Patriotism: The War on Stage

The visual arts communicated several brands of patriotism and used diverse images and forms to capture the imaginations of observers. The performing arts were similarly rich in patriotic expression. By the turn of the twentieth century, public entertainment was as diverse in Russia as in any Western country. Industrialization and increasing commerce brought Western cultural fashions to blend with traditional forms of Russian urban culture. At the same time, entertainment became increasingly democratized as people of high and low social strata mingled at theaters, the circus, and variety shows. These were the main places for cultural communication and consumption until the rise of the cinema in the 1910s. In 1914, all the performing arts reacted to the war with a massive outburst of patriotism. Just as in the visual arts, different understandings of patriotism soon developed, and its social aspects became more important as charity displaced jingoism.

Welcome to the Big Top: German Pigs, Wrestling with Wilhelm, and Other Patriotic Circus Acts

In the years before World War I, the Russian circus had become quite a heterogeneous art form. Performers not usually associated with the circus—tango dancers, actors, wrestlers—shared billing with the traditional equestrians and clowns as audiences became increasingly diverse. The various social groups were neatly kept apart in the circus building or tent, but everyone went to the circus. Ordinary people crowded the galleries and swarmed out to the street during intermissions; the bourgeois and aristocratic visitors to Petrograd's Circus Ciniselli, for example, sat in the first rows and boxes, and during the breaks they promenaded through carpeted hallways, viewed exotic fish in aquariums, and sipped champagne at the buffet.[1]

Patriotic circus pantomimes, which originated in France as reenactments of famous battles with scores of people and animals, were revived with great success. In Russia the first patriotic pantomimes had been staged both at the circus and in gigantic open-air productions during and after the war with Turkey in 1877–78. In the open-air show *The War with Turkey* in St. Petersburg's Krestovskii Park, for example, more than one hundred fully equipped footsoldiers and cavalrymen on horseback crossed a river on boats, built pontoon bridges for heavy artillery pieces, and attacked fake fortresses amidst the thunder and smoke of explosions. Sometimes even carrier pigeons took part in the action. On a smaller scale and with less technical extravagance, patriotic shows and historical reenactments were performed on urban fairgrounds well into the 1880s. The *balagan* (fair booth) of the St. Petersburg entrepreneur Vasilii Malafeev was especially famous for its dramatization of the battle against the Mongols on the field of Kulikovo in 1380.[2]

Technical wonders, patriotic imagery, and horseback acrobatics were the main ingredients of pantomimes during World War I. All major circuses opened the 1914–15 season with extravagant patriotic shows. In October 1914, the prestigious Circus Ciniselli produced the spectacle *Hero of the World War; or, For Tsar, Motherland, and Slavdom!* by A. Ia. Alekseev-Iakovlev. Under the direction of Scipione Ciniselli and with props and lighting effects provided by the Petrograd fairground entrepreneur Abram Leifert, seven scenes and a "brilliant apotheosis" offered a set of short dramatic pieces that reflected some of the main motifs of wartime patriotic culture. A Slavic dance introducing Serbia as Russia's brother was followed by reenactments of the massive street demonstrations in the capital on 20 July. Next came the departure of troops from a train platform, complete with moving train. Depictions of the still distant war showed the "barbarians of the twentieth century" killing "Russian patriots" in a border town and the famous exploit of the Cossack Koz'ma Kriuchkov remade into a spectacular horseback number. Finally the unity of Russia, France, Britain, and all the other allies was heralded in symbolic personifications. Seventy-five musicians and over two hundred players participated in the show, which was so successful that it was repeated many times, though the censor complained that some actors did not adhere to the authorized script.[3]

Similar spectacles, featuring increasingly sophisticated technical tricks and a growing variety of patriotic motifs, enlivened other major circuses as well. Petrograd's "Modern" Circus, which had to postpone its first show several times because foreign performers under contract could not travel to Russia, opened the season with the four-act pantomime *Bloody Knights,* in which a captured Cossack escaped and took a German officer prisoner, the Germans executed a Polish priest, and a German nurse killed a Russian officer. Satan, as Wilhelm II, ordered his generals to oppress the world with fire and sword, and to burn little children.[4]

Bloody Knights was so successful that the Circus "Modern" staged two more pantomimes immediately afterward. In *The Triumph of the Powers,* a "political sketch" by A. V. Bobrishchev-Pushkin, actors personified the warring countries. Later restaged at the Imperial Mariinskii Theater as a benefit show under the direction of the avant-garde director Vsevolod Meierhold, it featured allegorical sets and costumes designed by Sergei Sudeikin. England, for example, wore a headdress shaped like a ship, and France's cape was covered with Bourbon lilies. In *The Powers of Hell,* Wilhelm II, Franz Joseph, and the sultan were trundled into the ring in wheelbarrows, like loads of manure, while devils danced around them. The show closed with an "apotheosis" produced by Ivan Lebedev or Diadia Vania, the organizer and referee of popular wrestling matches.[5]

The public's fascination with Wilhelm II was so great that he even appeared in Ciniselli's popular children's pantomime *Cinderella.* Many years earlier, it had become customary to include various famous figures among the guests in the ballroom scene—Napoleon, Tolstoi, Bismarck—all played by children. After August 1914, Wilhelm and Franz Joseph showed up among the guests and were literally kicked out with the vociferous approval of the others.[6]

The patriotic pantomimes of World War I were thus more than reenactments of famous battles. To satisfy a more diversified audience, circuses added such elements as satire, abstraction, and allegory to their "realistic" battle shows. Of course, the fighting scenes were still impressive with the multitude of participants, the smoke, the noise, and the clear winners. But such scenes could now also be seen on (allegedly) more realistic newsreels at the movies, which in the eyes of the audience must have made circus pantomimes seem disappointingly artificial. The limitations of "realism" led to a transcendence of reality in the form of allegorical and satirical representations. It also resulted in an increased number of acrobatic acts, particularly in the form of the *dzhigitovka*, the classical Russian horseback number so closely related to Cossack prowess, as well as an increased use of technical tricks that reflected the general fascination with technology among Russian circus audiences. This fascination was most evident in the pantomime *The Great War of 1914 on the Ground, at Sea, and in the Air: The Deluge of Belgium* at Moscow's Nikitin Circus, which featured a real inundation of the ring and an air battle between planes and a zeppelin in the cupola. The aged Akim Nikitin, by the way, was one of the most actively patriotic of Russian circus directors. He staged many patriotic pantomimes and gave large amounts of money to charity.[7]

The standard finales of patriotic pantomimes were the "grand apotheoses," which usually pictured Russia and its allies in folkloric costumes or as an accumulation of such national symbols as flags, heraldic signs, and national anthems. After the military action, the maltreatment of the kaiser, and the technical wonders, these finales cast a quasi-religious aura over the shows, particularly since the national anthem had traditionally been played only on important holidays before the war. They eased the razzle-dazzle into a festive patriotic contemplation and put all the acts and attractions into an ideological frame, into the "popular system of the world" that Paul Bouissac has found in the circus. During the first months of the war, this system made good triumph over evil in both the feats of individual heroes and the display of national symbols, which remained neutral enough to allow everyone to share some feeling of patriotic community in the face of official and authoritative heraldry.[8]

Clowns had more difficulties with such a simplistic and positive interpretation of patriotism. Traditionally their role had been to comment on the latest talk in town, to criticize authority, to turn hierarchies upside down, to let the audience judge rulers, politicians, and other important people—to "redistribute power," in Joel Schechter's words. Under the conditions of censorship, this was a difficult though not impossible undertaking, as anecdotes of such famous clowns as Anatolii and Vladimir Durov had shown. Particularly famous was the story of the time Anatolii was forced to bow to the Odessa city governor, Zelënyi (which means "green"). The clown took immediate revenge: he showed a variety of animals bowing to a green boar, and then he rode through the city in a cart pulled by a green pig. How now could clowns suddenly support the interests of rulers? Even if they wanted to do so, how could they promote patriotism without giving up their chief raison d'être?[9]

The solution closest at hand was a simple transfer of criticism to authorities in the enemy camp. This meant the same dramatic elements, the same tricks as usual, but with a twist—clowns now implicitly closed ranks with a system they normally ridiculed. The main target was the kaiser, whom they attacked in monologues, jokes, puns, mimicry, and animal metaphors. The censor, however, prohibited attacks deemed too rude and direct. Crowned heads, even those of enemies, were not open to unrestrained abuse that might lead to the drawing of analogies. Thus many jokes and monologues were deleted from the scripts of the clown Eduard Korrado, who compared Wilhelm to pigs, dogs, and other animals.[10]

Working under censorship made some clowns more inventive. Not outspoken criticism and obvious jokes but subtle hints, even ambiguity were their trademarks. The musical clowns Bim and Bom (Ivan Radunskii and Mechislav Stanevskii), for example, devised a skit for Moscow's Salamonskii Circus in which Bom, dressed as the Turkish sultan and accompanied by a monkey, sang a patriotic ditty to the sound of a hurdy-gurdy. This portrayal of the sultan as a wandering organ grinder might not have passed the censor in written form. The quick-change artists Konstantin and Leon Tanti used no script at all when they appeared in a revue ridiculing the German army and Prussian Junkerdom in Efim Efimov's circus in 1915. That same year, Paul Kodanti entertained audiences at the Circus Ciniselli with a trained pig that happened to bear a striking resemblance to the commander of the German armies on the eastern front, General Paul von Hindenburg.[11]

The use of animals, particularly pigs, to attack the higher-ups was a technique most skillfully developed by the Durov brothers. When World War I broke out, Anatolii and Vladimir Durov were already fighting their own war. Both were famous, and both were vain and competitive. They were satirical clowns and animal trainers, but Anatolii leaned more toward satirical verse and political jokes, whereas Vladimir concentrated more on animal acts and even developed his own scientific method of training animals. Both of them saw World War I as a public relations opportunity. Vladimir happened to be on tour in Berlin when the war broke out. Once safely home, he lionized himself as a prisoner of war both in his performances and in a booklet titled *In German Captivity*. He recounted how the Germans called all Russians pigs, how the stereotypical cries of Hoch! (Up!) resounded everywhere, and how he got even. It seems he trained his landlady's dog to respond to the cry of "Hoch!" by lifting his rear leg and doing what came naturally. Perhaps he did—after all, Vladimir *was* in Berlin in 1914—but another of his stories is less plausible, for Anatolii told it too. On tour in Berlin long before the war, Anatolii/Vladimir asked a pig to choose between a loaf of bread and a helmet. The pig, in Durov's voice, answered: "*Will Helm*" ("I want the helmet"). This joke, according to the brothers, led to the clown's arrest.[12]

As the war wore on, Anatolii harped more insistently on the patriotic theme. In 1915 his *War of the Animals* was an overwhelming success at Petrograd's Circus Ciniselli. He loosed pigs and goats among geese and turkeys, and his running commentary on the chaos in the ring drew parallels with the real war. This act was based on a film that Durov had made in late 1914. *Napoleon Reversed* (*Napoleon naiznanku*), released by Drankov in Moscow, featured a monkey in the role of a new Napoleon (actually Wilhelm II), geese, ducks, dogs, and pigs as ordinary Germans, rats as German soldiers, foxes as European diplomats, and pigs as the German General Staff. The scenario is more spectacular than coherent: Thanks to the intrigues of the monkey-kaiser, fights erupt in Turkey (between dogs). In a peaceful German town, an art professor (also a monkey) appears and destroys all the artworks in the local gallery that he considers alien to the German genius (Anatolii was prescient as well as clever). An enemy spy (a fox) sets the city on fire and the train in which the population flees is shelled, with great loss of life. Elsewhere the pigs of the General Staff are awaiting news of their victory, but the message they receive tells them that the Gallic cockerel has annihilated the German army and proclaimed eternal peace.[13]

Both film and circus act presented a strange mixture of heraldic animals, pets, and livestock with more or less clear symbolism. Before the war, Durov had used pigs as the embodiments of high-ranking people in the reversed hierarchy of the circus; now pigs played the major villains in his wartime shows. This use of pigs blended with a nationalist motif that was popular in other countries as well and that could be found, for example, on postcards and in press cartoons: Wilhelm as a wild boar, his soldiers as pigs, his subjects as *kolbasniki,* or sausage eaters (who apparently ingest rather than embody the metaphor). Thus, pigs were so rich in both social and nationalist associations that the censor found it difficult to eradicate them completely.[14]

Insulting the enemy was only one way for clowns to express patriotism. After the first months of the war, domestic issues became salient again, and clowns skewered war speculators and profiteers, who were generally blamed for the worsening shortages and accused of immoral behavior. Instead of attacking state authorities, clowns now criticized a social evil related to the war. They became the advocates of a population suffering from the war and thus expressed what one might call social patriotism, loyalty to the people of the country rather than to a ruler or an ideology.

Criticism of profiteering and shortages was nothing new. During the war with Japan in 1904–5, for example, Anatolii Durov had attacked speculators in an act with trained rats. In 1915 he attacked them again, particularly in his "War Riddles," short riddles and wordplays that were taken over by other clowns as well. Criticism of speculators and deficiencies at home, of course, did not detract from attacks on the enemy. Anatolii Durov had both in his repertoire, as did his son Anatolii, who was jailed for ridiculing the tsarist air force in 1914 but was applauded for his patriotic diatribes against the German barbarians in 1915 and 1916. Because clowns had to react to the talk of the town, the contents of their acts depended heavily on the location where they were presented. Provincial towns, where Anatolii played in 1915 and

1916, were not likely to be the sites of large-scale speculation. Here people were more conservative, and their concern focused on the war's impact on their sons, brothers, and husbands. Conventional patriotic acts directed against the enemy still garnered loud applause. In the big industrial cities and the capitals, however, attacks against profiteers and speculators, some of whom were often sitting in the front rows, were a guaranteed success, because the rest of the audience could see the sumptuous lifestyle, the cars, and the expensive clothing of these people every day while everything they needed to sustain their own lives grew scarcer.[15]

Some clowns went beyond criticism of profiteering to ridicule patriotism or express war-weariness. In 1916 Sergei Al'perov and his son Dmitrii had to brave the anger of an officer in the audience who was offended by an irreverent reference to the St. George's Cross, the highest military decoration. In the same year a song by the clown Dmitrii Kol'petti told about the exhaustion of the German people and their pleas to Wilhelm for peace. In a later song titled "Dream" ("Son"), Kol'petti dreamed of a flight over a peaceful city, where everything was available in abundance:

> I'm comfortably stretching out
> In the Devil's airplane
> And taking off, a light-winged bird,
> The capital below me.
> Looking down, I rub my eyes:
> The capital—a paradise.
> No lines, and lots of goods all over,
> The warehouses are opened up
> With flour, soap, and even sugar.
> They're selling vodka and cognac.
> The people all are of good cheer,
> And not a single German here.
> I ask about our whereabouts.
> "The capital"—the Devil spouts.
> You Devil, don't you dare to fool me,
> If you don't want me to box your ears,
> And tell me, where are all the trials
> That we endured the last two years?
> "It's all been gone for quite a while,"

Explains the Devil with a smile,
"And changed forever and for good.
Now people live the best of lives.
There are no sick, no prisoners,
No profiteers and speculators,
There are no jails, no creditors,
No bloodsuckers such as landlords even.
And firewood is now plentiful. . . ."
I open my eyes—and all is gone.[16]

The joke about the St. George's Cross and Kol'petti's songs expressed war-weariness and at the same time transcended social patriotism with its concern for economic difficulties. By trivializing a major patriotic symbol, the Al'perovs attacked patriotism in its conventional sense and indirectly declared war against the war itself, its idea, not just its economic repercussions. They injected an ideological element into their show by desacralizing the highest official honor for patriotic behavior. Kol'petti, for his part, brought in a human vision, a longing for peace and an anarchic paradise that promised more than just material prosperity.

Clowns obviously had many ways to express patriotism—outward appearance, animals, and particularly "the word that flew and hit like a bullet," as Dmitrii Al'perov put it. They also introduced a social and even utopian component, defining patriotism less in abstract terms of motherland and nation than as a moral responsibility toward one's fellows. According to a contemporary journal, however, voices were raised against so-called intelligent clowns, those who allegedly talked too much about problems. After all, it was suggested, people still went to the circus to have fun and to forget their everyday problems. "They simply wanted to laugh," as one critic remarked. Thus if clowns wanted to satisfy their audiences (and the censors) and at the same time communicate their convictions, they had to walk a thin line. Another way out of this situation, however, was available to them: they could stick to a light repertoire and become active in charity.[17]

Clowns solicited donations of money and warm clothing either during their own acts or as participants in one of the many benefits that usually brought together a wide variety of entertainers. Some of them went to hospitals and played for the wounded. The Al'perovs even performed for German POWs. Benefit performances organized by

Moscow Artists for the Russian Army and War Victims at Nikitin's and Salamonskii's circuses were very successful. Here Bim and Bom appeared with such celebrities as the actors Ivan Moskvin and Ol'ga Knipper of the Moscow Art Theater. In fact, one of these performances in January 1916 was produced by Bim, who at the time was the director of the Salamonskii circus. The show offered everything from dramatic sketches to horseback acrobatics, a women's folk chorus, clowns, and illusionists. A wide variety of circus performers thus got a chance to show their patriotic spirit, which was otherwise difficult to convey in the circus ring.[18]

Acrobats who wanted to express patriotism could add a folkloric touch to their acts by alluding to typical Russian traditions or by wearing some sort of national dress. Vitalii Lazarenko, for example, who was famous for his leap over three elephants in early 1914, became known as "Jumper Cossack" during the war, a clear reference to the widely admired valor and patriotism of Cossacks. The troupe of the horseback acrobat Prozerpi caused a sensation in 1916 with its "Russian Troika." On a fast-moving sleigh ajingle with little bells, the acrobats formed a human pyramid; they jumped from a springboard in the center of the ring into the moving troika, and leaped from the sleigh to the horses and back again. Their stylized boyar costumes were echoed by the boyar caftan sometimes worn by Akim Nikitin, the patriotic founder of the first purely Russian circus, and a traditional Russian coat became the trademark of Diadia Vania, the folksy referee of wrestling matches.[19]

Wrestling matches were part of patriotic circus culture. Popular in the Russian circus since the turn of the century, they were promoted in particular by Diadia Vania and had a special place in circus performances, with their own rituals and stars. Soviet scholars interpreted such matches as both an outlet for aggressive emotions in a repressive state and an expression of a subconscious longing for strength and power in society as a whole, but especially among the intelligentsia after the Revolution of 1905. The writers Aleksandr Blok, Aleksandr Kuprin, and Aleksandr Grin were fascinated by the circus and in particular by wrestling, as many of their works attest.[20]

Wrestling, however, also includes the concept of justice, as Roland Barthes has shown: the wrestler who fights unfairly must pay for his or her misdeeds (after 1907 there were also matches between women in Russia). Perhaps this is why wrestling became so popular in Russia, where the century-old idea of *pravda*—justice, truth, and right all bound up in one word—was very strong. World War I shifted the idea of pravda to the international plane. At least in the eyes of Russian patriots, the war was also fought for justice, as the lubok "Russia for Justice" (Fig. 11) suggests. Wrestling matches could thus be seen as manifestations of patriotism.[21]

The view of sport as an outlet for nationalist emotions was not unusual in nineteenth- and twentieth-century Europe. As big attractions in the Russian circus during World War I, wrestlers and weight lifters provided a chance to identify Russian muscle power with the power and strength of the country as a whole. The wrestler who billed himself as the Russian Lion knew what he was about; so did Diadia Vania when he donned his folk outfit.[22]

A story that appeared in Diadia Vania's journal *Gerkules*, the principal publication in the field, provided the ideological frame for wrestling matches during the war. The story begins before the war with a fight between Karl Schwarz, the German champion, and Nikolai Moroz, a Russian wrestler. Before the match, the Russian audience insists on hearing the national anthem, and everyone joins in as it is played. During the match, Karl, who wears whiskers like Wilhelm II's, fouls Nikolai, and the audience screams: "Down with the German!" "Get him in a headlock!" "Kill the sausage eater!" Finally the referee and other wrestlers overwhelm the "brutal German." Disqualified, he goes to sit in his room at the Old Dresden Hotel, drinking, of course, beer. Several years later, Schwarz and Moroz accidentally meet again on the battlefield. Sportsmanlike Moroz challenges Schwarz to a match. Now the German has to pay for his misbehavior, and finally he dies from an old wound. This story transfers the nationalist clichés of German brutality, deceit, and beer-and-sausage culture to the world of sport, with obvious analogies to war. The graphic presentation of the story is also suggestive. At the top of the page is a drawing of a wrestler grappling with Wilhelm II; at the bottom is a vignette of a drum, a rifle with bayonet, and pairs of dumbbells.[23]

Not only Russia was wrestling for justice; its allies did their best to overwhelm the "German brute" as well. Belgian, French, and other wrestlers appeared on the pages of *Gerkules*, and even Maurice Maeterlinck, the Belgian poet, was honored as an amateur boxer who now (allegedly) was fighting the Germans. These fictions presented war as a sports event, as a match of good buddies against an evil enemy. Appeals for donations and the greetings of wrestlers who were serving in the army ate away at the illusion of an invincible Russia propagated by the journal and by the remaining wrestlers in the circus ring.[24]

The reality of the war hit the Russian circus very hard. More and more performers and horses were drafted, food for the animals became scarce, and some performers and at least one circus director were forced out of work because of their German citizenship. Thus the circus of Albert Suhr was dissolved as early as July 1914, and the clown Nikolai Buiakovskii was demoted to the position of lighting technician and bill poster. The requisitioning of horses was a particular problem. Pëtr Tarakhno, a clown who used to play for his comrades in the trenches, told a heartbreaking story about a horseback acrobat whose career was ended when she lost her only horse to the army. There were many such cases. Only performers and circus entrepreneurs who were citizens of an allied country, such as the Italian Rudolfo Truzzi, were able to keep all their horses. Because of the de facto closing of Russia's western border, few foreign performers could come to Russia, and the circus was peculiarly dependent on traveling performers and foreign stars. Directors thus had to improvise. Either performers could take on functions they were not really trained for or shows could concentrate on one sort of act, such as wrestling, which for a long period was the only attraction offered by the Circus Gorets in Smolensk.[25]

The Russian circus went through many changes during World War I. Pantomimes were revived and staged with great success in the first months of the war. With their crowd scenes, technical effects, acrobatics, and allegorical scenes, they offered action and movement, drama, military bravura, clear winners, and obvious patriotic messages. Clear winners could also be expected in wrestling matches. These shows presented an illusion of irresistible power and unlimited strength with definite social, moral, and nationalist overtones. During the war years, the idea of Russia fighting for a just cause and punishing the wicked Germans from a position of moral superiority was an integral part of these matches and their journalistic orchestration. Straightforward patriotism with strong national self-esteem and a clear concept of the enemy emanated from both patriotic pantomimes and wrestling matches. As the war progressed, however, pantomimes all but disappeared and more and more wrestlers had to abandon the circus ring for the front line. In the circus, as elsewhere, patriotism acquired new meanings when it was exposed to the realities of war.

Clowns had ways to show their patriotic convictions, but first they faced the problem of integrating something as serious and official as patriotism into their world of reversed hierarchies and unconditional laughter. They were used to attacking, not to selling an ideology. Attacks on the enemy, in particular on Kaiser Wilhelm, were consequently the easiest solution. Clowns could keep their jokes, animal acts, or funny songs and still make an implicit patriotic statement. Attacking the enemy was not the same as praising the tsar or promoting Great Russian chauvinism. Benefits and the increasingly fashionable political monologues gave clowns a means to express positively what they really understood by patriotism. For many of them, particularly after the first few months of the war, it meant loyalty to the people, not to abstract national symbols and an imperial ideology. When clowns attacked profiteers and expressed war-weariness, however, they exchanged the role of clown for that of the variety artist or political satirist. Instead of turning things upside down and playing with them, they took problems seriously and confronted their audiences with unexpected realities that were not always appreciated. People wanted to laugh, perhaps now more than ever. Most clowns, therefore, mingled conventional jokes with their political commitment.

The Russian circus as a world in microcosm thus presented patriotism in various ways during World War I. With its diversity of acts, the circus was flexible enough to combine different understandings of patriotism. It could react to changes in the popular mood and try to exert influence by direct interaction with the audience. Thus it helped to reconfirm a variety of patriotic values. In the circus ring it became clear that patriotism was not a monolithic idea, that it had breaks and different meanings, which often remained vague and ambiguous, just as in real life.

Balalaikas, Tangos, and Patriotic Songs: The Wartime *Estrada*

The broad diversity that characterized Russian cultural life and in particular urban entertainment in the first years of the twentieth century is best seen in the *estrada*, the variety show. Estrada encompasses everything from music, theater, and poetry recitations to dance, puppet shows, and the circus. It has been argued that it does not constitute a genre of its own, but rather is a conglomeration of performing arts. Yet estrada is a typical Russian phenomenon with roots in fairground culture, literary evenings, and the Russian theater of the nineteenth century. Combined with such later Western influences as the music hall, the *café-chantant* (or *shantan,* as the Russians called it), and the political cabaret, the Russian estrada of the early twentieth century was an art form that touched almost all levels of urban society.[26]

Shows were put on in restaurants, gardens, all sorts of theaters, people's houses, cabarets, nightclubs, the circus, and multipurpose halls in schools and other institutions. During the war, estrada shows even found their way into hospitals and out to the front line. The open stage encourages improvisation and interaction between performers and audience. Shows could be altered to include the latest talk of the town, cultural values could be exchanged and confirmed in direct dialogue, and new trends and fashions could emerge. Estrada shows were very diverse. An acrobatic act might come after a poem or a gypsy song and be followed by a play, a film, or a dance number. One show might concentrate exclusively on poetry, another on a gypsy singer. Consequently, there was no such thing as a typical estrada artist. Dancers, clowns, actors, and singers alike moved between their traditional spheres in the performing arts and the estrada; other performers focused on one particular field of estrada, perhaps folk music or ballroom dancing.[27]

The war had a strong impact on estrada. Attendance figures dropped sharply in the first days of the war in response to the general uncertainty, the draft, an initial moving up of the closing time to 11 P.M., and the prohibition of alcoholic beverages. But in the fall attendance went up again. The contents of many shows changed as new kinds of performances were developed. Stanislav Klitin's division of estrada into rhetorical, instrumental, vocal, choreographic, and acrobatic categories is less helpful than a model based on the various ways estrada responded to the war—a boom in Russian folklore and tradition, a strong escapist trend, an outpouring of intellectual criticism directed against both the enemy and internal deficiencies, mass-oriented manifestations of patriotism, and finally the creation of new forms of performances in connection with fund-raising activities.[28]

Recollections of common cultural traditions and myths are important contributors to the patriotic spirit of a society. The tendency to
look for one's national identity in a heroic and culturally pristine past
during times of uncertainty is therefore not unusual. During World
War I this interest found expression in Russian estrada as countless
folk singers, storytellers, and musicians became popular. What was
thought to be genuine Russian music filled the programs and even
overtook the fashionable gypsy songs. Heroic epics and folktales were
dug up in remote villages and presented to urban audiences.[29]

Folk choruses had existed in Russia since the 1860s. They sang folk
songs in urban taverns and coffeehouses, and one of them even toured
Western Europe, Africa, and America with a program that included
jingoist songs. The quality of this music was uneven. Some choruses
attempted to present authentic Russian songs, others offered a colorful
mixture of sentimental ballads, or "romances," and even gypsy songs.
The most original chorus, organized in 1911 by Mitrofan Piatnitskii,
consisted of real peasants in authentic costumes from various regions
of the country who contributed their local songs to the group's repertoire. They first sang for small audiences made up largely of musicologists and other urban devotees, but after their initial success, they
performed for a wider audience on a stage decorated like the interior
of a peasant house or a site in a village. Soviet research usually celebrated Piatnitskii's chorus as a genuine expression of the people's
artistic potential and as a deeply "patriotic enterprise" that could
blossom only after the Bolshevik Revolution. During World War I,
however, Piatnitskii gave more performances than the average two or
three per year suggested by Soviet works. In February 1915 alone he
gave four regular concerts and in December 1914 he gave three benefit
performances that were advertised on a poster showing a peaceful
village scene. Like his concerts, the poster offered the dream of an
ideal Russian world and appealed to a romanticized communal spirit
and a common cultural tradition—in other words, to typical patriotic
values.[30]

Most performers of folk songs were not so sophisticated as Piatnitskii. Although the wartime issues of journals such as *Var'ete i tsirk*
were full of ads for "Russian choruses" and "peasant" or "boyar"
singers," few of these performers had real folklorist ambitions. They
did not go out to the villages to collect local music but rather attracted
their audiences with "patriotic songs," "lavish boyar costumes," and

"precious jewelry"; they might don the bast shoes of peasants and thus appear as *lapotniki,* but their costumes made no pretense at authenticity. Condemned by Soviet scholars as inauthentic (which they were) and even harmful to the people (which they were not), these performers presented simplified images of country life, spiced with the dramas of ballads and gypsy songs, to the patrons of urban taverns and vaudeville houses, who cared little about the purity of the music or the preservation of folk art. For them this music meant entertainment in the spirit of the proverb "The song for the heart, the heart for the Motherland" (Pesnia—k serdtsu, serdtse—k Rodine). It was a nostalgic drift back to an ideal world of village culture, which still permeated the worldview of many Russian city dwellers. It consequently confirmed a nebulous feeling of belonging, of being part of a bigger sociocultural community, and thus paralleled on a lower artistic level what Piatnitskii offered for a more erudite audience.[31]

The superstar among the singers of popular songs was Nadezhda Plevitskaia. This self-made singer of rural background was instrumental in displacing the gypsy craze with the patriotic and sentimental songs of village life in the prewar years. Among her admirers were Nikolai II and a host of theater and opera personalities, such as the bass Fëdor Shaliapin and the editor of *Teatr i iskusstvo,* Aleksandr Kugel'. As one of the first Russian gramophone stars, she had the largest audience of any estrada artist of the time, triggering a "Plevitskomania" all over the country and among all social strata. During the war, Plevitskaia, like some of her colleagues, volunteered as a nurse for a couple of months, and on her own time she appeared in her Red Cross outfit and sang folk songs in hospitals for the wounded. Her recordings were played on gramophones in the trenches, on warships, and in officers' messes, offering nostalgic dreams of homey villages and peasant kitchens.

Plevitskaia had given a concert largely of soldiers' songs for a Moscow army unit as early as 1910, and in World War I her patriotic repertoire was particularly popular. Describing one of her benefit performances in Kislovodsk in 1915, Kugel' noted a tragic tone in her voice after her experiences as a nurse and the death of her fiancé at the front. In "O, Rus'!" she sang about village children being led into battle, their spirits high; Russia itself was described as their mother in peasant dress. In another song she reminded soldiers of the legacy of Jesus Christ and of their comrades killed in battle. With such lyrics of

popular heroism and death, Plevitskaia regularly moved her audiences to tears and perfectly reflected the general ambivalence toward the war in 1915. Her songs reflected a mood of retreat into the
shell of a secure communal identity and at the same time a hesitant
hope for victory. By expressing what many people were longing for or
afraid of, she conquered the hearts of mass audiences.[32]

Folk choruses and singers were only one part of the folkloric wave.
Russian folk instruments—the domra, the gusli, and particularly the
balalaika—also experienced a renaissance. As the most typical Russian instrument, the balalaika had been promoted since the 1880s by
the "musician-patriot" Vasilii Andreev and his Great-Russian Orchestra, which in 1914 was granted the privilege of styling itself "Imperial." Andreev had introduced balalaikas of various sizes, from con-
trabass to piccolo—a startling innovation—and he treated them as
orchestral instruments. On his initiative, balalaika courses were organized all over the country and other Great Russian Orchestras were
founded. During World War I many disabled soldiers participated in
these activities, and Andreev's benefit concerts were usually sold out.
All the proceeds of these shows went to the tsarina for support of the
military hospitals she sponsored.[33]

Pseudo folklore of the sort offered by Andreev's balalaika orchestra
was not the business of Ol'ga Ozarovskaia. This narrator and storyteller of heroic epics and old village tales had her biggest success
during the war. A serious student of folklore, she often went to the far
north of Russia to explore the oral traditions of folk poetry. On one of
her trips to the province of Arkhangel'sk she met an old woman by the
name of Mar'ia Krivopolenova, and took her with her to Moscow,
Tver', and Petrograd. Together they recited *byliny*, the old Russian
heroic epics, historical legends, and minstrel songs. Their performances on the stages of theaters, in schools, and in literary circles were
always enthusiastically received by the mostly intellectual
audiences.[34]

Often folk songs, instrumental music, and stories were combined in
one estrada show or mixed with other kinds of acts. Particularly at
benefit performances, balalaika players, storytellers, and folk singers
might appear together with stars of the opera and the stage. Thus at a
charity bazaar sponsored by the Ladies' Circle of the Petrograd School
of Army Medics in December 1915, members of the imperial opera
and the imperial ballet were joined by a Great Russian Orchestra, a

folk chorus, the balalaika soloist B. S. Troianovskii (a friend and student of Andreev), a gusli soloist, four interpreters of Russian songs, a teller of byliny, and the conservatory-educated folk singer M. I. Nelidova. This motley mixture obviously added an earthy, patriotic touch to the bazaar. Like many such events, it revealed a demand that apparently flourished among urban and intellectual audiences, especially in connection with war-related charity. The recollection of national values, the temporary shedding of cosmopolitanism, and the mobilization of indigenous cultural and financial potential were all on the agenda during the war. Folklore provided a point of cultural identification and gave some immediate ersatz meaning to the act of donating money for something as hard to imagine as a maimed human being.[35]

Not everyone, however, was interested in cultural traditions, national identity, or charity events. Many people either did not care about patriotism or simply wanted to forget the war and have fun. For them, estrada offered a variety of entertainments catering to escapist tendencies—the longing for faraway exotic places or the desire for an unrestricted and anarchic freedom. Despite the prohibition of alcohol, bars and nightclubs were booming, dance floors were packed, and a partying craze swept the country. Gypsy musicians and "Romanian" orchestras found a niche in this sort of nightlife, as did a rich assortment of demimonde hangers-on and nouveau riche war profiteers. In this decadent and exotic world shone such stars as Aleksandr Vertinskii, Iza Kremer, and the poet Igor Severianin.[36]

Among the fashionable nightclubs of the time, the most notorious were the Villa Rodé, Rasputin's favorite haunt, and the Akvarium in Petrograd, and the Strel'na and Iar in Moscow, the latter the nightly hangout of the philandering circus director Al'bert Salamonskii. Here the best gypsy bands with the most beautiful singers appeared, high-class prostitutes offered their services, champagne and wine flowed freely, and the latest dance fashions from abroad were celebrated. Only the rich could afford this kind of bohemian life. To get to the Strel'na or the Iar, which were located in a neighborhood that was then beyond the city limits, clients paid between 80 and 150 rubles for a cab on New Year's Eve of 1916–17. A bottle of wine or vodka sold for at least 100 rubles (at a time when a bottle of milk cost 30 kopecks), which included a substantial bribe to the police to circumvent the prohibition law. If a bribe did not work, liquor was sold discreetly in milk jars or lemonade bottles. This system functioned so well that only a few of the posh places really got into trouble with the authorities. One of them, however, was Petrograd's stylish Troitskii Theater, where in 1915 the prompter, the assistant director, and some other employees were discovered to be bootlegging cognac. After this incident, anyone who was offered a glass of cognac was likely to respond, "Oh, you work at the Troitskii?"[37]

Dancing was an entertainment that reached far beyond the expensive world of nightclubs. In a host of dance pavilions and halls, people of all walks of urban life indulged in foreign, especially American rhythms and tunes. The dance craze that was so conspicuous in England, France, and Germany during the war hit Russia with full force. With only a brief delay, the cakewalk and the fox-trot were adopted during these years, first by the haut monde and later by a wider public. Most important was the appearance of the tango, which remains one of the most popular dances in Russia to this day. Record companies quickly picked up the latest fads and multiplied them by the millions, using the gramophone's power as the new legislator of taste. Patriotism and the war were largely absent from the dance floor. After all, people at the time danced partly to transgress traditional mores and to revolt against a system of conventions of which patriotism was an integral part. The popular tune "Krovavoe tango Vil'-gel'ma" (Wilhelm's Bloody Tango) was not really an exception. Although its theme was patriotic, it played on the thrill of a *danse macabre* and the erotic aura of both tango and vampiric blood lust that were so familiar to contemporaries from countless motion pictures. More than patriotic prose, it was this poetry of decadence and death—the "feeling of the end of history," in Boris Groys's words—that made everything seem possible and lured so many people to the loose and sensual wilderness of the dance floors.[38]

Aleksandr Vertinskii became almost synonymous with decadence, apocalyptic pessimism, and refined high life during the war. The star of this salon poet and first Russian singer-songwriter began to rise sharply at the end of 1915, when he appeared at Petrograd's Pavil'on de Pari in the mask of a white Pierrot. This mask of the Italian commedia dell'arte had found a home in a variety of Russian theater productions and artworks. Its tragicomic features expressed the weltschmerz then in vogue among the intelligentsia and high society, and it superbly suited the sophisticated Vertinskii, who had been called "brother Pierrot" during his burdensome duty on a hospital train early in the war.[39]

Vertinskii was neither a first-class poet nor a very good singer, but he was good enough at both endeavors to create highly inspired stage shows. His lyrics—partly his own and partly adaptations of poems by such celebrated authors as Anna Akhmatova, Nikolai Gumilёv, and Igor Severianin—featured a world of broken love, palm trees, South Sea cruises, tropical bars, and narcotics. His *arietki* (little arias) "The Little Creole," "Lily-White Negro" (both dedicated to the film star Vera Kholodnaia), "Cocaine Girl," and "Snowy Lullaby" offered flights into surrealist fantasies. With their diminutives, they suggested a childlike innocence, a retreat into a sheltered childhood of euphoric dreams that stood in sharp contrast to the adult realities of the war. His service on the hospital train had taught Vertinskii those realities all too well. With Vera Kholodnaia, the other great purveyor of illusions during the war, he took his dreams to the wounded in a Moscow hospital. Some seventy maimed and bandaged men propped themselves up to hear Vertinskii sing a few of his songs and dance the tango with Kholodnaia between their beds. For hours after the stars had left, ambulatory patients tangoed up and down the hospital corridors.[40]

Vertinskii's was not the only star to rise during the war. Iza Kremer, a chanteuse and actress from Odessa who was famous for her ability to produce real tears on demand, sang about a "Negro from Zanzibar" and "Madame Lulu of the Boulevard de France" with great success in 1915–16. At the same time, the Ego-Futurist Igor Severianin, who was instrumental in starting the wave of exoticism with such poems as "Lilac Ice Cream!" and "Champagne Polonaise," recited his latest works about pineapples in champagne ("Overture") and "A Light Blue Evening" during his notorious "poetry evenings." Severianin not only transported his audiences to faraway places and ecstatic sensations; as an ardent anti-German, he also appealed to emotions quite of this world, though not without a decadent touch. He recited his patriotic "Poem on Belgium" several times at Petrograd's Stray Dog (Brodiachaia Sobaka) cabaret in 1914 to music by Nikolai Tsybul'skii, alias Graf Okontrer (Count On-the-Contrary), the establishment's eccentric pianist. Severianin's poem honored heroic Belgium by praising the famous oysters of Ostend. In view of the terrible sufferings that Belgium endured in the war, Vladimir Maiakovskii considered this culinary metaphor to be in poor taste.[41]

Escapism and weltschmerz were powerful themes of wartime estrada. Their popularity increased over the course of 1915 and 1916, as
the careers of Vertinskii and Kremer demonstrate. The more burdensome the war became, the more people wanted to get away from it.
Escapist estrada, however, was predominantly entertainment for a
small segment of the intelligentsia and the more affluent urban strata.
From this exalted milieu it filtered down to the lower classes through
gramophone recordings and motion pictures. Few people who could
afford this entertainment were hit hard by the war, and many of them
grew richer because of it. The widening social gap between those
making money from the war and those being sent to the slaughter was
also reflected in estrada. While one part of it provided entertainment
to the profiteers, another part addressed the war in a patriotic but
critical way.

An intellectually ambitious approach to patriotic themes was available in cabarets and theaters in miniature (*teatry miniatiur*), which had
emerged largely in reaction to an elitist dramatic art that many people
considered too realistic. Cabaret was thus an escape for the more
daring actors and a place for avant-garde experiments and new artistic
forms. The Bat (Letuchaia Mysh') cabaret was supported predominantly by actors from the Moscow Art Theater, while Petrograd's
Comedians' Stop (Prival Komediantov) was closely connected with
members of the Aleksandrinskii Theater. Not surprisingly, the programs of these places met high artistic standards and often featured
serious satirical drama in addition to music and literary readings.[42]

Most miniature theaters were less ambitious than cabarets and more
concerned with plain entertainment. They mushroomed during the
war in workers' suburbs, provincial towns, and the metropolitan centers alike. Their quality ranged from the artistic cabaret with an almost
exclusively dramatic repertoire to modest variety shows arranged
around the performance of a movie. Pëtr Solianyi, who under the
pseudonym Pëtr Iuzhnyi regularly wrote about the latest trends in
dramatic art for *Teatr i iskusstvo*, attributed the success of these theaters
to their casual character, their variegated programs, and the brevity of
the performances—all of which reflected the contemporary pace of
life and allowed for quick and inexpensive entertainment, "at any time
of the day and without the need to check coat and overshoes."[43]

Cabarets and most miniature theaters offered a broad spectrum of
patriotic entertainment in addition to their regular repertoire. De-

pending on the main emphasis of their program, they might present recitals of war poetry, patriotic farces and comedies, or nationalist monologues. Petrograd's Stray Dog, for example, featured a series of benefits with Russian music and old romances in November 1914. All the proceeds went to a hospital organized and supported by members of the cabaret. Charity and a touch of folklore, however, were only supplements to the Dog's primary draw—literary evenings and poetry readings featuring prominent Russian writers of the time.

Aside from Igor Severianin, the cabaret presented readings of poetry about the war by Vladimir Maiakovskii, Anna Akhmatova, Sergei Gorodetskii, Nikolai Gumilëv, and others. Antiwar verses, bittersweet transfigurations of the war, and jingoist lyrics were offered side by side, revealing many writers' ambivalence about the war. Maiakovskii, for example, conjured up the horrors of war in his poem "Mother and the Evening Killed by the Germans" at a time when he was painting his crude caricatures for Segodniashnii Lubok. He was obviously torn between hatred for the aggressors and compassion for the suffering soldiers. Since his work for Segodniashnii Lubok was confined to the early months of the war, his attitudes may have evolved over time. For Akhmatova, the war was simply a great human tragedy, which she deplored in such poems as "July 1914," "Consolation," and "Prayer." Gorodetskii saw the war as a cleansing process that would strengthen Russia through moral renewal and imperialist feats. Accordingly, he reproduced the whole array of right-wing imagery and national heroes, such as the pilot Nesterov in the poem "Air Warrior." Gumilëv, finally, romanticized the war as a challenging adventure (he actually enlisted in the army and wrote reports from the front for the newspaper *Birzhevye vedomosti*) yet avoided the excesses of jingoism. The cabaret could thus provide a place for literary discussion of the war and at the same time reflect the variety of attitudes toward patriotism within the literary world.[44]

The Comedians' Stop, which opened in April 1916 to fill the void left by the censors' closing of the Stray Dog, offered a program with stronger theatrical emphasis. Patriotism played only a minor role in these shows. Such directors as Vsevolod Meierhold and Nikolai Evreinov made the Comedians' Stop an important forerunner of the Russian experimental theater of the 1920s. In addition, and continuing a development started at the Stray Dog and Moscow's Bat, it fostered the creation of a children's theater through the revival of the puppet stage, which in its epigrammatic concision was meant to fulfill the cabaret's function of parodying elite theater.

By taking up the almost defunct traditions of puppet theater, in particular of the fairground Petrushka glove-puppet show, cabaret inherited popular and quite harmless nationalist clichés. *Nemets-doktor*, for example, the German doctor, had long been a favorite butt of Petrushka's ridicule. Petrushka teaches him to speak Russian or beats him to death with his club, and sometimes offers him to the cheering audience as a potato or a suckling pig. During the war it seemed natural to replace the doctor with Kaiser Wilhelm. Sergei Sudeikin, the chief set designer and decorator of the Comedians' Stop, drew a picture in which Petrushka is lifting his club over the kaiser's bewhiskered head. In a similar adaptation, another of Petrushka's standard victims, the Corporal, became the Feldwebel. Together with Franz Joseph, Wilhelm II also appeared as a marionette in shows by Nikolai Petrov, a director at the Aleksandrinskii Theater who began his estrada career early in the war in a Petrograd cabaret with the characteristic designation Petrushka and who later, as Kolia Peter, became one of the leading puppeteers of the Comedians' Stop.[45]

The puppet stage was not the only theatrical experiment of the time with roots in Russian folklore. The lubok also came to life on the cabaret stage. The Bat was particularly known for this kind of production, which featured a lubok-style picture drawn on a curtain that stretched the width of the stage. The figures' heads were replaced by holes through which the actors stuck their heads to sing songs related to the subject of the lubok. Comic sketches of army life or about Wilhelm and Franz Joseph were announced and commented on by a *conférencier,* or master of ceremonies, a figure new to the Russian stage, introduced at the Bat and brilliantly played by its director, Nikita Baliev.[46]

Small-scale patriotism—as a poem, a playful children's delight, or a folkloric fancy—was characteristic of cabaret's ambiguous and aesthetic approach to the war. Outspoken kaiser-bashing was absent. Discussion of the war in verses and in metaphors and its inclusion in theatrical experiments was as far as this sophisticated and cosmopolitan genre would go. Because a refined form of presentation was obviously more important than ideological content, a wide spec-

trum of views could coexist at literary evenings, everything from paci-
fism to classic Slavophilism. As the war progressed, however, charity
was all that remained of the Russian cabaret's contribution to patriotic
culture.

Less fussy about aesthetics and style were the two most ambitious
miniature theaters in the capital, the Troitskii and the Crooked Mirror
(Krivoe Zerkalo). Especially in the first months of the war, these two
establishments became famous for their hearty patriotism and witty
kaiser-bashing. Both houses offered mainly dramatic repertoires, with
a focus on parodies, farces, and satires. The artistic concept of the
Crooked Mirror, which was run by the actress Zinaida Kholmskaia
(Timofeeva), Aleksandr Kugel"s wife, was simply to make people
laugh. Thus it became a playground for several famous directors, who
would rather produce astute and biting plays there than at a regular
elite theater. If the cabarets were the places to try out new dramatic
forms and conduct highbrow literary discussions, the Mirror and the
Troitskii were the places to go for extravagant comic satire and dramatic wit. Full houses were the best evidence of the popularity of this
kind of entertainment.[47]

The Troitskii Theater presented comic pieces about the kaiser, his
army, and German culture with great success in the 1914–15 season.
Written in part by Arkadii Averchenko and other members of the
journal *Novyi Satirikon*, they had such titles as *The Fool* and *The German*,
which announced itself to be "A Joke." They made fun of German
petty-bourgeois values and shopkeeper's mentality, and Krupp appeared as a specter of the ultimate evil. *Hoch Patriots: Götterdämmerung*
launched a witty broadside against German culture and spirit as well
as a biting attack on the fashionable operas of Richard Wagner. This
"German patriotic opera" featured heroes of *Der Ring des Nibelungen* in
comically exaggerated situations and full of self-importance, thus expressing the aversion, particularly rampant at the beginning of the
war, to Wagner's work and its alleged Germanic imperialist
ideology.[48]

In the fall of 1914, the Crooked Mirror's program was not much
different from the Troitskii's. Almost without exception it offered patriotic farces. Aleksandr Kugel', for example, produced the "grotesque
harlequinade" *Marlborough Goes to War*. Based on a French farce about
the famous English general, which under the name *Mavrukh* became
one of the few Russian patriotic folk dramas in 1812, the play was

revived in September 1914. The plot deals with the eternal boastfulness of soldiers, who are shown with straw epaulets. If in 1812 the main character of the piece was Napoleon, in 1914 Wilhelm II and German saber-rattling were the natural targets. In a variation of the kaiser theme, the play *Tsar' Vasil'ian* combined Wilhelm's Russian nickname, Vas'ka, with the eighteenth-century folk drama *Tsar' Maksimilian*. With sets and costumes by the *Novyi Satirikon* cartoonist Remi (Nikolai Remizov) and the accompaniment of a hurdy-gurdy, the production was reminiscent of the balagan, the old Russian fairground show booth, where *Tsar' Maksimilian* had normally been played. As in the folk drama, popular fantasies and images of the ruler, in this case Wilhelm, were at the center of the plot. A whole range of comic figures appeared as well: Franz the old knight, Krupp the smith, and a Count Tseppelinskii. The political and diplomatic events leading up to the war were recapitulated from the perspective of an ignorant mass audience in "a very simple way," Aleksandr Kugel' declared, and with "lovely naiveté."[49]

Such patriotic farces and comedies were phenomena of the first few months of the war. They relied strongly on exaggeration, thus dramatizing what otherwise could be seen on satirical postcards, lubki, or the pages of *Novyi Satirikon*. Like the caricatures, the comedies largely disappeared in early 1915. This parallel development comes as no surprise if one considers the close collaboration between contributors to the satirical journal and the two miniature theaters. Patriotism obviously had its limitations for serious artists and actors alike. Repetitive caricatures of Wilhelm on paper and on stage simply became boring after a while. They revealed no new aesthetic insights and they could not arouse patriotic enthusiasm for a nebulous common cause. In the absence of any attempt to formulate positive ideals of national identity, attacks against the enemy remained little more than exercises in wit.

In the use of folklore for patriotic purposes and the recourse to proven patriotic subjects such as the Napoleonic War we see other similarities between the visual arts and the small theaters. Just as lubki experienced a renaissance during World War I and picked up the style of the 1812 broadsides, folk dramas, puppet shows, stylistic elements of the balagan, popular plays of the Patriotic War, and even the lubok itself were taken up and experimented with on the stages of miniature theaters and cabarets. It goes without saying that these folkloric productions were tailored to sophisticated urban audiences. They included a fair amount of cultural nostalgia in addition to the loose patriotic message of a common heritage and satirical attacks on the enemy.

Patriotic declamations, humorous verses (*chastushki*), and political monologues were parts of the standard repertoire of most miniature theaters during the war. Delivered by *kupletisty* and *zlobisty*, performers who recited comic verses (*kuplety*) or commented on the latest talk of the day (*zloba dnia*), these performances reached a much larger segment of the population than the comic plays. Kupletisty appeared not only in miniature theaters, but also in the shantan, gardens, cinemas, and circuses. Their merchandise was the biting word and the hard-hitting joke, which aspirants to the trade practiced at popular "humorists' competitions" in Odessa, where many of them came from, and at Moscow's Odeon Theater. Kupletisty were constantly in trouble with the censors, who demanded to see all scripts in advance and sometimes forbade whole performances. Performers learned to evade censorship by frequently changing the place of their performances or by using gestures to express deleted lines. That was how the young Nikolai Smirnov-Sokol'skii, winner of the Odeon competition in October 1916, managed to present the murder of Rasputin, a strictly forbidden subject. Patriotic verses were usually permitted, so long as their attacks on Kaiser Wilhelm were not excessively harsh or vulgar.[50]

Aside from the conférenciers of the cabarets, kupletisty and zlobisty were the estrada artists in closest contact with the audience. Confronting the audience at an almost conversational distance, they could address them directly and react to interjections from the floor. Thus some digressions from approved scripts (the main source for the historian) were possible. Like barometers of public opinion, kupletisty sensed the atmosphere during the war and reported it in their pieces. As early as the fall of 1914, they were expressing both escapist tendencies and patriotic solemnity, a dualism that became noticeable in most visual and performing arts only in mid-1915. Thus I. A. Rabchinskii, who appeared in several Petrograd theaters, openly invited his audience to forget about the war and joke with him; after all, the war would be won anyway. Sergei Sokol'skii, in contrast, who was widely considered to be the best kupletist of his day, summoned up the misery of war so convincingly that it was impossible for him to tell jokes.[51]

Sokol'skii, who died in 1918, was the most talented of a group of estrada performers who had created the so-called barefoot genre (*bosiatskii zhanr*) in the years after the 1905 Revolution. Inspired by the works of Maxim Gorky, they appeared in rags to comment on society and the world from the perspective of "Siberian hoboes." In this role, Sokol'skii presented his patriotic commentary with great success at the fair in Nizhnii-Novgorod in the fall of 1914 and at Moscow's Ermitazh vaudeville theater in the summer of 1916. His regular stage, however, was Valentina Lin's new theater in Petrograd. Sokol'skii dedicated his *Pliashushchaia lirika* (Dancing poetry), published in early 1916, to Lin. This book, containing most of Sokol'skii's patriotic poems in an elaborate art nouveau design, has so far largely gone unnoticed.[52]

At the time his book was published, Sokol'skii's repertoire was patriotic in a variety of ways. It included earlier texts straightforwardly praising Russian military heroes such as Koz'ma Kriuchkov and the pilot Nesterov, who was likened to a knight of the old Russian byliny whom people would remember through the years. As in the old sagas, Sokol'skii describes the hero's farewell to Kiev—incidentally, Nesterov's hometown. Images of the *dikoe pole,* the open prairie of the Russian south and natural habitat of strong knights, freely mix with the technical details of contemporary air battles and the horrifying drama of the pilot's kamikaze stunt. In other early pieces, Sokol'skii bewails the tragic lot of "fair Belgium" and its heroic king, who as the leader of a "free people" takes the defense of his country in his own hands but is finally forced to surrender. The country's sufferings will not be in vain, however, as history will show. Sokol'skii expresses a similar hope in a poem about Poland, which, as "Russia's sister," will realize its longings: having shed its blood in struggle against the Germans, Poland deserves its freedom and will rise again, just as it proclaims in its national anthem, which Sokol'skii wove into his piece. Ideas of national freedom and democracy escaped the censor's eyes in the cloak of patriotic compassion for the pitiable victims of German aggression.[53]

The long ballad "A Word about Russia" also envisioned national freedom for Russia, though with no overt mention of a democratic society. Directed against the "internal German," all the "Karls, Fritzes, and Vons" in the country, it drew an ideal picture of a "Russia for the Russians," a unified society of happy and industrious workers and peasants, a civilization that stood far above the Prussian "iron culture" (ideas also actively promoted by such liberals as Evgenii Trubetskoi).

This ideal world, however, was far from realization. The number of Baltic barons certainly dwindled during the war, but Russian society did not really unite in the war effort. In fact, it split, and Sokol'skii bitterly attacked the profiteers in his later pieces.[54]

Sokol'skii's "Jackals," the most famous monologue against profiteering in wartime Russia, was performed by many other artists. It relates a fictitious conversation with a wounded army captain who tells Sokol'skii about the horrors of the battlefield:

"The soldier does not fear the battle
But listen, what is terrible,
When you are completely forgotten
Sitting somewhere in a trench.
And in the darkness, in your hideout
The rapacious jackal finds you.
You lie there sick and listless
Among dead bodies as his prey
And see the grave-dog coming closer.
On such a night my hair turned gray."
He then fell silent. I was moved
And was unable to respond.
What can a poet tell a soldier?

                    .   .   .

He bids farewell and says to me:
"You're lucky, there are no jackals here!"
And off he goes. . . . And in the distance
Fades the clatter of his spurs.
Deep in the artist's chest, however,
Resounded this concluding phrase:
"There are no jackals." In the city
These animals never graze.
But those who in the name of greed
Open stores despite the crisis
And use the war for their advantage
To overcharge and force up prices,
Who even turn their motherland
Into a base and vile bazaar
And do not care about the danger
That's coming to it from afar,

> Tell me, are these not also jackals,
> These merchants, salesmen, rogues, and crooks? . . . [55]

Sokol'skii equally condemned an array of other evils, including anti-Semitism, which had a long tradition in the Russian Empire but became a particular issue during the war. About half a million Jews were conscripted for the Russian army, and many Jews studying abroad returned and volunteered as soldiers for the tsar. This show of patriotic loyalty impressed even staunch right-wingers and had a special impact on the artistic world. While the government continued its oppressive policies against the Jews, outlawing Yiddish and Hebrew publications in 1915 and forcefully resettling hundreds of thousands of Jews from areas near the front as potential German spies, film-makers were releasing such works as *The Jewish Volunteer* and *The War and the Jew*; a new journal, *Voina i evrei*, praised the heroism of individual Jewish soldiers; and a lubok was published showing Russian soldiers defending a Jewish graveyard against the Germans.[56]

Sokol'skii expressed his sympathy with the Jews in several monologues. The most famous, "Shindel'man," tells the story of Khaim Shindel'man, a brave Jewish soldier who volunteers for a dangerous reconnaissance job. He gets caught by a German, who tries to lure him into collaboration by talk of the sufferings of Jews in Russia. Shindel'man replies that Russia is his motherland, and although the Jews have suffered there, the land is watered by the tears of their mothers. How is it possible to betray such a country? After the war, all people in Russia will be brothers and will live in peace. Shindel'man tells the German that he is not afraid of being shot—and that is how he dies, "for his native Russia, for the Tsar!"[57]

In "The Law of the Jungle" Sokol'skii attacked "hooliganism," the breakdown of general mores, and the amorality of such urban entertainments as luxurious nightclubs with their private rooms and alcoves. He felt ashamed that some Russians enjoyed these pleasures while others were dying at the front. His monologues thus expressed not only the social patriotism promoted by circus clowns but also a moral rigor and civil ethos that went beyond the "mask" of social consciousness that the Soviet scholar Evgenii Kuznetsov discerned in the art of the "Siberian hoboes." In "Jackals" especially Sokol'skii developed a picture of the war that in its accusatory vividness is reminiscent of scenes in Erich Maria Remarque's *All Quiet on the West-*

ern Front. He went beyond his earlier pieces about heroism and society and introduced an existential component that resembled the humaneness and vulnerability expressed in Pasternak's "wounded soldier" poster (Fig. 36).[58]

Some less gifted kupletisty underwent a similar development: they started out with conventional patriotism in 1914 and turned to social criticism sometime in 1915. V. F. Bil'ianin, who was billed as Ernani, announced himself to be the "unique and distinguished parodist of the Crooked Mirror" and appeared there and in other miniature theaters as "king of the quick-change artists." His early patriotic repertoire overflowed with stereotypes of the kaiser, his barbarian army, and German beer-and-sausage culture. Everything of this sort disappeared from Ernani's act by 1916. In a much more lyrical tone, the monologue "Russian Dream" told about Death dancing over the trenches and deplored the discord in Russian society. In "Heroes behind the Lines" he pointed to Kuz'ma Minin, the hero of Russian unity in the Time of Troubles and a merchant by profession, as a patriotic model for contemporary merchants, who had turned out to be the curse of the country rather than its saviors. And finally, in "The Jew," which the censor deleted in its entirety, Ernani praised Jews' patriotism and told of prayers for the tsar offered up in synagogues.[59]

Ernani's ballads and Sokol'skii's poems document a change of patriotic atmosphere in 1915. If patriotism figured in kupletisty's acts at all, it was now a serious matter. Ardent calls for social solidarity replaced riotous jokes; images of "soldiers dying in the arms of Red Cross nurses for Russia and the tsar," one performer recorded, displaced the dream of Russian superiority on the battlefield. The horrors of the war thus gave rise to disillusionment and heightened moral activism at the same time. The satirists turned from patriotic symbolism to focus on the individual, whether a suffering soldier or a profiteer. These two polar opposites in a society splitting apart were after all real people, as audiences were all too well aware. Some theatergoers in Kiev hurled insults at people in the front rows when a kupletist skewered profiteers, and soon the entire audience exploded in a free-for-all.[60]

Kupletisty and all the other performers in cabarets and miniature theaters presented patriotism as a multiform aesthetic challenge. Patriotism for them was not just an internal conviction or a commonly accepted ideology but something that had to be consciously shaped in one's mind and discussed with artistic intellect as well as political and moral standards. Patriotism, consequently, was something dynamic that could change over time and react to the situation at hand. With growing economic and social hardships, *rodina* increasingly came to be identified with the people of the country, not with an abstract ideology of empire or Pan-Slavism. What to some conservatives may have looked like unpatriotic behavior or even defection to the enemy was nothing more than a good sense of realism, a stronger commitment to social and moral values, and an effort to keep the country from breaking apart.

Estrada also offered a completely different kind of patriotism that appealed to a broader audience. So-called patriotic concerts and narodnye gulian'ia (carnivals) with patriotic programs mustered the whole range of national and military symbolism and presented it in an orderly and ceremonial form. In this kind of entertainment, patriotism changed not at all; it remained static in the tight-fitting costume of convention and the stiff order of military bands.

By the turn of the twentieth century, narodnye gulian'ia in their traditional form had largely disappeared. Yet as with other forms of folk art, attempts to revive them as folklore shows occurred shortly before World War I. Domesticated forms of gulian'ia also took place in summer gardens and even indoors. These events were easier to control by the police than the traditional big outdoor fairs. Typically organized by charity organizations, they featured lotteries, Petrushka shows, clowns, military bands, and dance numbers. Allegorical processions that depicted Russian proverbs, say, were a particular attraction. Narodnye gulian'ia were an entertainment predominantly for the middle classes—people who could afford the admission charge and buy lottery tickets for charity. They were traditionally family events and thus had something to offer children as well.

In August 1914 a patriotic gulian'ie in Moscow's Renaissance garden combined all of these themes in a day-long extravaganza. It appealed to the youngest patrons with free toys and balloons. During a "grand gulian'ie" in the Moscow zoo shortly afterward, a children's troupe played Glinka's *A Life for the Tsar*, a patriotic opera if ever there was one. In the evening, adults could join in a "magnificent patriotic promenade" that called to mind prewar patriotic processions of the radical right, featuring a multitude of flags, portraits of the tsar, and banners bearing the images of national heroes. An army band and a string orchestra played Tchaikovsky's *1812 Overture*, and another historic war was glorified in the musical play *The Battle of Poltava* by Aleksandr Cherniavskii, a composer of gypsy songs and military marches and a popular accompanist of the Petrograd estrada. A fireworks display saluting the allied powers ended this patriotic potpourri.[61]

Far surpassing the gulian'ia in patriotic fervor and reactionary spirit were the "patriotic concerts" organized by Mariia Ivanovna Dolina, soprano of Petrograd's Mariinskii Theater and "soloist of His Imperial Highness." The daughter of an army officer, Dolina had received a German-Lutheran education in St. Petersburg. As a second career and in what looks like a revolt against her upbringing, she had become active in estrada as a promoter of national music long before the war. In the concert series "The Russian Song" she had presented folk music collected by ethnographers and musicologists together with songs by the Mighty Five—Modest Mussorgsky, Aleksandr Borodin, Nikolai Rimski-Korsakov, César Cui, and Mili Balakirev—who took their inspiration largely from folk music and legends and thus created the national school of Russian music.[62]

Dolina's patriotic concerts usually took place at the Circus Ciniselli, but she gave some of them at the Cadet School on the University Embankment and at the Army and Navy Hall on Liteinyi Prospekt. A rather mixed audience from all walks of life attended them, in part because tickets were distributed in such disparate places as factories and the Petrograd Medical Institute for Women, and admission charges ranged from 12 rubles to 32 kopecks "for workers." All the proceeds went to charity. Between 26 August 1914 and 24 April 1916, when the 102d concert closed the 1915–16 season, 304,178 rubles and 34.5 kopecks had been raised, with the biggest chunk of money (almost 60,000 rubles) earned by the first sixteen concerts, during the heady days at the beginning of the war. For this achievement, the tsar awarded Dolina medals and honors, and an army unit was named after her and supported by concert proceeds.[63]

Patriotic concerts raised funds for a large variety of beneficiaries, which were usually listed in the programs. Aside from the activities of the officers' wives who formed the ladies' committees of countless regiments, the shows supported hospitals, hospital trains, and orphanages. Their programs read like a Who's Who of Russian wartime charity. From members of the imperial family and the old aristocracy to obscure and often ad hoc groups of engineers' widows or the alumni of a certain school, the range of people who participated in humanitarian activities was extremely wide. Some concerts supported a more general cause, such as "the air force," "Serbia," or "Belgium." In these cases, the beneficiary was often a major theme of the show. A "Belgian patriotic matinée" on October 19, 1914, for example, featured at least ten songs and poems about the heroism and the beauty of this country, including the premiere of Igor' Severianin's "Poem on Belgium." The rest of the program consisted of national anthems, Russian folk music, songs in praise of the tsar, and a film released by the Skobelev Committee about a heroic attack by a Cossack.

Some six hundred musicians and artists appeared in the concerts. Regular participants included a "patriotic chorus" under Dolina's direction, the bands and sometimes the choruses of the Pre-obrazhenskii, Izmailovskii, Moskovskii, Volynskii, and Naval Guard regiments, the balalaika ensemble of the First Railroad Regiment, a gusli orchestra and chorus from Smolensk, and the string orchestra of the Preobrazhenskii Regiment, a veritable symphony orchestra that also played at the Mariinskii Theater. To this patriotic overkill were added such imperial opera stars as the bass Aleksandr Mozzhukhin and the tenor Aleksandr Matveev—ironically a great favorite in Wagner's operas before the war.[64]

Exercises in patriotic fervor, the concerts featured all the national symbolism and pillars of state and Russiandom appropriate to the ideological arming of a country at war. The national anthem was sung repeatedly. Occasionally announcements of decorations, rescripts of the tsar, and pastorals of the Orthodox Church were read. Honored through the presence of the bands of the Imperial Guard regiments, the Romanov dynasty and the Russian military were both celebrated for their heroic past. "Grand apotheoses" and patriotic tableaux vivants showed scenes from military history and such national heroes as Kutuzov and Suvorov. These tableaux vivants were lubok-like scenes performed by actors frozen in surreal poses, usually lit from below against a background of flags, St. Georges, or two-headed eagles. As a tradition, these patriotic shows date back to the nineteenth-century balagan and patriotic demonstrations by the radical right.[65]

Dolina's patriotic concerts were a peculiar phenomenon of wartime estrada. Concerts of patriotic and military music were nothing new, but Dolina's shows were unusual in their breadth and diversity. On the one hand, they maintained a democratic and populist character by gathering all strata of urban society for a common patriotic cause; on the other hand, they promoted reactionary ideas of hierarchy and traditional order. By combining opera excerpts with folk music, military marches and official-bureaucratic ceremonies with fairground traditions—all for charity—they thus created a new form of estrada entertainment original in its eclecticism.

Shows for charity became a special genre of wartime estrada. An organization called Artist—Soldatu (Artist for the Soldier), made up of Petrograd actors, musicians, and other performers, regularly sent gifts to soldiers at the front and supported its own hospital train through lotteries and concerts. These benefit shows were unlike the usual estrada fare; they brought together performers and performances that were not seen on the same stage elsewhere. As an art form appealing to a broad social spectrum and traditionally relying on the diversity of its presentations, estrada was the natural environment to accommodate the great outpouring of charity among Russian performing artists. It also allowed for less conventional and more direct forms of humanitarian activities.[66]

Performers had more immediate ways to reach soldiers than benefit shows. They presented estrada entertainment at the front, in hospitals, and at festivities honoring the recipients of decorations. November 26, for example—St. George's day—was traditionally a day of heightened charity activity during the war. Noble ladies sold champagne at concerts "for the support of the soldiers," and most theaters scheduled special shows on that day. The heroes who had received a St. George's Cross were invited to dinners and shows in their honor. Thus in 1915 the Petrograd People's House of Emperor Nikolai II, run by the Committee for People's Temperance and housing theaters for opera, drama, and estrada, held a banquet for soldiers (Fig. 44). An orchestra and army bands played throughout the meal. After the national anthem was played, the guests enjoyed a short opera, a comedy, and finally a show with jugglers, folk singers, and clowns. During the intermissions a special coupon purchased tea and cake. Everything was neatly organized. After the show, the soldier-heroes were invited to take their forks, knives, plates, and glasses as souvenirs, along with any leftovers, but were expressly forbidden to take anything else. Even entertainment in one's honor was regimented.[67]

Entertainers' visits to hospitals became known as "flying con-

44. Menu for a charity banquet at Petrograd's People's House. Gosudarstvennyi muzei istorii Sankt-Peterburga.

certs." We have seen the impression left by Vertinskii and Kholodnaia's tango; other artists played the balalaika or, like Plevitskaia, sang ballads and folk songs. Dolina also appeared at hospitals, though mostly at those for officers. The celebrated bass Fëdor Shaliapin founded and financed hospitals in Moscow and Petrograd, and he appeared there from time to time to sing arias and soldiers' songs for the wounded. Occasionally he also performed at other hospitals, but in 1915 his interest in this kind of direct charity diminished. Other performers soldiered on. When A. A. Aleksandrov, a little-known actor at Moscow's Korsh Theater, celebrated his 150th hospital show in January 1916, the wounded greeted him with an ovation and presented him with a briefcase and a letter pad inscribed to "the comforter of soldiers' pain."[68]

The Section for Factory and Village Theaters at Moscow's People's University recruited performers for shows at hospitals. As no stage was available, the players set up folding screens as sets and were ready to go on within five minutes after their arrival. The shows consisted of short dramatic sketches played by actors of such an illustrious house as the Moscow Art Theater, tales and stories read by the author Stepan Skitalets (Petrov), folk songs and ballads, and balalaika pieces. The musician P. I. Ivanov-Vol'skii was a frequent participant until he was drafted; then his music enlivened his encampment (Fig. 45).[69]

Estrada at the front was usually organized by entertainers serving in the army or the Red Cross, as in Plevitskaia's case. There is little evidence that estrada performers from the cities actually went out to the front line. Iurii Morfessi, a gypsy singer from Odessa, who visited the front near Riga, did not get beyond staff headquarters, where he and his troupe had dinner with the officers. Drafted performers who wanted to entertain their comrades at the front were thus forced to improvise a stage, arrange seating on either makeshift benches or the ground, and adjust their program to the available personnel and to the taste of the mostly uneducated audience. A folk chorus organized by the nightclub entertainer Cherviakov among the men of his outfit had great success in a hospital tent in early 1917. Cherviakov, in frock coat and tie, sang about "Wilhelm's dance with the loud-mouthed Turk," and for a rousing finale the chorus belted out the song every Russian knew as "Ta-ra-ra-bum-biia."[70]

A more elaborate estrada program was offered to a whole regiment

45. P. I. Ivanov-Vol'skii (*right*) and a friend make music at the front. Gosudarstvennyi muzei politicheskoi istorii Rossii, St. Petersburg, f. IX, no. 12494.

in the summer of 1916. About three miles from the German lines an open-air stage was constructed of sand and sod against a backdrop of small trees. As in an amphitheater, the soldiers sat on the surrounding hills; chairs were provided for the officers and nurses. A sergeant who in civilian life had worked as a conjurer began the show with some tricks and then came a Petrushka performance. A. M. Volzhin, who had played at Moscow's Sergievskii People's House, was in the middle of a tale when German planes attacked. When the planes flew off and the smoke cleared, Volzhin went on with his tale. The show came to an end with a performance of the regimental chorus and a couple of clown acts.[71]

Estrada performances at the front were welcome diversions for the troops, but the draft also deprived the audiences at home of their accustomed entertainment. Estrada suffered other material hardships during the war as well. The prohibition of alcohol lowered profits at the buffets, and theater directors minimized their losses by reducing salaries. Some houses even had to close when they were requisitioned as hospitals. In September 1915, just as the new season was about to begin, the threat of requisitioning such popular Petrograd miniature theaters as Nevskii Fars, Lin, and Troitskii led to an uproar in artistic circles and the press. The owner of Nevskii Fars, the delicatessen merchant G. G. Eliseev, declared that he would rather give away one of his other buildings or even build a new hospital than shut down his theater. The protests helped, and in the end no house had to close. A year later the Crooked Mirror and Nevskii Fars were requisitioned for a short time, but after another press campaign they were "found to be not suitable as hospitals." Tsarist authorities were obviously less implacable in requisitioning buildings than their Bolshevik successors.[72]

Russian wartime estrada was as varied as the society that produced and enjoyed it. It was fragmented and multifaceted, and thus eludes easy categorization. If the circus was a funhouse mirror that distorted and condensed reality into a world in microcosm but nevertheless contained what Paul Bouissac calls a "metacultural code," estrada was more like a plain mirror that reflected a world no longer comprehensible. Because the circus ring constituted a closed system and the various acts were part of a compact whole, it is possible to identify changes in patriotic attitudes and values during the war.

Estrada, in contrast, was an open stage both literally and figuratively. It did not encode and thereby condense a culture in symbolic action, but instead reflected the cultures of what Herbert Gans called the diverse "taste publics" of an increasingly heterogeneous society. Most city people had their choice of entertainments, regardless of social standing or class. This casualness, which was even more in evidence in the moviehouses, had its effect on estrada, where patriotism competed with other subjects and had to hook onto existing trends as a commodity of entertainment.[73]

Folklore accommodated patriotism relatively well and had long been a popular part of estrada. After 1914, this kind of entertainment experienced a boom, for it emphasized cultural traditions and national myths that fostered a patriotic spirit. The creation of a common national identity and a nebulous feeling of belonging was in this respect more important than the authenticity of the presentations. Serious ethnographers and fake peasant choruses, catering to audiences of varying sophistication, communicated the same communal spirit.

Escapist tendencies, too, had long existed in estrada, and they also experienced a boom during the war, especially after 1915. Instead of patriotism, however, they fostered sophisticated hedonism and ostentatious decadence. After all, the reality people wanted to escape was increasingly dark, whether on the battlefield or on the home front. Escapism consequently grew ever more escapist, and increasing numbers of people were eager to exchange the rodina of snow and birch trees for a tropical beach fringed with palms.

The same conditions that made people seek refuge in exotic places challenged others to increase their social commitment. Although members of the critical intelligentsia, actors, singers, and writers quickly trained their wit against Prussian militarism and the joke-figure Wilhelm in patriotic outrage at German aggression, they soon redefined their understanding of patriotism as a more positive and humanistic value. Performers in the cabarets and the booming miniature theaters, especially kupletisty, promoted patriotism as an attitude of civic responsibility and denounced profiteers, the "jackals behind the lines." Patriotism with this moral impetus and social consciousness offered a way to send a clear but not always appreciated message to the audience. It was certainly more honest than the nebulous patriotism available in "folklore" shows.

Similarly clear messages were sent in patriotic mass events. Patriotic gulian'ia and concerts largely reduced patriotism to historical clichés and national symbols taken over from the radical right. This encoding process is reminiscent of the circus, and it is indicative that that is precisely where many of Dolina's concerts were held. Like the apotheoses of the circus pantomimes, these concerts reaffirmed conservative values and strengthened the existing order. At the same time, they attempted to rally a broad spectrum of society behind a common patriotic cause. But this populist appeal with a monarchist core was successful primarily in the first months of the war, as the proceeds of Dolina's concerts demonstrate. In the long run, nationalist imagery and army bands simply became boring to people who had enough of the war in their everyday lives.

Estrada presented many patriotisms, from a nostalgic search for a common cultural identity to social criticism and even conservative monarchism. It also found expression in a wave of charity that transcended all ideological undertones. Many performers donated all or part of their proceeds or collected money from the audience. The charitable impulse led to the flying concerts at hospitals and the combination of highbrow and lowbrow entertainments in one show. As a faithful mirror of society, estrada thus reflected a widespread outpouring of charitable feelings that transcended social and class lines even as it exposed the fragmentation of the Russian public.

War in the Footlights: Patriotism's Grand Exit

When World War I broke out, Russian dramatic art was at a peculiar stage of its development. The realistic tradition of the Moscow Art Theater (Moskovskii Khudozhestvennyi Teatr, or MKhT), which had set the tone of Russian dramaturgy for about twenty years, was being challenged. Instead of attempting to bring "life as it is" to the stage, more and more plays focused on obscure details or emphasized symbolic meanings. Plots structured on problems of everyday life were increasingly replaced by those dealing with eternal truths and transcendent speculations. Naturalistic stage sets gave way to dainty decorativeness and a proclivity for fancy costumes and grand gestures. The promoters of this development were directors. They had become so powerful in the theater world that they created what has been called a *rezhissërskii teatr* (director's theater), in which the director's interpretation of a piece mattered more than the piece itself or its performance by the actors.[74]

The repertoire of the years immediately preceding the war, which changed very little after 1914, was characterized by such diverse subjects as the sexual question, otherworldly powers and the irrational, and apocalyptic issues. Love dramas, romantic pieces about the good old days, and pieces about modern decadence were performed cheek by jowl with somber plays about death and the end of the world. Alongside them, however, remained the classics of Shakespeare, Molière, and Aleksandr Ostrovskii.[75]

Matching these transformations on the stage was an equally important development in the audience: the blurring of class distinctions. Drama had ceased to be an entertainment solely for the intelligentsia and high society; now it was enjoyed by an emerging middle class, by state officials and officers, who were increasingly recruited from the lower classes, and even by some workers who could afford to pay for seats in the gallery. Wealthy refugees from the western regions of the country, too, began to frequent the theaters of the two capitals during the war. Thus the 1914–15 season even saw the opening of new theaters in Moscow. Throughout the country, the establishment of "people's theaters" after the 1880s, a movement particularly inspired by Aleksandr Ostrovskii, made drama, the "culture of bourgeois society," available to everyone who wanted to enjoy it. Undertaken as a didactic enterprise by the intelligentsia and well-meaning factory owners, people's theaters had become big attractions for workers and peasants, and their attendance figures far exceeded those of any other form of theatrical entertainment.[76]

Despite its democratic appeal, Russian drama was still an art form of the intelligentsia. The repertoire, the productions, and their messages reflected the attitudes of a group of people who saw themselves in the traditions of European theater, particularly German, French, and English theater. To such cosmopolitans, the outbreak of the war posed some serious problems—just as it did to their colleagues in London, Paris, Berlin, and Munich. Should they, for example, forswear everything German in the name of loyalty to Russia? Was it possible to put on a piece by Schiller and still be patriotic? How could patriotism be combined onstage with the high standards of contemporary dramatic art? These questions came under discussion during the war, but in August and September 1914 most Russian drama stages were simply scenes of exuberant patriotic outporings.[77]

When the war broke out, most of the regular playhouses were closed for the summer break, and only dacha or summer theaters (dachnye teatry) in vacation spots were open. At the news of the war, most of these houses introduced their programs with the national anthem, but they had no patriotic plays to offer, and their season was almost over anyway. By the opening of the regular theater season in September 1914, however, directors had had time to prepare appropriate shows. The MKhT removed pictures of German playwrights from the foyer, but its display of patriotism was only a prelude to the regularly scheduled performance of a play by the nineteenth-century dramatist Aleksandr Griboedov. In an amphitheater on the stage—used for an earlier Hamlet—actors and other theater personnel appeared with an orchestra and a chorus and sang the national anthem, then immediately went about their regular business. The most prestigious theater in the country was obviously not the place for boisterous patriotic spectacles.[78]

Other theaters were not quite so restrained. When the curtain at Moscow's Korsh Theater went up for the first performance of the new season, the audience saw a sky with gradually dispersing clouds revealing a Russian knight surrounded by the various peoples of the empire. On the backdrop hovered a double-headed eagle the width of the stage, holding the flags of Russia's allies in its talons. Above the eagle was inscribed "Great is the God of the Russian Land." Into this veritable tableau vivant a Russian soldier in full combat gear appeared, flag in hand, to the sound of a fanfare. He was followed by soldiers of the allied nations carrying their respective flags. During each appearance the pertinent national anthem was played. At the end, all participants looked up to the inscription while the audience enthusiastically applauded. This patriotic show was repeated several times at the Korsh.[79]

Similar enthusiasm met the opening performance at the drama theater of Petrograd's People's House, which happened to coincide with Russian victories in Galicia. A play titled *Suvorov* was staged by Aleksei Alekseev-Iakovlev, well known for his mass spectacles. Without much dramatic development, it featured a series of scenes and tableaux vivants in which the great general orated to his soldiers and the anthem was played. For those who did not get into the theater, a tableau vivant was set up outside the building depicting the patriotic demonstration on Palace Square on the day war was declared.[80]

The shows at both the Korsh Theater and the People's House displayed a peculiar tendency to appropriate popular art forms that were usually found only in the circus or estrada. The opening of the season demonstrated that authentic forms for expressing patriotism on the legitimate stage did not exist. Patriotic plays had to be written, and the writing took time. It also took longer to stage a play than an estrada show. Once patriotic pieces were available, theaters generally had to decide whether to put them on. Each house coped with the problem in its own way.

The MKhT did not offer a single patriotic piece during the war—such plays apparently being too weak for this temple of elite dramatic art. It did, however, stage classics with some relation to the contemporary period. The two founders of the theater, the directors Konstantin Stanislavskii and Vladimir Nemirovich-Danchenko, as well as the *Mir iskusstva* artist Aleksandr Benua, produced three short tragedies after pieces by Aleksandr Pushkin in a "Trilogy of Death," which were done in "apocalyptic tones." In early 1915, this program was a total flop, but later that year the audience received allusions to death and decay much more warmly. Il'ia Surguchev's *Autumn Violins,* a love story about an elderly woman, offered an aesthetic treatment of fall and falling leaves which was at the same time romantic-escapist and suggestive of the end of life. The mood among the audience had obviously become more somber and indecisive by the end of 1915, a phenomenon that influenced the programs of other theaters as well.[81]

Petrograd's Aleksandrinskii Theater, the oldest Russian drama theater, was something like a counterpart to the MKhT in the capital, although its repertoire alternated between naturalistic and experimental-symbolist productions. *King, Law, and Freedom,* by Leonid Andreev, the most famous Russian playwright of the time, was the only patriotic piece produced on its stage during the war. It dramatized the heroic defense of Belgium, an event that had so deeply moved Andreev that he wrote passionate newspaper articles about it in addition to the play. He was particularly impressed by the patriotism of the poet Maurice Maeterlinck, who had allegedly enlisted in the Belgian army to save his country from the Germans—a canard that came to be widely believed. In reality, Maeterlinck turned 52 in 1914 and was much too old to be accepted by the army. Nevertheless, the role of the patriotic poet very much suited Andreev's convictions at the time, which had turned from pacifist to staunchly patriotic. Like many other liberal intellectuals, he saw Germany as the embodiment of reaction, a foe that had to be defeated if Europe was to see peace (and Russia, by implication, an end to its reactionary regime).[82]

King, Law, and Freedom, which was hastily put together from the latest newspaper accounts and named after a line of the Belgian anthem, was widely considered to be the best and most serious patriotic play, although Andreev himself later described it as "bad journalism," and one of the most influential critics of the time, Nikolai Efros, found it trivial, too full of pathos, and too restricted to contemporary relevance. It was first performed at the end of October 1914 in Moscow's Drama Theater (Moskovskii Dramaticheskii Teatr) and had its Petrograd premiere in December at the Aleksandrinskii (Figs. 46, 47, 48).

46. Ivan Mozzhukhin as Clairmont in Leonid Andreev's *King, Law, and Freedom* at the Moscow
Drama Theater, 1914. Gosudarstvennyi tsentral'nyi
teatral'nyi muzei imeni A. A. Bakhrushina, Moscow.

At the same time it was made into one of the artistically most ambitious patriotic films. Directed by Pëtr Chardynin and released by
Khanzhonkov, this film was especially praised for avoiding the
graphic scenes that formed the main ingredients of most other patriotic movies.

47. Andrei Petrovskii as the German Supreme Commander in Leonid Andreev's *King, Law, and Freedom* at the Aleksandrinskii Theater in Petrograd, 1914. Gosudarstvennyi tsentral'nyi teatral'nyi muzei imeni A. A. Bakhrushina, Moscow.

The plot of *King, Law, and Freedom* is quite simple. Into a peaceful garden scene somewhere in Belgium comes the news of the German attack. The owner of the garden, a famous national poet (modeled after Maeterlinck), and his two sons go to defend their country. One son dies. The second son and the father are wounded and tended by the mother, who has enlisted as a nurse. She takes them home into the quiet garden. Count Clairmont (an embodiment of

48. The German War Council in Leonid Andreev's *King, Law, and Freedom* at the Aleksandrinskii Theater in Petrograd, 1914. Gosudarstvennyi tsentral'nyi teatral'nyi muzei imeni A. A. Bakhrushina, Moscow.

Belgium's King Albert), "a great hero and the soul of the Belgian people," appears to ask the poet's advice. After long deliberation, the two patriots decide to save the country by opening the dikes and drowning the German invaders. The last scene, played to the accompaniment of technical and lighting tricks, was warmly applauded in both productions. Likewise the appearance of Clairmont, played by the film star Ivan Mozzhukhin in Moscow and by Iurii Iur'ev at the Aleksandrinskii, was greeted by tumultuous applause, and caused the ladies in the audience to make "increased use of their handkerchiefs."[83]

From a dramatic point of view, the meaning of the piece was obvious. It built on a familiar and very popular patriotic motif and lacked any profound hidden message or symbolism. Everything was as clear as the newspaper articles on which it was based. Andreev's reputation and his civilized approach to the war theme in both senses of the word—that is, the absence of violence and the praise of a responsible citizen (the poet)—made the play a success. It offered a display of patriotism and civic duty to those who were cultured enough to despise the regular fare of patriotic shows as too crude, but who still were not cosmopolitan or apathetic enough to do without patriotism altogether. In other words, the piece exactly fitted the educated but not overly intellectual audience of the Aleksandrinskii Theater.[84]

Ambiguity was also characteristic of the repertoire of Moscow's oldest playhouse, the Malyi Teatr (Little Theater), during the war. Under the direction of Aleksandr Iuzhin-Sumbatov, one of the most famous contemporary actors, the Malyi had circumvented the general quest for new form and content by committing itself to the classics. The quality of its program was consequently declining and acquiring an epigonic touch. During the war, however, with the elimination of all German plays from the repertoire, Iuzhin in particular set out to meet the audience's need for diversion. In his opinion, overt demonstrations of patriotism could better be staged by the opera or the ballet. Its philosophical implications, for which the legitimate theater would be the right place, were too dreadful to be dramatized at the moment. No one wanted to be confronted by these difficulties now. The Malyi consequently offered French comedies along with the customary Shakespeare, Ibsen, and Ostrovskii.[85]

Patriotism and the war were almost negligible themes on the stages of the three Russian playhouses with the most elite aspirations but figured more prominently in houses that traditionally had a broader repertoire and a less intellectual audience. Petrograd's Suvorinskii Theater (also called Malyi Teatr) was one of those houses. An enterprise of the conservative publisher Aleksei Suvorin and some of his friends, it was initially famous for its productions of European classics and its leaning toward social-critical pieces. Around the turn of the century, some critics even compared it to the MKhT. In the years before the war, however, plays of this sort were dropped in favor of a colorful and more popular mixture of light entertainment—comedies, melodramas, and pieces about court and bourgeois life, all with elaborate staging. The Suvorinskii's audiences became correspondingly diverse, more prone to show off and have fun than to ponder profound questions. Among them one found state officials, bourgeois, guards officers, ladies of the demimonde, local artisans, and students.[86]

Patriotism at the Suvorinskii was as juicy and varied as one might expect from its prewar repertoire and an audience eager for light entertainment. The patriotic play with the greatest success was *The*

Shame of Germany: Cultural Beasts by Mamont Dal'skii, a celebrated actor, well-known rake, and friend and acting teacher of Fëdor Shaliapin. Like Andreev's *King, Law, and Freedom*, the play was based largely on newspaper accounts and caricatures. It did not delve into the deeper problematic of war, as one of its critics complained. But this was exactly what made it a success with the Suvorinskii's audiences. They shook with laughter at the cartoon-like Wilhelm with his oversized whiskers and his stern face. They reveled in the spectacle of beer-swilling German officers and in the dull and stupid officer played by Dal'skii, delivering boastful monologues. The audience also suffered through scenes in which German soldiers beat Russian women.[87]

The Shame of Germany has no coherent plot. As an agglomeration of clichés, it resembled the patriotic farces put on by the miniature theaters, though it was more than just funny. With its reference to atrocities, it aspired to a higher dramatic level, but that ambition was thwarted by the incoherence of the episodes. Yet its sensational appeal and crude exaggeration made the piece easy to play and easy to understand. After its premiere in late September it went on tour to Rybinsk and was taken over by a few Moscow theaters as well. The best proof of its entertainment value was its success at a summer theater as late as 1916.[88]

Most other patriotic productions at the Suvorinskii Theater followed the model of Dal'skii's play. As the critic Boris Bentovin repeatedly complained, they all lacked dramatic development. Such pieces as *Knights* and *The Taking of Berlin during the Reign of Elizabeth* were put together like slide shows, sketches of trench and hospital life interspersed with historical scenes, with no elaboration or character development. It was only late in 1915 that both dramaturgy and the war began to be approached more seriously, though not without the customary sensational touch.[89]

Following H. G. Wells, the play *Miraculous Beams* by the critic and playwright Fëdor Fal'kovskii featured a young researcher developing a long-range missile. Haunted by dark forces, in particular a German Baron Otto (an incarnation of contemporary spymania and at the same time a swipe at Baltic barons), the young man reflects upon the moral implications of his work. He finally decides to make his weapon available to all countries so that war will become unthinkable. Before he can act, however, he dies and takes the secret of his weapon to the grave. This prenuclear piece about a wonder weapon and mutual assured destruction was both thought-provoking and fascinating. Its warm reception showed that by late 1915 even the Suvorinskii's audiences had begun to prefer plays with more depth and fewer clichés.[90]

The audiences at the drama theater of Petrograd's People's House were even less class-conscious than the Suvorinskii's. This theater's offerings attracted all sorts of people and frequently played to standing-room audiences. Soldiers, officers, the middle class, students, workers, and curious intellectuals were treated to pieces by Russia's leading playwrights as well as to historical plays, fairy tales, and schmaltzy melodramas. The melodramas set the tone for most patriotic productions on that stage. Here heroism and lost love, jealousy and loyalty to the motherland were the dominant themes; Wilhelm and his barbarians were rarely seen. The critics usually praised these productions and forgave their shortcomings. After all, this theater could not be measured by the same standards as the traditional elite houses.[91]

The plays at the People's House appealed to patriotic feelings through their themes of everyday life. They used national symbolism, but the patriotic message was usually pitched at a human level. In *Resurrection*, for example, Jews were shown as good soldiers who fight for the might and glory of Russia. As we have seen, this was a rather controversial theme during the war. In the People's House production it was underlined and given immediacy by the reading of current newspaper stories about the war. A similar plea for social unity as a patriotic duty was made in *The Blaze of War*, in which the wife of a Russian officer overcomes her love for a German spy with the help of an idealistic musician, who is appalled by the aggression of a country that could produce Beethoven. His friend, a socialist student, is likewise outraged, and calls upon the audience to set aside all party differences and work together for the common cause. These two pieces appeared in late 1914; by 1915, the patriotic repertoire had been scaled down to short sketches presented as preludes to regular plays. *Behind the Red Cross*, by the renowned critic Vladimir Botsianovskii, features a nurse's fiancé who is jealous of his beloved's future patients. He overcomes his jealousy by joining the army. So easy, so neat, so heart-wrenching—that was patriotism at the People's House.[92]

Russian playhouses thus reacted to the war in a variety of ways. To a large extent they either ignored it with escapist fare or transcended it with plays about death and decay. Patriotism was on display only sporadically and disappeared almost completely in 1915. This phenomenon was not restricted to the world of theater, as other performing and visual arts attest, but it was particularly strong there. Aside from the weakening of an initial patriotic spirit, there were many other reasons for the decline of patriotism in the theater. Above all, drama was obviously not suited to patriotic propaganda. The borrowing of such forms as the tableau vivant and the paraphrasing of newspaper articles could not create a "patriotic drama" because they lacked the suspense of dramatic development. Contemporary critics recognized this problem and early in the war began to discuss the absence of a serious patriotic repertoire.

Nikolai Efros, for example, complained that the task of the theater was not to illustrate newspaper accounts. Pëtr Solianyi, while recognizing the low quality of patriotic plays, saw them at least as an interesting expression of the contemporary situation, which "the historian could study in peacetime." For him these pieces were something like an instinctive reflex of self-preservation in wartime, with no artistic aspirations. He might have added that with the exception of Andreev, almost no serious playwright in Russia had this reflex. Most of the pieces were hastily written by actors, critics, or scenarists; hence their low quality and often journalistic character. As ad hoc workshop productions, they were nothing but attempts to contribute to the initial patriotic wave and to provide what Solianyi called "spiritual support for the war effort."[93]

Solianyi also pointed to the difficulty of producing heroic battles and other mass scenes on the small space of a stage, where action was basically structured into entrances, exits, and dialogues. Tableaux vivants and bombastic monologues could not solve this problem; they simply transferred patriotic demonstrations from the street to the stage. Iuzhin-Sumbatov took the logical step of avoiding patriotic plays altogether at his theater. Vsevolod Meierhold, however, expressed the belief that in times of great social flux the theater must listen to its audiences and be guided by them. He called on playwrights to provide scenarios that could easily be adapted to changing circumstances. His idea was realized in the staging of the circus pantomime *The Triumph of the Powers* at the Mariinskii Theater. As the majority of patriotic plays showed, however, this kind of repertoire was not really opening up the stage to daring experiments or creating a new genre. Rather, it led to plays with formal inconsistencies and clumsy action. As Aleksandr Kugel' put it, "the war did not help the Muses."[94]

Critics debated not only the patriotic repertoire but also German influence on the Russian theater. In August 1914 most theaters banned German plays from their programs and all German and Austrian citizens were expelled from the Playwrights' Union, unless they were Slavs. A more profound contribution to the discussion came from Solianyi. In a series of articles he discussed the important role Germans had played in Russian theater history, even though they had "always remained strange and alien" to Russians, who preferred Shakespeare and the French theater. It had become clear, however, that the country of poets and thinkers had turned away from its traditions and adopted the religion of militarism. Solianyi's disappointment was echoed by others. But some pointed out that Schiller was not responsible for Wilhelm II and that Heine had made fun of Prussian militarism. Now, they asserted, the great classics were foolishly attacked as works of the enemy, while some houses simply changed the names of contemporary German writers to make them look Russian or French and staged their works with great success. The Austro-Hungarian Ferenc Molnár, a war correspondent for the *Berliner Tageblatt*, was only one such playwright.[95]

As in the other arts, the war affected theater more directly with serious material pressures and changes in personnel. The pages of the leading theater journals were full of complaints about higher taxes on tickets. In November 1915 an increase of between 20 and 100 percent, depending on the price of the ticket, led to a sharp drop in attendance figures and consequently in theaters' revenues. The immediate victims of this development were the actors, whose salaries were cut or contracts changed.[96] Problems arose in their daily work as well. By late 1916 stage makeup became all but unobtainable, because as a luxury item it was no longer imported. Furthermore, by 1915 the prices of canvas, nails, and other materials necessary for the construction of sets had doubled. I. I. Zhdarskii, the administrative director of Petrograd's Lin Theater, consequently developed a recycling program for old sets: he had them washed and painted again. The price of paint, however, had also doubled. The bold and flashy aniline dyes in particular, which were imported from Germany, had become extremely rare and expensive. As a consequence, wartime stage sets were generally less colorful, had fewer contrasts, and thus were less striking to the eye.[97]

The rising prices of all sorts of clothing were devastating to actors without season contracts, who had to provide their own costumes. In addition, heightened sensitivity to material inequalities had led to a widespread campaign in 1916 against expensive fashion. In the artistic world, this campaign was promoted by the actress Nadezhda Smirnova and the group Artisty Moskvy—Russkoi Armii i Zhertvam Voiny. Less illustrious actors without season contracts were outraged. How dare Smirnova, who had her pick of the extensive wardrobe of Moscow's Malyi Teatr, lecture them? They were forced to buy expensive outfits to appear onstage and then criticized as unpatriotic for wearing them.[98]

Many actors were drafted and some theater people were caught abroad by the war and had to make long detours to return home. Some drafted actors performed for the troops. Leonid Utësov, for example, who later became famous in estrada and as leader of a jazz band, was part of a group that put on patriotic shows for the regiment's officers. The female roles were filled by local women. After the play only the "actresses" were invited to dine with the officers; Utësov and the other men had to eat in the kitchen.[99]

Utësov's regiment was stationed near Odessa and had not engaged in combat, but frontline units also enjoyed theater. In their leisure time, soldiers organized so-called bivouac spectacles (*bivachnye spektakli*). On makeshift stages or simply on a hill and with minimal props—captured spiked helmets, improvised whiskers—they played popular comedies and original sketches about Wilhelm and the Germans (Fig. 49). One of these amateur groups even sent a letter from the Caucasian front to *Teatr i iskusstvo* asking for support in the form of old costumes, wigs, and particularly women's dresses. In another letter to that journal, an officer reported the great success of a regimental drama group that played in a real theater in a town near the front line. He wondered whether the Zemstvo Union could not support this kind of entertainment, which was so greatly appreciated by the soldiers.[100]

Organized theatrical entertainment for the troops did not exist in Russia during World War I. Although the leading journals reported the popularity of such entertainment in the French army, there was no organization in charge of theater for the Russian army, let alone a "theater officer" or a well-developed network of companies playing for the troops on a regular basis, as was the case on the German side. An investigation on Russia's northwestern front in 1917 indicated that

49. A bivouac spectacle. Gosudarstvennyi muzei politicheskoi istorii Rossii, St. Petersburg, f. IX, no. OF 149.

most soldiers were not used to this kind of entertainment and many did not grasp the meaning of even the most simple plays. This was the experience of Pavel Gaideburov, whose itinerant troupe performed at the front in the fall of 1917. It was not the first to do so. In the summer of 1916 members of Artisty Moskvy—Russkoi Armii i Zhertvam Voiny, among them the famous Ivan Moskvin, had visited the front in the Caucasus with gifts for the soldiers. They also played and read short episodes by Chekhov. Photographs and a letter to the editor of *Rampa i zhizn'* indicate that this was not the only time that members of the group played for the troops, but their sporadic performances reached only a very small segment of the army. As in Austria, where companies of Viennese actors toured the front, Russian troops were entertained by metropolitan actors. It goes without saying that there was an immense cultural gulf between these people and the simple peasant-soldiers who formed their audiences.[101]

Most actors, however, limited their work in support of the war effort to charity. Artisty Moskvy, Artist—Soldatu, and several theater companies coordinated and organized their activities. The MKhT, for example, supported its own hospital by donating 2 percent of its income and organizing readings and lectures for the wounded. Actors with the imperial theaters started a similar enterprise. Famous actresses such as Ol'ga Knipper and Nadezhda Smirnova solicited donations of money, warm clothing, and tobacco on the street and from door to door. The great tragedienne Mariia Ermolova gave poetry readings to support hospitals. Smirnova also organized song recitals in hospitals, and usually brought two stagehands to carry the accompanist's piano. People's theater companies gave complete performances of plays by Ostrovskii and Gogol in hospitals. Amateur theater groups of summer vacationers invited wounded soldiers to their shows in fashionable dacha districts. Although they shunned patriotic pieces because of their low artistic quality, many actors nevertheless found ways to express their patriotic feelings in acts of social responsibility and philanthropic commitment.[102]

The war hit Russian drama during a period of tremendous change and innovation. As the traditions of realism were questioned, so too were established aesthetic and dramaturgic principles. With the experiments of writers, directors, and actors, Russian theater combined an eclectic mix of artistic forms and styles. In principle, this situation could have favored the creation of a special form of "patriotic drama" as yet another theatrical experiment. For several reasons, however, this experiment failed. As an ideology, patriotism was simply too popular and too shallow to form the foundation of first-rate drama. Not surprisingly, all attempts to create a patriotic drama resorted to tabloid sensationalism or popular forms of entertainment, such as the tableau vivant and melodramatic spectacles. Consequently, these pieces were played predominantly in theaters that catered to people of all classes. The temples of elite culture largely avoided this kind of repertoire and offered their regular fare of sophisticated international drama. A leaning toward both apocalyptic and escapist pieces, however, did demonstrate the ambivalence with which intellectuals and parts of high society viewed the war.

For the intellectuals, drama also revealed serious tensions between a traditional cosmopolitanism and the patriotic demands of the war. It was not just the formal deficiencies of patriotic drama that repelled them but also its simple messages of good and bad, theirs and ours. In their eyes, Schiller was not an enemy simply because he was German. If they participated in patriotic demonstrations at the beginning of the war, it was against the new German "religion of militarism" and the "spirit of Krupp," not against idealist philosophy and the Weimar classics. Discussions on the pages of the leading theater journals showed that German pieces were excluded from programs more to please the public and to comply with an unwritten code condemning everything German than to express the genuine patriotic feelings of the directors and actors. These feelings came to the fore in a completely different way and were strikingly evident in the widespread charity work of theater ensembles and stars.

Charity was also instrumental in the creation of the first Russian front-line theater. Early in the war, theater in the army had been staged only by amateur groups of soldiers or drafted actors. In 1916 the first professionals from elite theaters in the capitals played for the troops while delivering gifts they had collected in the streets of Moscow or Petrograd. Actors, consequently, were in the forefront of applied civic responsibility. By making direct contact with the army, they supported the soldiers as well as they could, both materially and spiritually, and thus showed a patriotism characterized by human rather than jingoist concerns. Whether this attitude was influenced by the sociorealistic traditions of the prewar repertoire we can only speculate. It was, in any case, admirable in view of the difficulties actors faced in mounting a production even in an established theater.

Melodies for the Tsar: Operetta, Opera, and Patriotic Music

Music was an important component of patriotic culture but it had unique limitations as a communicator of patriotic messages. This *langage moins le sens*, as Claude Lévi-Strauss called it, lacks linguistic, visual, and dramatic qualities; a melody may evoke feelings of joy, grief, or fear, but only lyrics or dramatic interpretation can convey a specific meaning. Even music that is strongly rooted in cultural convention, such as a national anthem, does not necessarily generate uniform associations among its listeners. Because perceptions are so idiosyncratic, any discussion of music is necessarily subjective, and of course it lacks the particular sensual qualities of the sound. This is especially the case in regard to music that is no longer played and has been "recorded" only in the writings of contemporary listeners. A historical study of music, consequently, has to rely on the lyrics of a song or an aria, the dramatic "packaging" of music on the concert and other stages, and the cultural conventions surrounding it.[103]

It is these cultural conventions that helped so-called national music to invade nineteenth-century concert and opera stages. Seen as a constituent part of the "national character" (or *Volksgeist,* as Herder called it) and theoretically serving to distinguish one nation from another, national music was an important component of European nationalism. It developed alongside national literatures and national schools of history, reflecting the search for a distinct cultural and national identity among the educated classes and the bourgeoisie. This identity was thought to emanate both from a heroic past and from the people, rooted in the native soil. National music, then, was characterized chiefly by mythology and folklore.[104]

Heroic epics had a long tradition in Russia. They were told and retold long before nationalism existed. They evoked a world of supernatural beings and historical figures that gave moral guidance and shaped a common cultural consciousness. When in the nineteenth-century Aleksandr Borodin picked up the old tale of Prince Igor and Mikhail Glinka the story of Ruslan and Liudmila, the music of their operas became part of a familiar mythological tradition. It also acquired meaning. Audiences learned to associate certain musical motifs and tonal structures with heroic myths, and hence with national greatness and superiority.[105]

Folk traditions had an even greater impact on Russian national music. Real and invented folk tunes were and still are the great hits of the Russian opera and symphony repertoires; their popularity attests not only to the simple beauty of Russian folk music but also to the romantic longing for their roots felt by nineteenth-century Russian audiences and composers such as Glinka and the Mighty Five. The elevation of a folk melody into serious music allowed for a fictitious bridging of social barriers and appealed to a communal and eventually national spirit. An ideal state of Russianness was depicted on the opera stage in numerous rural and popular scenes. Peasants and the popular masses are the real heroes of such operas as Glinka's *A Life for the Tsar* and Mussorgsky's *Boris Godunov* and *Khovanshchina*, suggesting that Russian national identity rested as much in Russia's people as it did in its heroes. In any case, though folk tradition was in itself not national, it became widely accepted as such through its adoption into elite music. It thus acquired mythological quality as the alleged source of a national musical character.[106]

National music became national because of the readiness of nineteenth-century audiences and composers to associate heroic themes and folklore with national identity. What exactly individual listeners to national music associated with it, however, is beyond the historian's grasp. The role of national music in World War I is therefore up for speculation. As countless program notes and concert announcements attest, works by Glinka, the Mighty Five, Tchaikovsky, and other composers of national music were played extensively. But at the same time the first big successes of works by Igor Stravinsky and Sergei Prokofiev were anything but national in spirit. In addition, according to contemporary observers, music with a more emotional appeal as well as chamber music and authentic folk music became increasingly popular during the war, suggesting a retreat at least from heroic motifs and a turn to more intimate and escapist fare.[107]

National music, consequently, was only one of several styles on the wartime concert stage. The few new compositions of serious music referring to the war may have had patriotic titles, such as Sergei Vasilenko's *March to the Melodies of Cossack Songs*, Aleksandr Glazunov's *Triple Alliance: Paraphrase of the Allied Anthems*, and Aleksandr Kastal'skii's requiem *Brotherly Prayer for the Heroes*—the latter two based on the Russian and Allied anthems—but they were rather awkward attempts to combine serious music with current events and official state glory. They lacked nostalgic and mythical quality, and none of them has joined the repertoire of Russian national music.[108]

Operetta and opera are the two musical genres that provide the most meaning in music. They offer stage action, sets, and lyrics, which can impart patriotic motifs much more articulately than any symphonic work. On the surface, operetta would seem to be the ideal form. After all, it was closer to estrada and catered to a similarly broad audience, who wanted to be entertained and were not looking for eternal truths and artistic refinement. These spectators preferred to have their values confirmed (or transgressed) in the nostalgic and ideal world of musical love melodrama, fairy-tale-like plots of social justice and harmony, and the lush atmosphere of gypsy barons and royal adventures. With the outbreak of war, patriotism was added to this list of themes, but the new topic turned out to be somewhat problematic.[109]

In Russia, as in most countries at the time, operetta meant Viennese operetta. Johann Strauss, Franz Lehár, and Emmerich Kálmán were the favorites of audiences all over Europe. In Russia, 90 percent of the repertoire before 1914 was made up of pieces by these and other Austro-Hungarian composers. At the beginning of the war, this *Venshchina*, as it has been called, became associated overnight with "Teutonic aggression." An orchestra was booed when it played a Viennese waltz, and had to strike up the national anthem to calm the crowd. Posters announcing "Teutonic" operettas were painted over by self-styled patriots; the pieces themselves were taken off the programs. In addition, many of the regular patrons of operettas as well as many singers had to leave for the front. As a result, several operetta theaters closed in 1914. Others tried more or less successfully to cope with the new situation.[110]

French operetta offered a way out of the repertoire crisis. Pieces by Jacques Offenbach, Alexandre Lecocq, and lesser-known francophone composers were staged in the fall of 1914. Viennese operetta still appeared, though in disguise, in a trend that accelerated later in the war when the French repertoire was exhausted. Program notes and posters simply changed the names of composers; they gave them a Romance or Slavic ending or used freely invented pseudonyms. A theater in Rostov-on-Don, for example, announced the operetta *Poet and Peasant* by one Zupeiskii (Franz von Suppé, of course). With similar patriotic zeal the same establishment Italianized even the French composer Daniel Auber into Oberoni, because it mistook Auber for a German named Ober, a word familiar to Russian ears from such German borrowings as *oberkonduktor* (main conductor) and *oberleitenant* (first lieutenant). Other composers were better off. As in the case of Friedrich von Flotow, if their names had a Slavic ending, they were simply declared to be Russian. Not only the names of composers were changed; Viennese operettas suddenly featured characters called Jacques and Jean instead of Hans and Friedrich, while the scene of the action was moved from the Vienna Woods to the Bois de Boulogne.[111]

With the disappearance of the "Teutonic" repertoire and the

chauvinistic wave at the beginning of the war, the demand for genuinely Russian pieces increased, but such pieces hardly existed. Operetta had first come to Russia from France in the late 1860s, and it still relied almost completely on imports. The few Russian operettas written before World War I were either musical medleys, so-called mosaics, with heavy stress on gypsy themes and spectacular costumes, or they more or less copied and plagiarized their Parisian and Viennese models in both musical style and dramatic content. No wonder that the first attempts to produce Russian patriotic operettas failed miserably: a projected piece by a Petrograd troupe in August 1914, which should have included real German POWs playing themselves, was never heard of again after the first announcement. Another piece with the promising title *Volga Sorceress*, which was played in the Petrograd theaters Niagara and Fortuna, turned out to be nothing more than a hodgepodge of familiar folk songs, factory ditties, and tangos.[112]

The only patriotic operetta received favorably by the critics was a production by one of the leading operetta directors and composers, Valentin Valentinov. His *In Positions* appeared in August 1914 in Petrograd's Letnyi Buff Theater. In the spirit of "folk patriotism" (it used folk melodies), it featured the prayer of a Russian soldier dying of his wounds and musical allegories of the Allied powers. Royalty, a standard theme of operetta, was included in a mocking duet between Wilhelm II and Bismarck. In the finale, all the nations fighting against Germany were presented in lavish costumes. The audience received *In Positions* with warm applause, and the critic of *Teatr i iskusstvo* was surprised by the deeply felt patriotism of the piece, which apparently prevented him from noticing the motley action and the lubok-like character of the production.[113]

What was acceptable in the first days of the war provoked critical comments very soon afterward. Operettas with such titles as *The Hussars of Death, Whiskers,* and *The Battle Raged* were staged at Petrograd's Luna Park Theater. Crude one-act pieces focusing on the kaiser, they had little to do with operetta. They lacked even the kitsch and rich costumes for which people usually came to an operetta. It is indicative of the strong wave of patriotism among the lower middle classes in the fall of 1914 that these pieces nevertheless drew appreciative audiences. Most of their music was written by V. Shpachek, whose mediocrity was already recognized before the war, and their libretti by Epikur (A.

L. Rubinshtein?). The masterpiece of this duo, judging at least by the reaction of the audience at the Luna Park, was *To the Attack:* Marie, a boisterous French girl, cautiously approaches an unsuspecting German lieutenant and cuts off his whiskers in order to make her jealous fiancé laugh. She runs away, but the German finds the young couple. Only the sudden appearance of a French detachment saves them from certain death "and the audience from major boredom," as a critic disdainfully noted. The plot had all the dramatic ingredients for success: a love story, jealousy, comic figures in uniforms, suspense, and a happy ending. In other words, despite the critics' attacks, patriotism could be presented in an operetta as long as it was tied to the elements with which operetta audiences were accustomed.[114]

Further developments proved those critics right who had pointed to the incompatibility of war and operetta: by the end of 1914, operettas with patriotic content had completely disappeared. Operetta in general, however, boomed amid the social changes of the times and the growing demand for escapist fare. Wealthy refugees from the western provinces of the empire, who increasingly frequented the cabarets and theaters of the two capitals, flocked to operettas as well. They did not go to the theater to be immersed in war-related issues; they wanted to be transported to a dream world filled with melodies they could hum.

Opera, with its high artistic standards, appeals to more serious audiences. Like drama, opera conveys deep values, tragic passions, and eternal truths in a complex mixture of music and dramatic action. Light entertainment and contemporary issues hardly fit this art form, and not just for artistic reasons: the writing and staging of an opera are lengthy processes. Consequently not a single patriotic opera was written in Russia during World War I; yet patriotism did find a place in Russian opera houses.

The opening of the 1914–15 season at Moscow's Bolshoi Theater showed the limited possibilities of patriotism on the opera stage. In a decades-old tradition, the Bolshoi presented Mikhail Glinka's *A Life for the Tsar*—the classic Russian national opera—preceded by the national anthem. To enthusiastic applause the anthems of Russia's allies were played as well (and continued to be played at almost all performances that season). Patriotic feelings obviously ran high that evening. They even led to a surprising change in the opera itself—one that was never repeated. In the fourth act of *A Life for the Tsar*, which tells how the peasant Ivan Susanin saved the life of the young tsar

Mikhail Romanov during the Time of Troubles (1604–13), Ivan is killed by the tsar's Polish enemies. This scene was simply omitted from the Bolshoi's opening performance. Apparently it was deemed inappropriate at such a historic moment to show Slavic brethren as the bad guys. Instead the orchestra jumped right into the finale, "Glory, Glory to our Russian tsar," and the evening ended with exuberant ovations.[115]

Operagoers who perused the program for the new season's offerings noted that the war had brought changes to the Bolshoi's repertoire. Although German operas had enjoyed great popularity with Russian audiences before 1914, they were now conspicuous by their absence. Richard Strauss's *Elektra,* under the direction of Vsevolod Meierhold, for example, had been a big success in St. Petersburg's Mariinskii Theater in 1913. More important was the fate of Richard Wagner's operas, which had been fixtures at all Russian opera houses since the early 1890s and which were performed even by itinerant troupes in the provinces. Wagner strongly influenced large segments of the Russian artistic intelligentsia, including contributors to *Mir iskusstva,* Sergei Diaghilev's Ballets Russes, and such symbolist writers as Aleksandr Blok and Viacheslav Ivanov. Indeed, since 1907 the entire *Ring des Nibelungen* was presented every year to a reverent audience at the sold-out Mariinskii. Wagnermania reached its peak in the 1913–14 opera season with eight new productions, including the Russian premiere of *Parsifal.*

The war temporarily cooled Russians' enthusiasm for Wagner. His music became associated with the boastfulness of Wilhelm II and his plots were reinterpreted: the quest for the Nibelungs' ring came to be seen as symbolic of Germany's imperialist ambitions. In 1914 Wagner's yearly *Ring* was replaced by a Rimski-Korsakov series consisting of his "folk opera" *May Night, The Snow Maiden, Sadko, The Tale of Tsar Saltan,* and *The Legend of the Invisible City of Kitezh.* This motley assemblage hardly constituted a cohesive cycle of operas. Though most critics welcomed the patriotic impulse behind this "feast of Russian music," they also voiced their doubts about lumping together unrelated operas in such a "chaotic mishmash" (*vinegret*). Nikolai Evreinov went further and pointed out that it was Wagner, not Rimski-Korsakov, who had fundamentally transformed the operatic form.[116]

No Russian opera house played a work by Wagner during the war. The absence of the German repertoire led to new productions of Russian operas. A close look at the programs of the three Moscow operas between 1913–14 and 1915–16, however, reveals that Russian operas were performed more frequently only in the first war season. They accounted for almost 71 percent of all performances in 1914–15, up from 58 percent the year before, only to drop to 58 percent again in 1915–16. Under existing conditions, a shift away from the Russian repertoire could mean only an increase in French and Italian works. These changes in popularity were also reflected in the leading operas of the two seasons: Glinka's *A Life for the Tsar,* which topped the 1914–15 season with 46 performances out of 510, moved down to seventh place in the following season with only 20 performances. Verdi's *La Traviata* moved up from eleventh place to the top in 1915–16 with 38 performances out of 553, followed by Tchaikovsky's *Pique Dame* and *Eugene Onegin*. When we see that Borodin's *Prince Igor* dropped from sixth to thirteenth place in 1915–16, it becomes obvious that operas with clear patriotic content had lost some of their appeal and that, with the exception of Wagner, the regular opera fare was regaining its pre-war position.[117]

The 1915–16 opera season was notable also for increases in total attendance and in number of performances. One critic attributed this "run to the opera" to war-related escapism, the influx of wealthy refugees into the cities, and the rising living standard of certain "well-known classes of society"—in other words, speculators and war profiteers. The delicate balance between opera's artistic and social functions thus began to shift. As the war progressed, the opera became more a place to see and be seen than a place for intellectual and artistic pleasure. The change was financially successful but aesthetically disappointing, at least for the critics.[118]

If there was one melody that was by definition patriotic, it was the national anthem. It had a specific function as a musical evocation of state and tsar. A national symbol like the flag or the imperial coat of arms, the anthem was nevertheless also a piece of music and thus subject to different associations. Its power to touch its audience is therefore difficult to judge. Like other national symbols, the anthem could be used simply to feign patriotism. It could also elicit deep feelings and move people to tears or solemn contemplation. Even staunch cosmopolites could be touched by its melody.[119]

"God Save the Tsar," Russia's anthem since 1833, invokes God's protection for a strong and Orthodox tsar who rules for the glory of the

Russian people and arouses fear in their enemies. It was played on all imaginable occasions during the war. Indeed, it was played so often that one can safely assume a certain attrition in its ceremonial grandeur and emotional evocative power. During the patriotic street demonstrations that usually broke out after Russian victories, the anthem was sung repeatedly when marching columns met or reached certain places in town. It could be heard at circus pantomimes, estrada shows, and concert halls. Until the 1915–16 season, opera houses and some theaters made the anthem a regular part of their performances. Playing or singing the anthem could be a reflex against anything that smacked of Germanism, from a Viennese waltz unthinkingly played by an orchestra to a film that in the absence of a sound track turned out only after a while to be a German production.[120]

The national anthem was played so often that in time it suffered from efforts to improve it. When one touring chorus came to the line about the fear the tsar aroused in Russia's enemies, they sang "fear" in threatening fortissimo, then ostentatiously paused. The choir of Petrograd's Ecclesiastical Academy emphasized the tsar's Orthodoxy. A supposedly clear national symbol was thus openly reinterpreted and used to promote special interests. Its original message was apparently too weak to carry itself. And so it was: countless pleas rang forth for God to save the tsar, but the tsar himself was all but absent from patriotic culture. Cultural convention rather than devotion to the ruler, then, must be seen as the driving force behind performances of the national anthem. Like the flag, it was a patriotic prop without much specific meaning.[121]

Music's main role in patriotic culture was to provide a patriotic atmosphere. Since melodies and musical styles allegedly expressed a Russian national character, they had long been associated with national identity. As background and complement to the direct patriotic messages of song lyrics and stage action in opera, operetta, and estrada, music appealed to irrational feelings of excitement and belonging to a familiar cultural milieu and tradition. But while audiences may have drawn collective comfort from a piece of music they recognized as "Russian" or "Slavic," individual listeners could attach their own private dreams and emotions to it. Patriotism in music, then, was a matter of both cultural convention and innermost feeling. It permitted a search for the national soul but also for one's own, and thus eludes completely rational and definitive conclusions.

The Russian performing arts fought the war on several fronts. Circus, estrada, theaters, and orchestras experienced substantial material pressures, and working conditions worsened for most performers during the war. In addition, many entertainers contributed to the common cause by participating in various forms of charity—benefit shows, "flying concerts" at hospitals, performances at the front, even voluntary deductions from their salaries. Nevertheless, the press sometimes denounced the full theaters and circuses as unpatriotic when people were dying in the trenches. *Teatr i iskusstvo* and other journals dismissed these attacks as wrongheaded. One need not destroy one's own culture in order to give one's all for the war effort, they argued. Not even the "barbaric" Germans did that.[122]

The Russian performing arts offered wartime entertainment in the form of escapism and patriotism, tailoring different forms and styles for an increasingly pluralistic society. Because of their immediacy and the communicative interaction between entertainers and audiences, the performing arts both reflected and influenced the mood of the time. An uneven triad of jingoism, escapism, and charity coexisted throughout the war, with one or the other prevailing at different times and among different social groups. At the most general level, jingoism was dominant early in the war, charity took over by 1915, and escapism increased in popularity as time went on. As circus pantomimes, patriotic gulian'ia, operettas, and the programs of theaters with more heterogeneous audiences show, jingoism was a matter particularly for the lower and middle classes. They flocked to these events during the first months of the war but then lost interest and began to prefer the escapist fare of clowns, romances, and gypsy barons. This is not to say that jingoism automatically involved support for the entire social and political order. After all, many people in the audience enjoyed the grand spectacles (as they later did the melodramas). For the intelligentsia and metropolitan high society, satirical plays, patriotic operas and concerts, and a few weak patriotic dramas offered an initial patriotic kick, but personal experience of the war soon turned their thoughts to death and decay or escapist indulgence in decadence.

A deep rift in the understanding of patriotism appeared most strongly in the performing arts. Conservative patriotism, or patriotism defined as loyalty to the existing state and power structure, competed with progressive patriotism, or loyalty to the Russian people and one's fellow citizen. In their antagonism toward the foreign enemy, both brands of patriotism underscored their Russianness by reliance on folklore. The conservative variant relied excessively on the traditional national symbols of flag and anthem and the traditional forms of patriotic display, such as pantomimes, tableaux vivants, and processions. The progressive variant embodied a patriotism of word and action, of social consciousness and philanthropy. Of course, to complicate matters further, the aesthetic conservatism of traditional patriotic culture need not imply political conservatism, just as charitable activities do not necessarily reflect progressive political ideas. Patriotism, therefore, was not a static ideology of the nation-state, but one that could acquire new meanings. In Russia, where it was promulgated predominantly by society (*obshchestvo*), it revealed divergent understandings of the common good. The initial enthusiasm against the enemy covered up these differences, but by 1915 it had become clear that not all loyalties were tied to the tsar, and that the motherland was neither a fetish nor immune to change.

3

Violence, Schmaltz, and Chivalry: The War in the Movies

Film was, in theory, the medium best suited to convey patriotic ideas. For its combination of visual imagery and performance it has aptly been called a "graphic drama" and a "moving painting."[1] As a technical and deeply democratic medium, it was particularly appropriate to a war of airplanes and submarines and massive armies. Russian films attracted vast audiences from all walks of life in both the cities and the countryside. The film industry boomed during the war and established itself as an important part of the entertainment business.

The Russian film industry of the 1910s was a jungle of foreign companies and newly emerging native producers and distributors, all in merciless competition. Since the release of the first Russian movie by Aleksandr Drankov in 1908, foreign firms such as Pathé and Gaumont had opened branches in Russia, while Russian entrepreneurs such as Aleksandr Khanzhonkov were claiming their own share of the market. The outbreak of war shifted the balance and accelerated the development of Russian film. By closing Russia's western border, the war virtually locked out foreign competition. Unlike Great Britain, which was flooded by American films during the war, the Russian film industry had to replace the absent Western products. As a consequence, new companies were founded, new studios were built, and even a film school was established in 1916. Khanzhonkov alone quintupled his output, and the total number of Russian films produced during the war rose to over 1,200—an average of about a movie a day.[2]

As soon as the war broke out, German films were withdrawn or shown under new names—though theater owners could expect angry audiences when such manipulations were discovered. In September 1914, for example, Moscow moviegoers noisily protested against a film they discovered to be German and walked out en masse. By 1915, an official ban on all German films caused the industry tremendous difficulties. A large number of films distributed in Russia before the war were of German origin, and quite a few producers and distributors were Germans. The company of Thiemann & Reinhardt almost became the target of an anti-German riot in Moscow before a quick-witted Russian cameraman changed the name on the building to Pathé, that of the French company that had once owned the studio. Paul Thiemann's successful Russian Golden Series, however, could not be saved; it ended when Thiemann was exiled to Ufa, in the east, in 1915. German theater owners also ran into trouble. Their licenses were not renewed for the 1914–15 season, and if they continued to show films, the authorities closed their theaters or exiled them. The jittery anti-German atmosphere led the president of the Duma, M. V. Rodzianko, to call the police on 21 August 1914, when he saw a man in a German uniform riding a bicycle on one of the Petrograd islands. At the police station it turned out that the man was acting in a film then being made "in a thoroughly patriotic spirit," as the police report stated.[3]

The elimination of foreign competition contributed enormously to the development of the Russian film industry. The de facto closure of the border, however, also entailed impediments to development. Film stock and other necessary materials imported from the West were already running out in 1914. The journals constantly lamented the "film famine" and the consequent rise in the prices of available materials; those prices often doubled in less than a week. Kodak's Moscow branch ran out of supplies and thereafter made deliveries only sporadically, after advance payment. Only late in 1915 did it receive more regular shipments via Vladivostok. Less painful for the industry but still a nuisance was a wartime tax on movie tickets, which was footed by theater owners and audiences alike. The temporary requisitioning of movie houses as hospitals and restrictions on the use of electricity during evening hours also took their toll.[4]

Despite the material pressures, film producers and theater owners engaged in charitable activities. In the first months of the war, several theater owners opened hospitals, some with as few as five beds, in private apartments and office buildings. Big companies such as Khanzhonkov supported their own larger hospitals. The biggest one, with sixty beds, was sponsored by the film industry as a whole. Special collections for its support were taken up before the shows, and theaters were asked to donate 10 percent of their box office receipts. The filmmakers' initial charitable impulse, however, soon waned. Donations for the hospital dropped from some 6,000 rubles in September 1914 to only 1,000 in February 1915—a time, incidentally, when the wartime boom was in full swing. Business, it seems, was more important than patriotic responsibility, and admonitions in the press failed to make a dent in this new reality. Aside from a few free film shows in hospitals, the film industry did not even come close to the impressive contributions of performing artists. A competitive environment and a volatile market called for the concentration of all financial resources on the procurement of famous actors and the production of as many box office hits as possible.[5]

With the sharp increase in film production, movie houses mushroomed. Countless theaters opened in provincial towns, and mobile units visited fairs and remote areas to bring educational programs on agriculture and the war to villagers. The boom was most evident in the capital, however, and Nevskii Prospekt became the prestigious address of the best movie palaces. By 1917 twenty-five theaters, some of them still in existence today, operated along the Nevskii; some three hundred others were in operation elsewhere in Petrograd. The movies had thus become the main form of entertainment for large segments of society. As in Great Britain, the film industry profited directly from the wartime ban on alcoholic beverages: instead of going to the tavern, people now went to the movies.[6]

Everyone went to the movies. At the picture palaces aristocrats rubbed shoulders with workers, bourgeois with the demimonde. Social barriers vanished before the silver screen. All Russia flocked to escape into a world of celluloid dreams, curiosities, and the cozy anonymity of the dark auditorium. The film historian Neia Zorkaia has pointed out that it was precisely this escapist function that made the movies so attractive during the war. What people actually experienced in the darkness of the theater is, of course, impossible to know. Their attitudes toward certain subjects as well as their tastes and predilections can only be surmised from the few available box office figures and the sketchy information provided by contemporary film journals. According to these scarce sources, the innovative films that did well among the urban middle and upper classes bombed in the provinces, where the less sophisticated audiences seem to have preferred films that focused on themes familiar from everyday life. Not surprisingly, provincial audiences were also drawn to war films, which fed their interest in a phenomenon that personally affected many of them.[7]

Films produced during the war were of three principal types: newsreels (*kinokhronika*), patriotic feature films, and—the vast majority—the usual fare that had been popular before the war. It was this "civilian" repertoire that laid the foundations of the Russian cinema, established its fame and high artistic level, and became associated with the first Russian film stars and directors: Vera Kholodnaia, Vera Karalli, Ol'ga Gzovskaia, Vitol'd Polonskii, Ivan Perestiani, Ivan Mozzhukhin, Evgenii Bauer, Iakov Protazanov. Embodying the spirit of the time, these films brought to life the types of heroes and heroines familiar from popular literature—the social climbers, the fallen women, the scheming aristocrats, the brutal businessmen. The stars became the faces of the new mass medium.[8]

Prewar Russian films had leaned heavily on literary classics. With the war came an emphasis on psychological drama, unhappy love, treason, seduction, espionage, crime, and the pursuit of wealth. Even pornography was available (the so-called Parisian genre). All of these films featured violent murder scenes, and many of the love stories ended in suicide or insanity. Typical ingredients were a lavish lifestyle and big-city decadence. At the highest artistic and technical level, Evgenii Bauer explored feelings of doom and exposed his characters' souls as they played out their fates in the gilded cages of their salons, winter gardens, and boudoirs. These almost interchangeable environments, paralleling the songs of Aleksandr Vertinskii, contributed to a general picture of the world-weary Russian fin de siècle.[9]

Few other directors' films matched the stylized beauty and psychological depth of Bauer's. Indeed, most films were completed very quickly, usually in seven to ten days, and shooting often began without a finished script. So-called *boeviki* (hits) were cranked out in huge numbers and sometimes in series. The notorious *Sonka, the Golden Hand*, for example, appeared in six installments in 1914 and 1915 and was a big draw. It tells the story of a young adventuress who gets by on her wits in the criminal underworld. As Neia Zorkaia has shown, all movies of this type relied on similar elements—they used the same set pieces, the same montage techniques, the same plot structure. Temptation, seduction, the fallen victim, alienation, blackmail, guilt, collapse, the paying of a moral debt —these ingredients were mixed together so often in so many variations that all audiences found them easy to digest.[10]

Both Bauer's art films and the melodramatic serials offered fantasies far removed from the real world the audiences knew. The kino-khronika, in contrast, provided some reality, or at least the illusion of it. Shown before the main feature, these newsreels and documentary films allegedly functioned as important sources of information and were eagerly watched, but their news value was virtually nill. As in all the other warring countries, battle scenes were almost always staged somewhere behind the lines, sequences were cut liberally and reused many times, and old footage of the Balkan Wars of 1912–13 was presented as late news. The film journals complained about these practices repeatedly but nothing changed. As long as the impression of reality was maintained, audiences were satisfied.[11]

Battle scenes were staged primarily because preparation to film a real attack would give the enemy strategic information and because logistical problems were difficult to overcome. Cameras were heavy and hard to handle under fire, and the presence of a film crew impeded troop movements. Moreover, cameramen tried to set up their equipment on a rise in order to get a clear shot, and there they were natural targets for enemy fire. George Ercole, an English cameraman who worked for the Skobelev Committee, was twice wounded in action and was awarded two St. George's Crosses for bravery. Another cameraman, who went by the pseudonym N. (probably Pëtr Novitskii of the Skobelev Committee), complained that audiences could not distinguish between the elaborate battle scenes in fictional films and his documentary footage. Once he was wounded when he was filming an attack under a barrage of enemy shells, but when his pictures were exhibited in Moscow, people surmised that he had produced the explosions with dynamite.[12]

The Skobelev Committee had the exclusive right to take motion pictures at the Russian front from the beginning of the war until December 1916. Its war film department was led by Feliks Karu, who had no preparation for his new assignment. (After February 1917 he tried to leave the country and take the department's money with him.) Karu had to hire personnel from such companies as Pathé and Gaumont, which were ready for the task but had lost out in their bids for filming rights at the front. He operated with only five cameramen, one of whom was permanently assigned to army headquarters. The remaining four men were far too few to cover major events along the long Russian front line. Russian movie audiences were well informed about the war on the Franco-German front, which Pathé and Gaumont newsreels covered extensively, but their own western and southern fronts were almost terra incognita to them. The Skobelev Committee's incompetence incensed Aleksandr Khanzhonkov, who relentlessly attacked the committee's monopoly in his journal *Vestnik kinematografii*. With no real action shots to publish, Khanzhonkov had to resort to wounded soldiers in Moscow hospitals, nurses being trained, and technicians assembling prostheses. Despite its weak performance with newsreels, the Skobelev Committee expanded its activities in 1915 to include the production of patriotic feature films. For this purpose it opened a new studio in Moscow and engaged, among others, the famous director Wladyslaw Starewicz.[13]

Most of the Skobelev Committee's newsreels were shot behind the lines and at army headquarters. These shots offered little excitement, but such as they were, they were authentic. At least one father recognized his drafted son on the screen. As in the newsreels released by the Bild- und Film-Amt, the equally disingenuous German counterpart of the Skobelev Committee, regiments paraded, pompous generals made a show of being busy, and soldiers dug trenches or celebrated Christmas in a forest. Such scenes did not need to be staged. The only real battles filmed between 1914 and 1916 were the taking of Przemysl in Galicia and the fall of Erzurum in Turkey. These sequences were spliced with staged scenes in longer documentary films. Nevertheless, the newsreels were then considered to be the best source of first-hand information about the war for both future generations and "the stupid and illiterate soldiers," as Captain Ia. P. Levoshko, the Skobelev Committee's director, remarked in an interview. The committee did in fact provide its films to screens near the front line; so did other companies. In 1916 Iosif Ermol'ev, a temporary coproducer of the committee's films, and Vladimir Vengerov pooled their resources and sent a car to the front with Western newsreels. In anticipation of Bolshevik propaganda techniques, the car was equipped with a projector, a generator driven by the engine, and a roll-out screen. Everything could be set up in twenty minutes, and letters to the journal *Sine-Fono* attested to the great popularity of the *kinemo-avtomobil* among the soldiers.[14]

Very few Russian newsreels and documentary films have been preserved. In 1991 a feature shown on German television included some footage from the Caucasus front and obviously drew extensively on the Skobelev Committee's documentary hit *The Storming and Capture of Erzurum*. More than fifty copies of this film were distributed. To cash in on the film's popularity, the Skobelev Committee sold the distribution rights to two influential Moscow theater owners, who then could charge what the market would bear to rent the film to other exhibitors, who in turn raised ticket prices. Instead of fulfilling its function as a nonprofit organization by providing pictures from the front for the public at cost, the committee thus used its monopoly to compete in the overheated film market.[15]

As an Eastern (and therefore fascinating) city that Russia had wrested from the Turks twice in the nineteenth century, Erzurum was a familiar theme in Russian patriotic culture, particularly through Pushkin's account of his journey there during the war of 1828–29.[16] Now it had fallen to Russia again, and Russians flocked to see the film about it. Though *The Storming and Capture of Erzurum* showed "everything except the capture of Erzurum," as some theater owners complained, it did contain many authentic scenes of the campaign and only a few staged episodes.

In the long takes so characteristic of early films, audiences saw Russian soldiers marching endlessly along narrow mountain paths. They could marvel at the men's ability to cope with the inhospitable landscape of the barren winter plateau. These scenes, shot at -22°C (-8°F), were a very exhausting affair for the cameramen. Easier to film were cavalry attacks of fast-riding Cossacks, which were staged behind the lines, the Cossacks riding toward the camera and passing it at close range in scenes that were to become standard features of American Westerns. Takes of the captured city are in the tradition of nineteenth-century panoramas and contemporary travelogues. The Armenian churches and Turkish mosques, the destroyed houses and deserted streets all convey a surrealistic melancholy, at least to today's viewer.

More naturalistic are scenes of soldiers gathered with their tin cups around a pot of soup, turning serious faces to look curiously into the camera. The end of the film offered a patriotic apotheosis in a tableau vivant showing Russia as a proud woman in a rich boyar costume and a soldier sitting at her feet holding a flag bearing the Turkish crescent and the inscription "Erzurum." As the film unfolded, the piano player in the movie house played somber or stirring music to fit the action on the screen and perhaps produced sound effects of explosions and horn signals; the last scene cried out for "God Save the Tsar," and no doubt it was provided.[17]

Patriotic feature films mixed elements of documentaries with regular film fare. Produced by the dozens in the first months of the war, these films largely disappeared in 1915. Of about one hundred feature films made between August and December 1914, fifty were devoted to patriotic subjects. And of twenty Moscow theaters sampled, only five did not show such films in November 1914. By March 1915, however, only five were still presenting patriotic films. Clearly interest in this kind of picture had waned. To be sure, patriotic films were generally low in artistic quality and typically were shot without much care. They might show a pilot taking off in one plane and landing in another. But these films were produced in record time. A film about the hero Koz'ma Kriuchkov, for example, based directly on newspaper accounts, was shot in two days under the direction of Vladimir Gardin for Thiemann & Reinhardt's Russian Golden Series. Kriuchkov was played by R. V. Boleslavskii (Riszard Boleslawski) of the Moscow Art Theater, who would not permit his name to appear in the opening credits (three asterisks were substituted) because he feared for both his reputation as a serious actor and his position in a theater headed by Stanislavskii, an outspoken enemy of film.[18]

Patriotic films took the forms of love melodramas, spy and detective stories, and action movies. The early films in particular, such as the one on Kriuchkov, resembled moving lubki; they had no dramatic development. Like the broadsides, these films offered satirical episodes and caricatures of the kaiser and his Austrian and Turkish colleagues. This very theme contributed to their disappearance in mid-1915, when the ridiculing of crowned heads was banned. The full array of clichés, standardized heroes, and slapstick tricks brought satirical lubki and postcards to life.[19]

A typical representative of the lubok war movies is *Off with the*

German Yoke. Released by Pathé in September 1914, it begins with Wilhelm and his generals boastfully galloping on hobbyhorses before a row of German soldiers. The stern faces and huge beer bellies of the generals stand in comical contrast to their childish jumping and the tiny wooden horses between their legs. In a later scene set in Wilhelm's war council, an aide-de-camp unfolds a map of Europe and begins to cut out countries. Wilhelm then distributes the countries to his officers, who exuberantly hop away on their hobbyhorses. Only one of them makes a long face. He has received Luxembourg, the tiniest scrap of paper. This first part of the film offers a consistent story about Wilhelm's expansionist ambitions, but the remainder lacks all coherence. We see a familiar motif for the German air force: German pilots blow soap bubbles and watch them fly. Then three soldiers, Russian, British, and French, look over a fence into a yard where German soldiers are parading in single file. The Briton pushes the last German in the row, and they all fall down like dominoes. The next episode shows a laughing Koz'ma Kriuchkov with some German soldiers wriggling on his lance. The panopticon ends with a still picture of a thumb between index and third finger—the familiar "finger" that was given to Wilhelm on postcards.[20]

Vulgarity, incoherence, and cheap laughs were the stock in trade of lubok war movies. Instead of catching the drama available in a good joke and translating it into cinematic action, they duplicated the static expression of cartoons lined up in a comic strip. By quoting the familiar aesthetics of the traditional picture stories and by going beyond the bounds of good taste, lubok war movies appealed to a broad spectrum of audiences, no matter that serious film journals panned them. Although attacked for their bad taste, their bad influence on lower-class viewers, and their bad style, they were produced in large numbers in 1914 and were superseded only slowly by more elaborate patriotic films.[21]

Patriotic films with actual plots can be grouped around several themes. The most prominent linked patriotism to a love story in which the lovers were either separated by the war or torn by conflict because one of them belonged to the enemy country. Films of this sort were not much different from the usual love melodramas, but the dangers of war added a new thrill and unleashed seemingly unlimited possibilities in the fantasies of screenwriters. In *In the Beams of German Antiaircraft Searchlights*, which was filmed and released by Mark Naletnyi in 1915, the pilot Sokolinskii (from *sokol*, falcon) meets the ballerina Viktoriia in Moscow's Iar nightclub. He invites her to an air show in which he performs daring stunts. Their unfolding love story is interrupted by the war. The two lovers meet again near the front line—he as an air force pilot, she as a nurse. When Sokolinskii has to fly a night reconnaissance mission over a German fortress, he is in danger of being detected by antiaircraft searchlights, so Viktoriia comes to his aid. On a snowy field near the fortress, which is within the range of the lights, she undresses and performs a wild dance, half-naked, to distract the Germans. Thanks to her courage, her lover returns safely. The next day, however, he finds Viktoriia lying frozen to death in the field. A simple love story turns into a surreal and maniacal sacrifice for the lover and the motherland, all surrounded by the technology of the first war in the air.[22]

Wartime love stories typically featured women as nurses. In late 1914 Khanzhonkov produced two highly praised films that dealt with the tribulations of young nurses and soldiers. *The Nurse* and *Glory to Us, Death to the Enemy* featured Ivan Mozzhukhin in his first movie roles and were directed respectively by Pëtr Chardynin and Evgenii Bauer. The biggest hit was *Under the Thunder of Cannons: Prussian Rapists*, released by A. E. Khokhlovkin in October 1914 and written by Ol'ga Bebutova, a writer of popular novels. In this film Fritz Müller, the son of a German factory owner in Russia, falls in love with Vera, the daughter of the factory's Russian bookkeeper. Vera, however, loves the young accountant Sorokin and repels Müller's advances. Müller threatens to fire her father. Suddenly the war breaks out. Vera enlists as a nurse; Sorokin joins the Russian army and is taken prisoner by a German unit under Müller's command. In a letter to Vera, Müller informs her about Sorokin's situation, which only she can change by giving herself to him. To save her lover's life, Vera appears in the German camp. From a bedroom window she sees Sorokin tied to a tree. Her heroic attempt to jump out of the window is thwarted by Müller as Sorokin looks helplessly on. Suddenly a shepherd boy creeps up to him and severs his ropes, and Sorokin jumps to the window, frees Vera, and kills Müller. He is in turn overpowered by other Germans and is led away to be executed. At that moment Cossacks appear and save his life. Virtue, bravery, and the omnipotence of Cossacks thus overcome the wickedness of a foreign rogue.[23]

Difficulties of quite a different kind had to be mastered by other star-crossed couples. International love affairs were anything but desirable in wartime, and several films showed where the lovers' final loyalty had to rest. *The Traitor,* a Gaumont film, tells the story of Max Werner, a German who is married to Madeleine, a French woman, and has lived in France for many years. Once the war begins, he conducts a "diplomatic correspondence" with coded letters and temporarily leaves his wife for a "business trip" to Switzerland. He returns as the Germans are approaching Paris and shows no regrets. Suspicious of his activities, Madeleine finally opens a letter addressed to him and finds a communiqué from the German secret service. Everything becomes clear to her. When Max enters the room, she shoots him with a revolver. The final scene shows her calling the police and reporting: "I killed my husband." The way to resolve a conflict between love and patriotism was made clear in such films—loyalty to the abstract idea of patriotism was more important than love for a human being.[24]

Complementing the motif of the foreign lover or husband as a traitor was the theme of nefarious seduction by a foreigner (the motif of "denationalization," as Jeffrey Brooks has called it). The danger of this kind of "national" seduction was particularly high in border regions with mixed populations. Aleksandr Drankov's *Alsace* tells the story of a French boy whose parents are involved in the French resistance against the Germans after 1871 but who is himself misled when a German girl "makes him fall in love" with her. The war breaks out and his parents move to Paris, but he, pressured by his girlfriend, enlists in the German army. Yet when he hears shouts of "Death to France!" he begins to regret his decision. When he shouts "Glory to France!" he is beaten up by a German mob. Covered with blood, he drags himself to his mother and dies. After the Germans are expelled from Alsace, the parents visit their son's grave and say: "Be happy, son, the French are here." The boy who temporarily abandoned his country for love is reunited with it in death. In addition to the sexual danger of foreigners, this film depicts ideas of blood and soil in a most literal fashion. Instead of a final unification with his loved one, the hero sheds his blood and is buried in his native soil.[25]

Films featuring the war with Turkey revealed Russians' old fears of the "Orient" and at the same time their fascination with the stereotypes of it. Treason and espionage as well as seduction and sexual oppression were the regular ingredients of these films. *The Bloody Crescent,* produced by Drankov from a script by Bebutova, focused exclusively on the sufferings of a Russian woman in a Turkish harem. Depicted as weak and silly, the Turks come across as less despicable than the Germans—indeed, as the victims of German scheming and wickedness. In *Turkish Espionage: The War and the Woman*, released by G. I. Libken in 1915, a young French woman who has learned to fly a plane falls in love with a Serbian pilot. To be near him she enlists as a nurse with the International Red Cross, and she is sent to a Turkish hospital. As she consoles a dying Turk, a prewar friend of her Serbian lover, she finds the secret plan for an attack in his pocket. She attempts to get away but is intercepted and thrown into a Turkish dungeon. Escaping in the uniform of a fallen Turkish officer whose documents she uses to commandeer a Turkish plane, she heroically crosses the front line and informs the Serbs about the imminent attack. Serbia repels the attack and the young lovers marry. Modern technology and the quick wits of a modern woman thus win out over "Oriental" male brutality.[26]

The most highly praised film on the "Oriental" theme was *Enver Pasha, the Traitor of Turkey*, which drew largely on actual events surrounding Turkey's entry into the war. Directed by Protazanov and released in early 1915, this film was one of the last in Thiemann & Reinhardt's Russian Golden Series. Its lavish sets reflect a Russian fantasy of a Turkish castle, with its fountains and hidden harem rooms. The story begins before the war in Berlin, where Enver Pasha works in the Turkish embassy. As an influential member of an ascending political party (the Young Turks) back in Turkey, Enver is courted by Wilhelm and showered with honors in efforts to ensure his loyalty to Germany in the coming war. He falls in love with the demimondaine Alisa, the girlfriend of Wilhelm's adjutant. When the Balkan War breaks out, he leaves Berlin and his paramour for his patriotic duty. By 1914 he has become all-powerful in Turkey. When the German general Liman von Sanders tries to persuade him to join Germany in the war, Enver rejects him out of fear of a war with powerful Russia. The Germans then send Alisa to seduce him into the war. But Enver's favorite in the harem, jealous and suspicious of Alisa, finds a letter about her mission. She gives it to Enver, and finally he understands that he was just a German tool. He sends a eunuch to kill Alisa. At the same time he is plagued by a vision: Turkey is destroyed in a war with Russia and a golden cross appears atop the mosque of Aja Sophia (better known under its Christian name, Hagia Sophia).[27]

This film identifies cowardice, sexual dependence, and weakness as primary Turkish characteristics. As in other films on the Oriental theme, *Enver Pasha* also conveys ideas about Russia's cultural, moral, and religious superiority. Yet it is German deceitfulness that leads Enver into the abyss, and thus he is an object of derision and sympathy at the same time, especially because he eventually understands his mistake. The message of this film is ambiguous. On the one hand it shows Russia as a civilized European nation, culturally distinct from the "Orient." On the other hand, Turkey seems too weak to be a real threat to Russia, for the real enemy is clearly in the "civilized" West. Yet the film implies that Germany is Turkey's real enemy and Russia its true friend. Notions of patriotism based on an identity constructed in opposition to a different culture thus mix with long-held traditions of Russian "protective" aims vis-à-vis the Ottoman Empire.[28]

Espionage and treason fitted nicely into a wave of detective novels and films that swept over the Western world and Russia alike. Many of these films merely adapted the war to an established taste, but some contained more elaborate patriotic messages. In *The Secret of the Krupp Works*, produced in 1915 by Mark Naletnyi and featuring actors from Moscow's Bat cabaret, an unemployed Belgian engineer, Albert Delaroche, is hired by the German spy von Holz to work for the Krupp armaments firm. When he goes to Germany to work in his special field, the construction of a powerful cannon, he leaves behind his fiancée, Madeleine. At Krupp's, spies intercept Madeleine's letters and seduce him with the young beauty Martha Stahl (Steel). One day, however, Delaroche is reminded of his fiancée when he sees a painting by Madeleine's artist brother Henri. At that moment Henri arrives to check on Albert for Madeleine and deliver a letter from her. Understanding his situation, Albert complains to Krupp and is allowed to see Madeleine, and at the same time he is told that war is imminent. Reunited with his love and ashamed of his moment of weakness, Albert destroys all the plans for his wonder cannon, replaces them with fake ones, and flees back to Belgium with Madeleine. Love of a compatriot, seduction by a foreigner, espionage, modern technology, and heroic Belgium combine in this film to make it more than just another spy movie. Such a cross section of patriotic themes was seldom available in such compact form.[29]

The representation of Belgium as the first and most vulnerable victim of German aggression and brutality was one of the most popular patriotic motifs not only in the visual and performing arts but also in the cinema. The film version of Leonid Andreev's *King, Law, and Freedom* (discussed in chapter 2) was not the only movie to play on Belgium's bravery, its famous king, and German cruelty. Most prominent among these offerings was *The Belgian Lily,* a partly animated film directed by Wladyslaw Starewicz. Starewicz had already made a successful patriotic trick film for Khanzhonkov in 1914, *The Stepson of Mars,* in which Bismarck sits on a cloud and drinks beer as Wilhelm II (a marionette) flies by on a sausage-blimp. *The Belgian Lily,* produced in 1915 for the Skobelev Committee's new feature film department, was more serious.[30]

At the opening of the film a little girl in a white dress finds a pale dead flower in a forest. In the next scene she sits in the study of her grandfather, an old man with a big bushy beard, who begins to tell the story of the lily. The animation begins at this point with a picture of the white lily next to a creek. In this sunny paradise the water flows, insects dance around the flower, frogs sing an ode to spring, a dragonfly plays a cello, and one frog sings an aria as another conducts the musical performance. (The latter two obviously stand for Maeterlinck and King Albert.) Paradise is threatened, however, by beetles living among the roots of a nearby tree; they are cleaning gun barrels, carrying halberds, and drinking beer out of big mugs. Their leader is a stag beetle whose mandibles call to mind the horns on Germanic and Viking helmets.

The beetles attack with cars, halberds, and artillery, but the "free lily" heroically stands in their way and refuses to move. The stag beetle pulls his saber and decrees the lily's death. The flower is cut down by the halberds and falls into the creek, becoming a bridge for the bad beetles. In the meantime, other beetles shaped like pine cones have come to the frogs' aid. The leader of the frogs (King Albert) opens floodgates somewhere in the distance, and waves of water (in the form of cotton) come streaming down to overwhelm the bad beetles. The animation is interrupted for the girl's question: Will the lily bloom again? The grandfather points to the flower's roots and says they will eventually sprout. In the final, animated scene, the lily does indeed bloom again, surrounded by the dragonfly and butterflies. Underneath, a pine-cone beetle plays the harmonica and dances a Cossack dance, symbolizing Russia's help and sympathy for Belgium.

The possibilities of animation enabled Starewicz to include more symbolism and to manipulate subconscious fears much more effectively than he could have done in a regular film. Relying extensively on pairs of opposites to convey a crystal-clear message, and making intelligent use of the limitations of black-and-white film, he used black for the villainous stag beetle and his army and white for the noble lily, the girl's gown, the cotton-water swallowing the evil forces. Romantic scenes of idyllic nature were set against the brutal and destructive technology of automobiles and artillery; civilized musical culture contrasts with preparations for war and excessive drinking of beer; the sun shining on the lily contrasts with the dark caverns of the tree roots where the beetles go about their destructive business. The frogs evoke the Russian fairy tale of the Frog Princess (*Tsarevna liagushka*), who has the good powers, in our case the Russian allies, on her side. The association of the girl in white with the broken lily forces comparisons with the "rape" of Belgium by the German army, and, as it was commonly believed, the rapes of Belgian women by German soldiers. *The Belgian Lily* is thus a masterpiece of early animation, full of symbolism and meaning, executed with a high degree of cinematic skill.

Though their plots are similar, *The German Barbarians in Belgium* does not approach *The Belgian Lily* in quality. Released by the Skobelev Committee in 1915, this nonanimated film placed the Belgium theme within the wave of terror movies (*film uzhasov*) then being produced about German atrocities. A German officer forces a Belgian boy to shoot his father; a German attempts to rape the boy's mother; shells explode as the family is liberated by the English. The film appeals to audiences' pleasure in vicariously experiencing men's worst instincts and women's worst fears.[31]

In war terror movies the German "brutes" and their "satanic" leader transgress all moral and religious bounds. Most of these films center on one outrageous episode, which is supplemented by a variety of less terrifying and more conventional atrocities. Thus *The Horrors of Reims*, released by Grigorii Libken, culminates in a German officer's attempt to rape a nurse on the altar of the famous cathedral. He is stopped by a clergyman holding a cross against him. The shelling of the cathedral and the Germans' drinking bouts within it pale beside this scene, which violates religious, moral, and patriotic values all at the same time.[32]

Wilhelm II depicted as Satan was a motif familiar in the visual and performing arts, and it also appeared in the titles of films depicting the kaiser's wickedness. In *The Breath of Antichrist* by Grigorii Libken, a peaceful Polish village and a loving couple are set against Wilhelm's murky deliberations on chemical warfare. After the customary horrors when the Germans destroy the village and many of its people, the kaiser's hell breaks loose as a cloud of poison gas creeps toward the Russian lines. The wind shifts, however, and the Germans themselves are hit by the "miasmic breath" of their ruler.[33]

The rumor that Wilhelm drank human blood actually circulated among the peasants of Kostroma province during the war, and it formed the basis for *The Antichrist*, a film produced by a studio that called itself Liutsifer. Introduced as the Prince of Darkness, Wilhelm is held responsible for all the atrocities committed by his soldiers, some of which are shown in the film, including attacks on Belgian civilians. The most impressive of these episodes is a sexual assault on a young woman by the crown prince himself. The visibility of a stockingless female leg in this scene prompted one critic to condemn the film as "plain pornography." Not unexpectedly, *The Antichrist* was a big hit, particularly in the provinces. During the first day of its run at the Triumf movie house in Buzuluk, it was shown without interruption from seven o'clock in the morning until midnight, "the longest session in the history of the Russian cinema," according to *Sine-Fono's* reporter.[34]

War terror films played extensively on the audience's fascination with the unknown and therefore dangerous aspects of the war. The psychological function was clearly more important than the historical authenticity of the episodes. In this respect, it should be noted that "German horrors" were already being advertised in a film produced at the very outbreak of the war, before any atrocities had been reported. Fantastic technology, brutality against women, and assaults on religion conveyed a sense of defenselessness, of being at the mercy of an unscrupulous enemy, but also of being on the side of right. Such clear transgressions of the most basic human values stirred emotions seldom experienced in everyday life behind the lines. They played on a fascination with the role of victim, the fear felt before a deadly blow, and thus made the war almost physically comprehensible to viewers' imaginations. At the same time, they depended on a reaction of relief triggered by this experience, an overflowing of emotion in an aggressive willingness to stand up against any atrocity committed by the foreign brutes.[35]

Such an overflowing of emotion into patriotic action was also the goal of a film produced by the Skobelev Committee, *The Poor Chap Died in an Army Hospital,* which was especially popular among lower-class audiences and became the second most watched movie of 1916. Based on a popular soldier's song that had become a great hit of Nadezhda Plevitskaia's, it was anything but a terror movie. As a classical melodrama, it appealed to familiar and comprehensible feelings. It opens with a young peasant living in a peaceful village with his family. He volunteers to serve the tsar in the war and risks his life to save a wounded officer. Later he is himself wounded, and "far from home and without the blessing of his mother, the young lad dies in a hospital." Arriving too late to see him one last time, his wife finds only the grave of her beloved and collapses in despair.

Nikolai Saltykov played the young soldier with great expressiveness. He showed the suffering and the emotions of the wounded at great length and effectively rolled his eyes toward the sky at the moment of death. These scenes, however, did not spark patriotic determination in the audiences. By the fall of 1916, they recognized themselves in the film. People sat with tears in their eyes as the piano player played the soldier's theme and the grief-stricken young woman on the screen bowed over the grave. *The Poor Chap* thus became the cinematic counterpart to Leonid Pasternak's poster of the wounded soldier. With its images the reality of the war made its way into the temples of dreams and escapism.[36]

The Russian film industry boomed during the war. With foreign competition banned, it developed its own styles and stars, and began to produce an immense number of films. The majority of these productions focused on crime, love, and psychological drama. They featured a world of social mobility (in both directions) that reflected the heterogeneity of their audiences. At the same time, they fed dreams of enormous wealth, beautiful women, and a lavish lifestyle along with fear of death, decay, and danger. These films created and satisfied all kinds of fantasies, allowing people to escape from their daily lives and the problems of the war.

War and patriotism were present in the movies in two forms: as a more or less authentic kinokhronika and as an ingredient of feature films with a variety of messages. Moviegoers viewed newsreels and documentary films as important sources of information and watched them with great interest, unaware that logistical and technological problems caused most of their battle scenes to be staged behind the lines, or that the Skobelev Committee, which had a monopoly on such films, was so understaffed that it could cover only a small fraction of the events on the long Russian front line. The French newsreels imported to fill the gaps familiarized Russian audiences with events on the Franco-German front and provided themes that in time showed up in patriotic feature films.

Feature films with war themes were produced both as patriotic propaganda and as plain entertainment. They were anything but the "extension and reflection of moral and patriotic feelings" that a contemporary journal had demanded.[37] Rather they were the crude and sensationalist fruits of savage competition among film companies. Superlatives of terror, baseness, brutality, and schmaltz advertised artistically weak and overhastily produced lubok farces, patriotic spy and detective movies, nationalist love affairs and melodramas, and thrilling and apocalyptic "terror films." These films drew extensively on patriotic traditions in the visual arts and the regular peacetime repertoire of the Russian cinema. Many adopted patriotic themes from postcards and lubok art, and thus became virtually "moving lubki," with little dramatic development and a stark cartoon style. Others, more elaborate and artistically demanding, blended with the traditional spy and adventure movies, love stories, and psychological dramas and enriched them with such patriotic issues as conflict between love for the nation and love for a person, atrocities committed by the enemy, and sympathy for a devastated ally. During the fall of 1914, the lubok films, a phenomenon peculiar to the first months of the war, were displaced by more sophisticated patriotic films. Even these films, however, declined in box office appeal during 1915 and 1916, and their plots became increasingly apocalyptic and pessimistic.

The war on film was an absolute novelty in Russian cultural life. A few newsreels had appeared during the Balkan Wars, but such a massive outpouring of documentary and patriotic feature films was unprecedented. Because World War I was the first war fought extensively on celluloid, the reality of war changed for many people. It became a commodity of the entertainment industry, to be enjoyed in the comfort and safety of a movie theater. The real dangers of the battlefield were turned into imagined threats, bloody horrors, and moral transgressions. The war could even be turned on and off. After all, people chose to go to the movies, and they also chose between war films and escapist fare.

As patriotism thus became a consumer item on the screen, feelings of us against them, of Russian moral and religious superiority were mixed with trivial stories of love and crime. Patriotism, once a quasi-religious dogma, became a theatrical set piece with widely variable roles and emphases. It could be understood as a moral dimension of a thrilling action or as something extraordinary, to be found only in connection with love affairs, spies, or heroism. In an art form that allegedly conveys the highest degree of realism and trustworthiness, this confusion of messages inevitably led to a decrease in clarity and an erosion of propaganda value. Patriotism in Russian films was thus multifaceted and almost casual, an appendix to the booming entertainment of an increasingly diverse society.[38]

Conclusion: National
Identity and Revolution

During World War I, patriotism in Russia was as variegated as the society of which it was a part. Because it changed over time in both form and content, it eludes simple definition. Nowhere was this more evident than in cultural life. The visual and performing arts and the cinema created a variety of patriotic "image worlds" and expressed them with all the richness characteristic of a rapidly transforming culture. Expressions of patriotism, however, dwindled in all of them between 1914 and 1917. After an initial outburst of flag-waving enthusiasm, which barely survived the catastrophic defeats at Tannenberg and the Masurian Lakes in the fall of 1914, Russian patriotism quickly became more differentiated, simultaneously reflecting separate and even disparate loyalties within society. It ranged from vilification of the enemy and glorification of Russia to strong social criticism and activism. Sometimes it was rejected outright in favor of escapist fare.

Older forms of Russian nationalist display—circus pantomimes, tableaux vivants, lubki, raëk—were enthusiastically revived during World War I, and patriotic culture came to depend heavily on folklore and nostalgia. It also drew on the satire of caricatures, cartoons, and farces, all legacies of the 1905 Revolution, and spread to new media that were becoming integral parts of an emerging mass culture. Postcards, posters, and films played important roles in the distribution of patriotic motifs and in wartime entertainment in general. Posters and films in particular were later used extensively to promote patriotism in World War II, as were the new forms of theater, estrada, and films designed to entertain troops at the front, all of which appeared for the first time during World War I as genuine products of patriotic culture. In addition, patriotic culture prefigured propaganda techniques that served the Bolsheviks well only a short time later. Cars, trains, and ships carrying movie equipment and graphic messages became as important as posters in the propaganda struggle of the Civil War.

Genres customarily associated with urban popular culture played more important roles than elite cultural forms in patriotic entertainment. As the possible foundations of loyalty to a society that ultimately binds the individual to the group, patriotism and nationalism flourish especially in a situation of mass communication, in which culture functions as the transmission belt. According to Ernest Gellner, nationalism can exist only in industrial societies with a high degree of mobility, literacy, and individualism. These factors may explain why patriotic culture in Russia was a phenomenon predominantly of the cities, where the lines of communication were short and quick, and why the urban lower classes responded to the war with more nationalistic fervor than the peasants in remote provinces could muster. They may also explain why popular and elite cultures initially converged in patriotic imagery.[1]

The images that Russians were accustomed to associate with patriotism and that they encountered or produced in all genres of patriotic culture can be grouped around a few main themes. External motifs—those focused on the enemy or on Allied countries—expressed patriotism by inference. Among them were clichés that could be found in all Allied countries during World War I. Kaiser Wilhelm, German *Kultur* and barbarism, and the fate of Belgium were as popular in New York and London as they were in Moscow. On the one hand, they called up the actual circumstances of the war; on the other, they reflected the close cultural connections of Russia with the West at the time and Russia's aspiration to be accepted as a civilized European nation.

External motifs of genuinely Russian origin were usually extensions of traditional stereotypes of neighboring countries. As in the other warring nations, enemy leaders became convenient personifications and focal points of broader sets of clichés. Long-held perceptions of the Orient as exotic and as a target for expansion, for example, influenced the image of a pitiful and silly sultan living amidst fantastic luxury. Images of a weak and crumbling empire, expressing imperial rivalry with Austria, were projected onto the figure of the old and frail Franz Joseph. The dominant role of Wilhelm in this trio and his alleged satanic character reflect Russians' perception of Germany as the most dangerous enemy, the one against which the greatest patriotic efforts had to be directed. The dehumanized image of Wilhelm also incorporated the traditional Russian clichés of Germans' militaristic boastfulness, cruel pedantry, and ungenerous small-mindedness.

External motifs were not numerous. Though they appeared in many variations—Wilhelm as another Napoleon, Belgium's King Albert as the embodiment of heroism—the concentration of these motifs in a few catchy keywords expressed the wartime situation of us against them, of a world of heroes and villains, with no need for further elaboration. This simplistic perspective led to a curious unity among the Russian social classes as popular and elite cultural forms used the same external motifs. The evidence of postcards and other stylistically broad visual materials indicates that kaiser-bashing and sympathy with Belgium were popular among all strata of society. This social unity against a foreign enemy turned out to be brittle, however, when Russians sought to define their own national identity in internal patriotic motifs.

Patriotic imagery reveals that Russians had a pretty clear idea against whom they were fighting in the war, but not for whom and for what. If a nation is a community imagined by its members, as Benedict Anderson convincingly argues, then Russia was not a nation during World War I. There was no commonly accepted national symbolic figure such as Uncle Sam or John Bull or the Deutsche Michel. The flag and the national anthem were so abstract and omnipresent that their meaning was open to individual interpretation or simple disregard. To a large extent, they had become ritualized as ornaments appended to theater, circus, and estrada shows; they were completely absent from such intelligentsia entertainments as cabarets and satirical journals.[2]

The tsar, the monarchy, historical military heroes, and mythological knights were not commonly accepted points of identification, either. Prominent on the political right and in official propaganda efforts by the Skobelev Committee, they also figured in patriotic entertainments designed for the lower classes. It should be noted, however, that Koz'ma Kriuchkov and other clever Cossacks were much more popular than the tsar and his generals. Seemingly closer to life, they offered more appealing and recognizable personifications of Russian military prowess than the traditional focus of Russian peasant loyalty, the person of the tsar.

The shrinking status of the tsar as a quasi-divine authority was matched by a notable absence of customary religious motifs, except for St. George and a few allegorical lubki. Otherworldliness was more prominent in transfigurations of military heroes in the tableaux vivants and "grand apotheoses." Superstition in the form of the White General and similar wonder-workers also reflected the decline of traditional national-religious values. Holy Russia and the saints of the Orthodox Church were no longer so convincing as valid sources of spiritual authority. Religion thus contributed only marginally to a common national consciousness.

The increasing secularization of the Russian lower classes that accompanied urbanization and the dissolution of traditional social identities thus found expression in patriotic culture as well. The shifts of national symbolism and the decline in loyalty to a traditional system and to a system of traditions had not yet resulted in the invention of generally valid alternative points of identification. Church and village were being displaced by cinema and city; a life space clearly defined was turning into one full of uncertainties, one that permitted a diversity of worldviews but lacked a widely accepted integrative ideology of the nation or civil society. By spotlighting the very question of national consciousness and loyalty, the war sped up this process of change by adding a national component to the ongoing social transformation. It contributed to the collapse of the old regime in February 1917 through more than its economic hardships. It accentuated what one might call a national identity crisis within Russian society.[3]

As widespread points of reference for patriotic feelings, Russian history and traditions appeared like a nostalgic reaction to these changes. History and traditions as internal motifs, however, offered conflicting images—military heroes jostling singing peasants. The artistic intelligentsia had discovered folklore long before the war, but enthusiasm for it gained momentum after 1914 in a renaissance of lubok art and a wave of byliny and old Russian tales in estrada shows.

What looked like a nostalgic drift back to the good old days, however, was also a reaction to the absence of more convincing focal points of patriotic identity. While some philosophically inclined intellectuals imagined a democratic civil society emerging in Russia after the war, others dreamed their Pan-Slavic dreams. Many intellectuals, however, chose Russian cultural traditions as their patriotic point of reference, one that allowed them to be Russian without having to support the existing state or ruler.[4]

Emphasizing one's national culture has been a traditional way to express nationalism for people without their own nation-state. Czechs, Poles, Germans, and Italians perceived themselves as cultural nations over most of the nineteenth century in opposition to the foreign rule or political nation under which they lived. They used their cultures and literatures to promote their national unity, to emancipate themselves from the states of which they were parts. Traits of this "Risorgimento nationalism," as it has been called, could also be observed in Russian patriotic culture. In a similar emancipatory effort, albeit with no clear political direction, large parts of Russian society, from Russian nationalists to the liberal intelligentsia, set themselves off from the existing state. Though they were not struggling for their own nation-state, they were nevertheless looking for forms of community legitimized by historical and cultural bonds rather than dynastic and imperial traditions, which had become alien to them and thus had lost their validity.[5]

Folklore and escapism, nostalgia and a longing for distant places are psychologically related and presuppose a similar state of mind. As in the other warring countries, Russians fled en masse from wartime reality. High society and parts of the intelligentsia in particular turned their backs on patriotism. Reflected in a display of luxury and decadence, their disaffection came to the fore in escapist trends on the stages of some legitimate theaters, on dance floors, and in the songs of a few celebrated estrada and nightclub stars. Disaffection could be found in other social groups as well. The cinema especially, but also such other new mass media as phonograph records, offered dreams of a beautiful and peaceful world, a world of wealth and luxury, to a more democratic audience. The cinema also provided escapism of quite a different sort, however. Films about vampires, murder, and suicide, apocalyptic visions of death and decay, which were otherwise available only in elite culture, modern literature, and philosophy, allowed for a flight from reality. This indulgence in murky pessimism and an almost palpable longing for the end of this world was peculiar to Russian wartime films. They orchestrated the Russian fin de siècle as a presentiment of the *fin de l'empire,* a phenomenon to be found elsewhere only in Austria, where such artists as Egon Schiele, Georg Trakl, and Gustav Mahler made death a central theme of their works and captured the atmosphere of a society dancing on its grave.

Escapism increased as the war dragged on, and other reactions to its growing burdens became evident in changes in patriotic motifs and themes and in a qualitative split of patriotism into active and passive forms. With the Austro-German victories in the late spring of 1915, jingoist imagery largely disappeared from the visual arts: heroic lubki vanished, extravagant patriotic circus pantomimes and jingoist plays disappeared. Now postcards with sentimental scenes of life at the front and caring nurses—a prime motif in all wars and countries—became popular, traditional sociocritical caricatures displaced antikaiser cartoons in satirical journals, and clowns and kupletisty began to attack speculators, war profiteers, and anti-Semites.

The shift toward more naturalistic depictions of the war and increasing criticism of people who did not share in the common effort was accompanied by a wave of charitable activities. Instead of propagating jingoist slogans and making fun of the enemy, entertainers of all kinds collected money and warm clothing, performed for the soldiers at the front, and gave "flying concerts" for the wounded in hospitals. Through their activities they expressed a social patriotism centered on human beings rather than birch trees. At the same time, they set an example of applied civic responsibility that matched the efforts among Russia's allies and stood in sharp contrast to the incompetence of official relief activities.

Diametrically opposed to this socially conscious active patriotism was passive enjoyment of patriotism as mass entertainment. To some extent passivity is characteristic of all consumers of culture—after all, audiences usually watch and listen—but the messages these audiences received might have stirred them to action. Few seem to have been designed to do so. A kupletist might convey a clear patriotic message, but an acrobat in a peasant costume or a nationalist drawing in a journal conveyed patriotic values only marginally and indirectly. In films patriotism came to resemble a variable set piece that was more an artistic convention than a call to conscious action. It was to be enjoyed as a thrill or a sentimental feeling alongside other impressions. Thus patriotism lost its uniqueness as a quasi religion and turned into a consumer item.

Historians will never be able to enter fully into the minds of people of the past. Yet they will always try to do so. During their futile attempts, they may learn that human life is too rich and too accidental to be subsumed under any explanatory construct. I do not offer "patriotic culture" as such a construct. I do not and cannot hope to plumb the patriotic feelings of individual Russians. I do not claim to have found a handy formula for patriotism in Russia during World War I, a formula that would allow one to draw clear-cut conclusions for the country's future development (or provide easy recipes for today's patriots). On the one hand, the Russian Revolution certainly did not happen as an inevitable consequence of the absence of a commonly recognized national identity, of a lack of that national cohesion which Russian Slavophiles and conservatives so cherished but were unable to actualize. On the other hand, the revolution would hardly have occurred without the dispersion of loyalties in Russian society. Nationalism, had it drawn on one unifying (albeit fictitious) national identity—whether Holy Russia and the tsar or some kind of Russian republic—might perhaps have overridden social fragmentation and economic distress, as it has done so often, notably in Germany since the nineteenth century. In February 1917, however, a unified national identity remained elusive, and Russians split their votes in the plebiscite that, according to Ernest Renan, stands at the origin of a nation.[6]

As an individal attitude and a social convention, patriotism is so complex that it cannot be reduced to the categories of cause and effect. I have therefore described its various representations and explored their meanings. The phenomenology and internal development of patriotism reveal its dynamism, and its attachment to a particular time and culture has filled it with life. In the end, however, any investigation of phenomena as puzzling as patriotism and as rich as Russian culture has to remain open-ended. Both live on and elude final appraisal.

Notes

Introduction: Patriotism and Its Metaphors

1. For an impression of the first days of the war on the streets of the capital, see the photos by Karl Bulla in A. Arnshtam, *Voennyi al'bom no. 1* (n.p., n.d.); police reports in TsGIA SPb, f. 569, op. 10, d. 154, which attest to the spontaneity of patriotic outbursts in St. Petersburg; and the detailed descriptions in *Peterburgskii listok*, 13–24 July 1914. For a discussion of Russia's social, political, and cultural situation at the outbreak of the war, see Hans Rogger, "Russia in 1914," *Journal of Contemporary History*, no. 4 (1966): 95–119.

2. For a detailed bibliography of studies on the military aspects of the war, see G. Khmelevskii, *Mirovaia imperialisticheskaia voina, 1914–1918: Sistematicheskii ukazatel' knizhnoi i stateinoi voenno-istoricheskoi literatury za 1914–1935 gg.* (Moscow, 1936). For social and cultural approaches, see Arthur Marwick, *The Deluge: British Society and the First World War* (New York, 1965); Modris Eksteins, *Rites of Spring: The Great War and the Birth of the Modern Age* (New York, 1990); Richard Wall and Jay Winter, eds., *The Upheaval of War: Family, Work, and Welfare in Europe, 1914–1918* (Cambridge, 1988) Paul Fussell, *The Great War and Modern Memory* (London, 1975); and Jürgen Kocka, *Klassengesellschaft im Kriege* (Göttingen, 1973). Noteworthy for its use of mass culture to recreate a "myth of the war experience" (though Russia is conspicuously absent) is George L. Mosse, *Fallen Soldiers: Reshaping the Memory of the World Wars* (New York, 1990). On the new interest in the war in Russia, see S. Polozov, "Avgust chetyrnadtsatogo," *Russkaia mysl'*, 29 September 1989, 13;

Jutta Scherrer, "Vom schwierigen Weg in die Demokratie: Laute Gedanken zu Rußlands neuer Vergangenheit," *Kursbuch*, no. 103 (1991): 178–88.

3. The need to clarify historical points of reference in newly emerging European nationalisms has been stressed by Peter Glotz, *Der Irrweg des Nationalstaats: Europäische Reden an ein deutsches Publikum* (Stuttgart, 1990), 68. On the history of Russian nationalism between World War I and the post-Soviet period, see the review essay by David G. Rowley, "Russian Nationalism and the Cold War," *American Historical Review* 99 (1994): 155–71; and Stephen K. Carter, *Russian Nationalism: Yesterday, Today, Tomorrow* (London, 1990). In his introduction (p. 3) Carter points out the connection between nationalism and ideological decline in the post-Soviet situation.

4. Carlton J. H. Hayes, *Essays on Nationalism* (New York, 1937), 2–6; Leonard W. Doob, *Patriotism and Nationalism: Their Psychological Foundations* (New Haven, 1964), 6; Earl L. Hunter, *A Sociological Analysis of Certain Types of Patriotism* (New York, 1932), 22–26; Eric Hobsbawm, *Nations and Nationalism since 1780: Programme, Myth, Reality* (Cambridge, 1990), 87–88. For a general overview of the earlier literature on patriotism and nationalism, see Karl W. Deutsch, *Interdisciplinary Bibliography on Nationalism* (Cambridge, Mass., 1956). Since the 1970s, discussions of nationalism have all but ignored patriotism. Reacting to the world's political changes, they address such issues as national movements, regionalism, and the anthropological and ethnic-cultural foundations of nationalism. The broad range of these discussions can be appreciated in the excellent study by Anthony D. Smith, *Theories of Nationalism*, 2d ed. (London, 1983), especially chaps. 7–10; for a brief summary, see the Introduction in Hobsbawm, *Nations and Nationalism.*

5. Leopold Haimson, "The Problem of Social Stability in Urban Russia, 1905–1917," *Slavic Review* 23 (1964): 619–42; 24 (1965): 1–22.

6. On nationalist philosophy during the war, see Ben Hellman, "Kogda vremia slavianofil'stvovalo. Russkie filosofy i pervaia mirovaia voina," in *Studia Russica Helsingiensia et Tartuensia. Problemy istorii russkoi literatury nachala XX veka,* ed. Liisa Byckling and Pekka Pesonen (Helsinki, 1989), 211–39. On official propaganda, see Iu. Aliakritskii, *Propaganda v armiiakh imperialistov* (Moscow, 1931), 10; Peter Kenez, *The Birth of the Propaganda State: Soviet Methods of Mass Mobilization, 1917–1929* (Cambridge, 1985), 9–10.

7. Victor Turner, *Dramas, Fields, and Metaphors: Symbolic Action in Human Society* (Ithaca, 1974), 13; David E. Nye, *Image Worlds: Corporate Identities at General Electric, 1890–1930* (Cambridge, Mass., 1985).

8. Ruth Benedict, *Patterns of Culture* (Cambridge, Mass., 1961), 253; Ernest Gellner, *Nations and Nationalism* (Ithaca, 1983), 7; Lawrence W. Levine, "The Folklore of Industrial Society: Popular Culture and Its Audiences," *American Historical Review* 97 (1992): 1372–73, 1381.

9. The problem of cultural translation is discussed in depth by Clifford Geertz, *The Interpretation of Cultures* (New York, 1973), 14–16 and passim.

10. On Russo-German relations and national stereotypes in general, see, among many others, Hans Lemberg, "Der 'Drang nach Osten.' Schlagwort

und Wirklichkeit," and Günther Stökl, "Die historischen Grundlagen des russischen Deutschlandbildes," both in *Deutsche im europäischen Osten. Verständnis und Mißverständnis*, ed. Friedhelm B. Kaiser and Bernhard Stasiewski (Cologne/Vienna, 1976), 1–17 and 18–34; Walter Laqueur, *Russia and Germany: A Century of Conflict* (Boston/Toronto, 1965), 13 and passim; Georg von Rauch, "Streiflichter zum russischen Deutschlandbilde des 19. Jahrhunderts," *Jahrbücher für Geschichte Osteuropas* 12 (1964): 5–47. On General Skobelev and his role as a popular hero, see Hans Rogger, "The Skobelev Phenomenon: The Hero and His Worship," *Oxford Slavonic Papers* 9 (1976): 46–78.

11. Heinz-Dietrich Löwe, "Political Symbols and Rituals of the Russian Radical Right, 1900–1917" (unpublished paper). On the role of self-stereotypes in national identity see L. M. Drobizheva, "Izuchenie natsional'nogo samosoznaniia v SSSR," paper presented at the symposium "Pre-Modern and Modern National Identity in Russia/Soviet Union and Eastern Europe," School of Slavonic and East European Studies, University of London, April 1989.

12. For a general discussion of Russia in the war, see Hans Rogger, *Russia in the Age of Modernisation and Revolution, 1881–1917* (London/New York, 1983), 251–71.

13. The numbers of participants in patriotic demonstrations and their social composition are mentioned in reports by several Petrograd police precincts (TsGIA SPb, f. 569, op. 10, d. 154, ll. 8–15, and op. 13, d. 1182zh, ll. 29–29 ob., ll. 34–34 ob.) as well as in *Peterburgskii listok*, 13–24 July 1914, and *Petrogradskii listok*, 9, 17, 21, and 26 October 1914 and 10 and 12 March 1915. According to these sources, the patriotic crowds at the center of St. Petersburg in the first days of the war numbered more than 10,000 but later shrank to "several thousand" or just "a thousand."

Picturing Patriotism: The War for the Eye

1. The interpretive value of pictures for cultural historians is discussed by Randolph Starn, "Seeing Culture in a Room for a Renaissance Prince," in *The New Cultural History*, ed. Lynn Hunt (Berkeley, 1989), 205–6.

2. Jeffrey Brooks, *When Russia Learned to Read: Literacy and Popular Literature, 1861–1917* (Princeton, 1985), esp. 151–52; S. S. Dmitriev, *Ocherki istorii russkoi kul'tury nachala XX veka* (Moscow, 1985), 101–7.

3. Many studies of lubki have been published, most of them concentrating on the early prints; see V. S. Bakhtin and D. M. Moldavskii, *Russkii lubok XVII–XIX vv.* (Moscow, 1962). Two short but competent studies are G. S. Ostrovskii, "Lubok v sisteme russkoi khudozhestvennoi kul'tury XVII–XX vekov," *Sovetskoe iskusstvoznanie* 2 (1980): 154–68; and E. G. Itkina, "Der russische Volksbilderbogen," in *Lubok: Der russische Volksbilderbogen*, ed. Wolfgang Till (Munich, 1985), 9–19; see also Paul Roth, "Der Lubok: Von der Papierikone zum ROSTA-Fenster," *Publizistik* 18 (1973): 154. For the distribution of

lubki, see S. V. Obolenskaia, "Obraz nemtsa v russkoi narodnoi kul'ture XVIII–XIX vv.," in *Odissei* (Moscow, 1991), 167.

4. Obolenskaia, "Obraz nemtsa," esp. 171–73.

5. The lubki of 1812 owe some of their fame to Lev Tolstoi, who mentions them in *War and Peace*. See E. P. Ivanov, *Russkii narodnyi lubok* (Moscow, 1937), 63; A. F. Nekrylova, *Russkie narodnye gorodskie prazdniki, uveseleniia i zrelishcha: Konets XVIII–nachalo XX veka*, 2d ed. (Leningrad, 1988), 114; Iu. M. Ovsiannikov, *Russkii lubok* (Moscow, 1962), 29–30; Walter Koschmal, *Der russische Volksbilderbogen (Von der Religion zum Theater)*, Slavistische Beiträge, vol. 251 (Munich, 1989), 101; Vladimir Denisov, *Voina i lubok* (Petrograd, 1916), 18–20, reproductions nos. 9 and 11; see also John E. Bowlt, "Russian Painting in the Nineteenth Century," in *Art and Culture in Nineteenth-Century Russia*, ed. Theofanis George Stavrou (Bloomington, Ind., 1983), 120–21, and Roth, "Der Lubok," 154.

6. Koschmal, *Der Russische Volksbilderbogen*, 100–101; Denisov, *Voina i lubok*, 23–26; Brooks, *When Russia Learned to Read*, 65–66; G. Miasoedov, "Russkii lubok kontsa XIX–nachala XX veka," in *Illiustratsiia*, comp. G. V. El'shevskaia (Moscow, 1988), 241.

7. The principal study and collection of lubki appeared in 1881: D. A. Rovinskii, *Russkiia narodnyia kartinki*, 5 vols. (St. Petersburg, 1881–93); selected parts of this seminal work have been reprinted and edited by Walter Koschmal as *Russkija narodnyja kartinki*, Specimina Philologiae Slavicae, vol. 84 (Munich, 1989); the 1913 Moscow exhibition was organized by Mikhail Larionov and Nataliia Goncharova (Ovsiannikov, *Russkii lubok*, 53). For the decline of the lubok as a popular artistic genre, see Ostrovskii, "Lubok," 166; Miasoedov, "Russkii lubok," 241, 247. On growing literacy, see Brooks, *When Russia Learned to Read*, esp. 27–34.

8. Brooks, *When Russia Learned to Read*, 314; *Affiches et imageries russes, 1914–1920* (Paris, 1982), VI; Ovsiannikov, *Russkii lubok*, 54; Denisov, *Voina i lubok*, 2–4, 28, and the review of that book by R. [= A. A. Radakov?], "Voina i lubok (Broshiura Vl. Denisova)," *Teatr i iskusstvo* 20 (1916): 302–3. Koschmal, *Russische Volksbilderbogen*, 102, notes a renaissance of the lubok as agitational art during and after the revolution, but overlooks the wartime boom.

9. See *Kartinki—Voina russkikh s nemtsami* (Petrograd, [1916]), sheets 85, 72, 74, 35; for their old versions, see Bakhtin and Moldavskii, *Russkii lubok*, nos. 24, 28, 73, and Denisov, *Voina i lubok*, 17 and no. 3. On German models see Wilhelm Fraenger, "Deutsche Vorlagen zu russischen Volksbilderbogen des 18. Jahrhunderts," in *Lubok: Der russische Volksbilderbogen*, ed. Wolfgang Till (Munich, 1985), 39–41, 50–51.

10. See *Voennyia kartiny* nos. 5 and 2 in PPDLC (no. 3502 H); J. F. Kowtun, *Die Wiedergeburt der künstlerischen Druckgraphik: Aus der Geschichte der russischen Kunst zu Beginn des zwanzigsten Jahrhunderts* (Dresden, 1984), 74–75; Platon Beletskii, *Georgii Ivanovich Narbut* (Leningrad, 1985), 109–11; Denisov, *Voina i lubok*, 28; Miasoedov, "Russkii lubok," 246–47. On Biokhrom, see *Sine-Fono*, no. 4–5 (1914): 38. For a contemporary commentary by the artistic editor

of the journal *Lukomor'e* see Gerasim Magula, "Voina i narodnyia kartiny," *Lukomor'e*, no. 30 (1914): 17.

11. Brooks, *When Russia Learned to Read*, 131; Mark Etkind, *A. N. Benua i russkaia khudozhestvennaia kul'tura kontsa XIX–nachala XX veka* (Leningrad, 1989), 205; Kowtun, *Die Wiedergeburt*, 74–75; Anna Lawton, ed., *Russian Futurism through Its Manifestoes, 1912–1928* (Ithaca, 1988), 12, 14; Camilla Gray, *Das große Experiment: Die russische Kunst, 1863–1922* (Cologne, 1974), 27, 111–12; E. Murina, "A. V. Lentulov," *Iskusstvo*, no. 2 (1957): 35–38. I have found no evidence to support Stephen White's assertion in *The Bolshevik Poster* (New Haven, 1988), 3, that Segodniashnii Lubok was founded by the Russian government.

12. For Maiakovskii's texts for the lubki of Segodniashnii Lubok, see his *Polnoe sobranie sochinenii v trinadtsati tomakh* (Moscow, 1955), 1:355–64; Magula, "Voina," 17; Vladimir Botsianovskii, "Novyi lubok," *Teatr i iskusstvo* 18 (1914): 810–12; Kowtun, *Die Wiedergeburt*, 75; E. F. Kovtun, *Russkaia futuristicheskaia kniga* (Moscow, 1989), 150, 155. All of Segodniashnii Lubok's lubki and postcards used for this book are in the Slavonic Library of the University of Helsinki.

13. My assumption that Maiakovskii was drawing more pictures than have so far been acknowledged is based on the fact that the unsigned postcards "Kazaku zhena Polina . . . ," "Vot kak nemtsy u Suvalok . . . ," "Kak nachnët palit' vintovka . . . ," "Shël v Varshavu . . . ," "Frants-Iosif s voiskom rad . . . ," and "Plyli eti mesiatsem . . . " contain a set of parallel lines, most of them blue, that can also be seen on a postcard signed by Maiakovskii ("Nemka turka u Stambula . . . "). At the same time, red horses and the sharp lines of figures and landscape in "Ekh i grozno, ekh i sil'no . . . " link this lubok to "Sdal avstriets russkim L'vov . . . ," which has been attributed to Aristarkh Lentulov (Miasoedov, "Russkii lubok," 250). Since the latter two pictures are so similar in style and coloring, the attribution by *Affiches et imageries russes*, 117–18, of the first to Lentulov and the second to Maiakovskii (who drew in a more dilettante style anyway) makes little sense.

14. See the quotation of S. P. Bobrov in Kowtun, *Die Wiedergeburt*, 59, and Magula, "Voina," 14–16; Ovsiannikov, *Russkii lubok*, 54; V. Okhochinskii, *Plakat* (Leningrad, n.d.), 71–72.

15. Miasoedov, "Russkii lubok," 243; Denisov, *Voina i lubok*, 27. Some of the other publishing houses are Levin, Shrotte, and Freiberg in Riga; Strel'tsov, Mashistov, the brothers Evdokimov, Konovalova, Morozov, Korkin, Beideman & Co., Krylov & Co., Chelnokov, and Postnov in Moscow; Gubanov in Kiev; and Kiugel'gen, Glich & Co. in Petrograd. Lubki from Postnov and from Korkin, Beideman are in PPDLC and GMISP, respectively. Unless I indicate otherwise, all other lubki referred to hereafter are in the collection of the Slavonic Library of Helsinki University and as photographs in my own collection. For a list of lubki editors, see Ivanov, *Russkii narodnyi lubok*, 13–14 (n. 1).

16. "Leib-gusary presleduiut otstupaiushchikh nemtsev v raione Krakova" (Strel'tsov, *Evropeiskaia voina* no. 15, n.d.); "Vziatie Peremyshlia" (Gubanov,

Voina Rossii s Germaniei i Avstriei no. 35, 1915); "Porazhenie avstro-germanskikh voisk u reki San" (Sytin no. 23, 1914) (PPDLC).

17. "Voina Rossii s nemtsami. Zverstva nemtsev" (Krylov, *Al'bom velikoi voiny* no. 2, n.d.); "Zverstva turok i kurdov" (Morozov, n.d.); Aleksandra Kalmykova, "Russkiia lubochnyia kartiny v ikh prosvetitel'nom znachenii dlia naroda za poslednee 75-letie nashei zhizni," in *Polveka dlia knigi: Literaturno-khudozhestvennyi sbornik, posviashchennyi piatidesiatiletiiu izdatel'skoi deiatel'nosti I. D. Sytina* (Moscow, 1916), 191.

18. "Pobeda Angliiskago flota v morskom boiu u ostrova Gel'golanda" (Sytin no. 14, 1914); "Voina v vozdukhe" (Sytin no. 45, 1914) (GMISP); see also "Voina v vozdukhe.—Podvig Pegu" (Sytin no. 41, 1914) and "Geroiskii podvig i gibel' znamenitago lëtchika Sht.-Kapit. P. N. Nesterova" (Korkin, Beideman, *Velikaia evropeiskaia voina* no. 173, n.d.).

19. "Rol' zhenshchiny v voine. Podvig sëstry miloserdiia" (Sytin no. 73, 1915) (GMISP); "Ranenye v Moskve" (Sytin no. 60, 1914) (GMISP). On the tradition of unscathed Russian heroes see A. F. Nekrylova, "Komicheskii batal'nyi lubok v sostave raëshnogo obozreniia," *Russkii fol'klor* 25 (1989): 55. On the absence of blood in war reports in general, see Paul Fussell, *Wartime: Understanding and Behavior in the Second World War* (New York, 1989), 268–69; and Mosse, *Fallen Soldiers*, 129.

20. Wilhelm is beaten with a birch branch by a Russian soldier in "Meniu Vil'gel'ma" (Krylov no. 14, n.d.); he is shown as a barking street dog with whiskers and spiked helmet being taught a lesson by the rifle butt of a Cossack in "Nauka nemtsu" (Mashistov, 1914); and he is stung by a Cossack's whip while an English sailor and a French soldier pull his ears in "Chto Vil'gesha, milyi drug . . . " (Postnov, 1914). In "Nemetskaia khitrost' i kazach'ia smekalka" by P'er-O [Sergei Zhivotovskii] (Sytin no. 66, 1914) a German with sausages hanging from his belt is trying to fight Cossacks with the help of trained police dogs, but the Cossack uses a beautiful female dachshund to lure the police dogs into a barn, where he locks them up.

21. "Podvig kazaka Lavina" (Sytin no. 36, 1914) (PPDLC).

22. The example from the Napoleonic Wars is in Obolenskaia, "Obraz nemtsa v russkoi narodnoi kul'ture," 173. See also Okhochinskii, *Plakat*, 71. A collection of Kriuchkov lubki in GMPIR, f. 5, nos. 11756–11782, gives an impression of the dissemination of the theme.

23. "Vrag roda chelovecheskago" (Sytin, 1915); this unsigned lubok was much appreciated by contemporaries (see Kalmykova, "Russkiia lubochnyia kartiny," 192; also Denisov, *Voina i lubok*, 29). For more recent reproductions, see *Affiches et imageries russes*, 123, and Frank Kämpfer, *"Der rote Keil": Das politische Plakat. Theorie und Geschichte* (Berlin, 1985), 15.

24. "Rossiia i eia voin" (Chelnokov, n.d.). For a discussion of the Muromets tale and for the role of Mother Russia in Russian folklore in general, see Joanna Hubbs, *Mother Russia: The Feminine Myth in Russian Culture* (Bloomington, Ind., 1988), esp. 153–60.

25. Iu. M. Lotman, "Khudozhestvennaia priroda russkikh narodnykh kar-

tinok," in *Narodnaia graviura i fol'klor v Rossii XVII–XIX vv. K 150-letiiu so dnia rozhdeniia D. A. Rovinskogo* (Moscow, 1976), 251.

26. On borrowing religious motifs for political purposes, see White, *Bolshevik Poster*, 5–7.

27. For lubki on the fairground, see V. G. Babenko, *Artist Aleksandr Vertinskii: Materialy k biografii. Razmyshleniia* (Sverdlovsk, 1989), 16–17; V. A. Nevskii, *Velikaia evropeiskaia voina: Sistematicheskiia programmy dlia narodnykh chtenii—vecherov po istorii i geografii voiuiushchikh derzhav* (Buzuluk, 1915), 39–42. This handbook for multimedia evenings with slide shows, readings, lectures, singing, and acting was designed to teach villagers about the other countries taking part in the war. On lubki as a medium for the sensational and curious, see Lotman, "Khudozhestvennaia priroda," 262; distribution is discussed in Brooks, *When Russia Learned to Read*, 66–67.

28. Kowtun, *Die Wiedergeburt*, 77; Gerald Janecek, *The Look of Russian Literature: Avant-Garde Visual Experiments, 1900–1930* (Princeton, 1984), 10.

29. Nekrylova, "Komicheskii batal'nyi lubok," 52. On raëk, see A. M. Konechnyi, "Raëk v sisteme peterburgskoi narodnoi kul'tury," *Russkii fol'klor* 25 (1989): 123–38; Nekrylova, *Russkie narodnye gorodskie prazdniki*, 95–125.

30. Nekrylova, "Komicheskii batal'nii lubok," 53–56; Brooks, *When Russia Learned to Read*, 103–4; N. I. Savushkina, *Russkii narodnyi teatr* (Moscow, 1976), 132–33.

31. Catriona Kelly, "Petrushka and the Pioneers: The Russian Carnival Puppet Theatre after the Revolution," in *Discontinuous Discourses in Modern Russian Literature*, ed. Catriona Kelly, Michael Makin, and David Shepherd (London, 1989), 75; E. M. Kuznetsov, comp., *Russkie narodnye gulian'ia po rasskazam A. Ia. Alekseeva-Iakovleva* (Leningrad, 1948), 99–100; A. M. Konechnyi, "Peterburgskie narodnye gulian'ia na maslenoi i paskhal'noi nedeliakh," in *Peterburg i guberniia: Istoriko-etnograficheskie issledovaniia*, ed. N. V. Iukhnëva (Leningrad, 1989), 44–45; idem, "Raëk v sisteme," 133. Attempts by members of the intelligentsia to reconstruct "traditional" carnivals continued into the 1920s and finally succeeded under the auspices of Obshchestvo Izucheniia, Populiarizatsii i Khudozhestvennoi Okhrany Starogo Peterburga; see A. G. Levinson, "Popytka restavratsii balagannykh gulianii v nepovskoi Rossii (K sotsiologii kul'turnykh form)," in *Odissei* (Moscow, 1991), 146–57.

32. TsGIA SPb, f. 569, op. 14, d. 161, ll. 20–21 ob.; Nekrylova, *Russkie narodnye gorodskie prazdniki*, 97; A. Rennikov, *Lunnaia doroga: Razskazy* (Petrograd, 1916), 114–16.

33. Denisov, *Voina i lubok*, 37–40. Anti-German raëk pictures, especially in the 1880s, are discussed in Obolenskaia, "Obraz nemtsa v russkoi narodnoi kul'ture," 177–78.

34. F. I. Shol'te, comp., *Grimasy voiny, 1914–1915 g.: Plakaty, karikatury, lubki*, 2d ed. (Petrograd, 1916), 49.

35. I. F. Masanov, *Slovar' psevdonimov russkikh pisatelei, uchënykh i obshchestvennykh deiatelei* (Moscow, 1958), 3:296; O. V. Tsekhnovitser, *Literatura i mirovaia voina, 1914–1918* (Moscow, 1938), 243.

36. On patriotic journals for soldiers, see L. G. Beskrovnyi, *Ocherki po ist-ochnikovedeniiu voennoi istorii Rossii* (Moscow, 1957), 437–40. *Voin i pakhar'*: *Ezhenedel'nyi voenno-narodnyi illiustrirovannyi zhurnal* was published and ed-ited in Moscow by I. I. Savostin; *Il'ia Muromets: Ezhenedel'nyi zhurnal dlia soldat* was edited by L. M. Savëlov and published by A. I. Mamontov in Moscow.

37. For a colored Easter supplement with pictures of air battles and Easter eggs, see *Il'ia Muromets*, no. 15 (1916); on Mazurovskii, a member of Pe-trogradskoe Obshchestvo Khudozhnikov, and his patriotic pictures, see V. I. Lapshin, *Khudozhestvennaia zhizn' Moskvy i Petrograda v 1917 godu* (Moscow, 1983), 13–14, 313.

38. *Il'ia Muromets*, no. 3 (1915): 11, 13; *Voina* was a supplement of the journal *20-i vek*, edited by N. Volyntsev and published by I. Bogel'man. The issue on the war in the air is no. 11 (1914).

39. Most of these front-page pictures were produced by the artist A. Panin; the examples are from *Voina*, nos. 13, 15, 17 (1914) and no. 27 (1915). On Skobelev, see Rogger, "Skobelev Phenomenon."

40. On *Niva*, see Brooks, *When Russia Learned to Read*, 111–14; E. A. Diner-shtein, "Fabrikant" chitatelei: A. F. Marks (Moscow, 1986), 25–51; *Oglavlenie "NIVY" za 1915 god*, III-V. Other artists who worked for the journal were M. I. Avilov, a war correspondent; S. F. Kolesnikov; E. E. Lansere, a contributor to *Mir iskusstva*; V. V. Mazurovskii; and N. S. Samokish, a professor at the Pe-trograd Higher Art School (Lapshin, *Khudozhestvennaia zhizn'*, 19–20, 30, 40–42). On Vladimirov, see "Batalist I. A. Vladimirov," *Niva*, no. 46 (1915): 841–42; for his pictures, *Niva*, no. 42 (1914): 811, and no. 46 (1915): 841–42.

41. [V. P. Krymov], "Ot redaktsii," *Stolitsa i usad'ba*, no. 16–17 (1914): 21; Epikur [A. L. Rubinshtein?], "Interesno zhit'! Malen'kii fel'eton," ibid., no. 23 (1914): 10. For reports about a patriotic exhibition and the ice sculpture, see ibid., no. 28 (1915): 27 and no. 30 (1915): 26. The drawings by Lodygin are ibid., no. 70 (1916): 18 and no. 79 (1917): 12.

42. About *Lukomor'e* see Tsekhnovitser, *Literatura i mirovaia voina*, 113–14; Beletskii, *Narbut*, 111–15. As an employee of a commission dealing with war trophies, Narbut had ample time to work for *Lukomor'e*, according to G. K. Lukomskii, *Egor Narbut: Khudozhnik—Grafik* (Berlin, 1923), 12; cover of *Lukomor'e*, no. 28 (1914). On the use of animal metaphors see Johannes Holthusen, *Tiergestalten und metamorphe Erscheinungen in der Literatur der rus-sischen Avantgarde (1909–1923)*, Bayerische Akademie der Wissenschaften, Philosophisch-Historische Klasse, Sitzungsberichte 1974, no. 12 (Munich, 1974), esp. 19–20.

43. Shol'te, *Grimasy voiny* (a publication of the journal *Argus*); *Karikatury "Voina i Pem"—Caricatures "La Guerre et Pême,"* 2d ed. (Petrograd, 1915); V. B. Lekhno, *Voina. V sharzhakh i karrikaturakh periodicheskikh izdanii* (Moscow, n.d.). An impression of the international exchange of caricatures can be obtained from *International Cartoons of the War*, ed. H. Pearl Adam (London, 1916), which contains two cartoons from *Lukomor'e* (nos. XXV and XXVI).

44. John E. Bowlt, "Nineteenth-Century Russian Caricature," in Stavrou,

Art and Culture, 226–27, 230–32; Georg Piltz, *Geschichte der europäischen Karikatur* (Berlin, 1976), 235–36.

45. "Bitaia karta," *Novyi Satirikon*, no. 41 (1914); for Nikolai II as king of spades see Lapshin, *Khudozhestvennaia zhizn'*, 103. On Averchenko and *Novyi Satirikon*, see the introduction by L. A. Evstigneeva in *Poety "Satirikona"* (Moscow/Leningrad, 1966), 8–48; "*Krasnyi perets" i drugie*, Stranitsy istorii sovetskoi satiricheskoi grafiki (Moscow, 1990). On Bilibin, see G. V. Golynets and S. V. Golynets, *Ivan Iakovlevich Bilibin* (Moscow, 1972), 101–38, and John E. Bowlt, *The Silver Age: Russian Art of the Early Twentieth Century and the "World of Art" Group* (Newtonville, Mass., 1979), 233–46.

46. See the cover of *Novyi Satirikon*, no. 36 (1914). Remizov sided with the Whites after October 1917 and had to emigrate (White, *Bolshevik Poster*, 114).

47. For Radakov's later work, particularly his posters for the literacy campaigns of the 1920s, see White, *Bolshevik Poster*, 104–5, 116; see also "Esli nemtsy vozmut Parizh!" *Novyi Satirikon*, no. 36 (1914): n.p. For a general overview of Radakov's work, see *A. Radakov, A. Iunger* (Moscow, 1989).

48. Nicoletta Misler, "A Public Art: Caricatures and Posters of Vladimir Lebedev," *Journal of Decorative and Propaganda Arts* 5 (Summer 1987): 63. On the Tass windows, a revival of the Rosta windows of the 1920s, see White, *Bolshevik Poster*, 123–24. Pictures by Lebedev are in *Novyi Satirikon*, no. 39 (1914): 8; no. 41 (1914): 3; no. 43 (1914): 6; no. 44 (1914): 5. Al'tman's drawing is in no. 38 (1914): n.p.

49. *Novyi Satirikon*, no. 1 (1915): 3, and covers of no. 5 (1915) and no. 8 (1916).

50. These figures come from a sample of 194 caricatures in journals and albums. They are supported by a sample of 360 satirical postcards that yield precisely the same results. On Napoleon, see Bowlt, "Nineteenth-Century Russian Caricature," 226–27; Harold Dwight Lasswell, *Propaganda Technique in the World War* (London, 1938), 89–90.

51. Robert Lebeck and Manfred Schütte, eds., *Propagandapostkarten* (Dortmund, 1980), 21. On individualism, see Jeffrey Brooks, "Competing Modes of Popular Discourse: Individualism and Class Consciousness in the Russian Print Media, 1880–1928," paper presented at the 19th National Convention of the American Association for the Advancement of Slavic Studies, Boston, 5–8 November 1987, 3.

52. On the problems of postcards as historical sources, see Marie-Monique Huss, "Pronatalism and the Popular Ideology of the Child in Wartime France: The Evidence of the Picture Postcard," in *The Upheaval of War: Family, Work and Welfare in Europe, 1914–1918*, ed. Richard Wall and Jay Winter (Cambridge, 1988), 359. Editions and provincial publishers are discussed in N. S. Tagrin, *Mir v otkrytke* (Moscow, 1978), 50–51. Tagrin's collection of postcards, one of the world's largest, is now in GMISP.

53. Tagrin, *Mir v otkrytke*, 34, 42–45; Serge Zeyons, *Les Cartes postales* (Paris, 1979), 26; White, *Bolshevik Poster*, 9. I am indebted to Andrei Dvorkin of St. Petersburg for the opportunity to browse through his substantial collection of Russian prerevolutionary postcards.

54. The standard division of World War I postcards into patriotic, documentary, and satirical cards is in Zeyons, *Cartes postales*, 48, 98–101.

55. On postcards in the role of lubki, see Denisov, *Voina i lubok*, 33. The use of postcards to convey information about the war was also common in Germany; see, for example, the collectors' album *Gloria—Viktoria: Der Völkerkrieg in Wort und Bild nach Daten geordnet. Ein Postkartensammelwerk* (Munich, n.d.), which includes more than 250 cards dealing with places hit by the war, military technique, and so forth.

56. "Kruzhok dam Petrogradskoi voenno-fel'dsherskoi shkoly," in TsGIA SPb, f. 569, op. 14, d. 161, ll. 4–21 ob.

57. On the technically more advanced French patriotic fantasy cards see Huss, "Pronatalism," 337–40. The so-called *Fürstenpostkarten* of Wilhelm II are discussed in Bernhard Wördehoff, "Der frankierte Kaiser: Posen fürs Volk," *Zeitmagazin*, no. 44 (October 1990): 40–46; see also Klaus-D. Pohl, "Der Kaiser im Zeitalter seiner technischen Reproduzierbarkeit: Wilhelm II. in Fotografie und Film," in *Der letzte Kaiser: Wilhelm II. im Exil*, ed. Hans Wilderotter and Klaus-D. Pohl (Berlin, 1991), 12–14.

58. On publishers who specialized in reproductions of fine art, see Tagrin, *Mir v otkrytke*, 53. Vladimirov's works are "Sledy Germantsev" and "Batareia na Visle" (Liubanskoe Obshchestvo Popecheniia o Bednykh, nos. 42 and 44, 1916).

59. Apsit's postcards include "Nashi sanitary na peredovykh pozitsiiakh," "Zheleznyia serdtsa," "Russkiie dobrovol'tsy vo Frantsii," and "Ukhod za ranenym vragami v nashikh lazaretakh" (all Viktoriia, n.d.); on Apsit, see White, *Bolshevik Poster*, 25–26.

60. For an album of war silhouettes see M. Lisovskii, *Siluety voiny. 1914–1915: Risunki uchastnika*, 2 vols. (Petrograd, 1915–16). Examples of silhouette pictures are "Vesti s rodiny," "Geroiskaia skhvatka kazaka K. Kriuchkova" (both Khmelevskii, n.d.), and "Gordost' materi" (Iskusstvo, no. 208, n.d.).

61. *Vestnik kinematografii*, no. 100 (1914): 14. On Samokish-Sudkovskaia, see N. I. Baburina, *Russkii plakat: Vtoraia polovina XIX–nachalo XX veka* (Leningrad, 1988), 117, 121, 124. Samokish-Sudkovskaia produced one of the very few postcards depicting a Russian knight. This card, titled "Velikaia voina," is reproduced in Anne Goulzadian, *L'Empire du dernier tsar: 410 Cartes postales, 1896–1917* (Argenteuil, 1982), 232.

62. On the multifaceted role of nurses in the war, see Richard Holmes, *Acts of War: The Behavior of Men in Battle* (New York, 1986), 98–100. On *Russkoe slovo*, the most widely read Russian newspaper during the war, see Louise McReynolds, *The News under Russia's Old Regime: The Development of a Mass-Circulation Press* (Princeton, 1991), 256–63. All Red Cross cards carried the following note: "2–3 postcards sold help to produce a gas mask."

63. On patriotic letters, see Tsekhnovitser, *Literatura i mirovaia voina*, 244.

64. Of the 360 postcards I investigated, 119 featured Wilhelm alone. For his prominence on cards of Russia's allies, see, for example, John M. Kaduck, *Patriotic Postcards* (Des Moines, 1974), 47; and Serge Zeyons, *Le Roman-photo de*

la Grande Guerre: Les Cartes-postales "Bleu-Horizon" (Paris, 1976), 11–12, 20, 38–46.

65. Richard Stites, *Russian Popular Culture: Entertainment and Society since 1900* (Cambridge, 1992), 89.

66. On Iunak's artistic individuality, see Ivanov, *Russkii narodnyi lubok*, 63; P. P. Ershov, *Konëk-gorbunok. Stikhotvoreniia* (Leningrad, 1976), 59.

67. On the cockroach motif, see "Prussaki" (Chelnokov, Moscow, n.d.).

68. For an explanation of the gesture, see Barbara Monahan, *A Dictionary of Russian Gesture* (Tenafly, N.J., 1983), 86–87; for a more detailed discussion of publishers of satirical postcards see Hubertus F. Jahn, "Patriotic Culture in Russia during World War I" (Ph.D. diss., Georgetown University, 1991), 58–65.

69. A. Bogachev, *Plakat* (Leningrad, 1926), 8; Okhochinskii, *Plakat*, 73; Kenez, *Birth of the Propaganda State*, 112; Jay Leyda, *Kino: A History of the Russian and Soviet Film*, 3d ed. (Princeton, 1983), 89.

70. Among the best works to emerge from this research are Baburina, *Russkii plakat*; White, *Bolshevik Poster*; and Kämpfer, *"Der rote Keil."*

71. Kämpfer, *"Der rote Keil,"* 161–62; Kenez, *Birth of the Propaganda State*, 9; Stephen White, "The Political Poster in Bolshevik Russia," in *Sbornik No. 8: Papers of the Eighth International Conference of the Study Group on the Russian Revolution Held at Hertford College, Oxford, January 1982* (Leeds, 1982), 25.

72. Frank Kämpfer, "Das frühsowjetische Plakat als historische Quellengruppe: Ein Beitrag zur Erkenntnistheorie des politischen Bildes," *Forschungen zur osteuropäischen Geschichte* 25 (1978): 157–58. GMISP holds countless posters announcing benefit performances.

73. For reproductions of the "red cross" poster by N. Piskarëv ("Vystavka kartin i skul'ptury 'Khudozhniki Moskvy—zhertvam voiny' " [Levenson, Moscow, 1914]), see Baburina, *Russkii plakat*, 42, and Lapshin, *Khudozhestvennaia zhizn'*, 35.

74. Viktor Vasnetsov, "Vo vsekh zalakh Rossiiskogo blagorodnogo sobraniia . . . " (Levenson, Moscow, 1914); for reproductions, see Baburina, *Russkii plakat*, 161, and Lapshin, *Khudozhestvennaia zhizn'*, 36.

75. Dolina's concerts are discussed in chap. 2.

76. Examples are S. A. Vinogradov, "Na pomoshch zhertvam voiny" (Levenson, Moscow, 1914), reproduced in Lapshin, *Khudozhestvennaia zhizn'*, 34; G. D. Alekseev, "Na prodovol'stvennuiu pomoshch' maloimushchim g. Moskvy" (Obshchee Delo, Moscow, 1916), reproduced in Klaus Waschik, *Seht her, Genossen! Plakate aus der Sowjetunion* (Dortmund, 1982), 17; A. E. Arkhipov, "Na peredovykh pozitsiiakh rabotaet tol'ko Krasnyi Krest . . . " (Levenson, Moscow, 1914), reproduced in Lapshin, *Khudozhestvennaia zhizn'*, 12. Pasternak's poster is analyzed in Baburina, *Russkii plakat*, 163–67; White, *Bolshevik Poster*, 14–15; and Leonid O. Pasternak, *The Memoirs of Leonid Pasternak* (London/New York, 1982), 69–70.

77. Kämpfer, *"Der rote Keil,"* 172. For examples of war loan ads in the press, see *Rampa i zhizn'*, nos. 12 and 48 (1916): inside covers; and *Stolitsa i usad'ba*, no. 54 (1916): inside cover and no. 72 (1916): 14–15. A large number of war loan

posters are reproduced in *Affiches et imageries russes*, 3–9; see also Joseph Darracott, *The First World War in Posters from the Imperial War Museum* (London/New York, 1974), 68; Maurice Rickards, *Posters of the First World War* (New York, 1968), nos. 8, 95, and 186.

78. On the exchange of exhibitions, see Joseph Darracott and Belinda Loftus, *First World War Posters*, 2d ed. (London, 1981), 7. A picture of the London exhibition, which took place in January in Hampstead, is in Marwick, *Deluge*, insert at 150; on the English show at the Petrograd Academy of Arts, see Okhochinskii, *Plakat*, 72, and Lapshin, *Khudozhestvennaia zhizn'*, 19 (the poster of the exhibition). The article, by Z. Vengerova, was "Steny angliiskikh gorodov," *Niva*, no. 43 (1915): 785–89.

79. Cheptsov's poster is reproduced and compared with others with similar motifs in Rickards, *Posters*, nos. 7–14; see also Darracot and Loftus, *First World War Posters*, 63–64.

80. For reproductions of the two Russian posters, see *Affiches et imageries russes*, 9, and Kämpfer, "Der rote Keil," 177–79; for Baden-Powell's poster, see Darracot and Loftus, *First World War Posters*, 13.

81. For examples, see Kämpfer, "Der rote Keil," 176–77. Vladimirov's and other posters are reproduced in *Affiches et imageries russes*, 5–7; Darracot, *First World War in Posters*, 68; and Lapshin, *Khudozhestvennaia zhizn'*, 13.

82. For reproductions of these posters, see Rickards, *Posters*, nos. 185, 186, and 95; Lapshin, *Khudozhestvennaia zhizn'*, 12; *Affiches et imageries russes*, 7.

83. For examples of commercial posters, see Baburina, *Russkii plakat*, 104–59. On movement in posters, see Kämpfer, "Der rote Keil," 124–26.

84. See the opinion of the anonymous author of "Voennyi zaëm," *Niva*, no. 50 (1916): 834; see also Viktor Shklovskii, quoted in Lapshin, *Khudozhestvennaia zhizn'*, 10–11. On the difficulty of measuring the effect of posters, see Darracot and Loftus, *First World War Posters*, 8. The difficulties of the Russian war loans are discussed in A. L. Sidorov, *Finansovoe polozhenie Rossii v gody pervoi mirovoi voiny (1914–1917)* (Moscow, 1960), 156–61.

85. On the importance of aesthetic conventions in the use of posters, see Kämpfer, "Der rote Keil," 51.

86. Baburina (*Russkii plakat*, 78, 80–81) mentions horror movies in general, without specifically discussing those that feature the horrors of war.

87. All of the film posters mentioned hereafter are found in GMISP.

88. On personification of the enemy in posters, see Carl Hundhausen, "Über das politische Plakat," in *Politische Kommunikation durch das Plakat* (Bonn, 1975), 27–28. Western examples are in Darracot and Loftus, *First World War Posters*, 41; Kämpfer, "Der rote Keil," 173.

89. Baburina, *Russkii plakat*, 160.

90. GMISP has a collection of patriotic coins, buttons, and wartime calendars by Sytin, Mamontov, Kibbel', and the Skobelev Committee. For Russian military stamps, see W. Schmidt, *Images of the Great War*, vol. 2, *An Illustrated Catalogue of Delandre's Non-French Military Vignettes, 1914–1917* (n.p., 1985), 68.

91. On a nation's flag as its primary symbol, see Raymond Firth, *Symbols:*

Public and Private (Ithaca, 1973), 338–41. Street collections and the propaganda train are described by W. Mansell Merry, *Two Months in Russia: July— September, 1914* (Oxford, 1916), 96–97, 117. On Bolshevik agitprop trains, see Kenez, *Birth of the Propaganda State*, 59–62; on German counterparts, Karl Wehrhan, *Gloria Viktoria! Volkspoesie an Militärzügen* (Munich, 1915), 11–21.

92. John M. MacKenzie, "Introduction," in *Imperialism and Popular Culture*, ed. MacKenzie (Manchester, 1986), 4.

2. Performing Patriotism: The War on Stage

1. Jewgenii Kusnezow [E. M. Kuznetsov], *Der Zirkus der Welt* (Berlin, 1970), 191; Iu. A. Dmitriev, *Tsirk v Rossii: Ot istokov do 1917 g.* (Moscow, 1977), 263; see also B. F. Geier, "Tsirk," *Organ*, no. 126 (January 1915): n. p.; M. N. Medvedev, *Leningradskii tsirk* (Leningrad, 1975), 49.

2. Mosse, *Fallen Soldiers*, 146; Kusnezow, *Zirkus der Welt*, 53–59, 153. On the show in Krestovskii Park in particular and public amusement parks in the capital in general see A. M. Konechnyi, "Shows for the People: Public Amusement Parks in Nineteenth-Century St. Petersburg," in *Cultures in Flux: Lower-Class Values, Practices, and Resistance in Late Imperial Russia*, ed. Stephen Frank and Mark Steinberg (Princeton, 1994), 121–30. Patriotic shows on the fairgrounds are discussed in the uncensored version of the memoirs of A. Ia. Alekseev-Iakovlev, compiled by A. M. Konechnyi as "Peterburgskii 'balagannyi maestro' A. Ia. Alekseev-Iakovlev," 22. I am grateful to Mr. Konechnyi for entrusting this typescript to me.

3. TsGIA SPb, f. 569, op. 14, d. 20, ll. 69–69 ob.; see the poster for *Geroi mirovoi voiny 1914 g., ili za tsaria, rodinu i slavianstvo!* in MTsI; on the success of the show, *Organ*, no. 123 (October 1914): n.p.; see also Dmitriev, *Tsirk v Rossii*, 280, who gives the wrong subtitle: "For Faith, Tsar, and Fatherland." On Leifert's show booth on Petrograd's Field of Mars, see Kuznetsov, *Russkie narodnye gulian'ia*, 88–100.

4. Dmitriev, *Tsirk v Rossii*, 280; on Circus "Modern," *Organ*, no. 121 (September 1914): n.p. See the poster for *Krovavye rytsari* in MTsI; "Tsirk 'Modern': Otzyvy sovremennoi pechati s 1908–1915 g." (typescript), 20, MTsI; also Iu. A. Dmitriev, *Vitalii Lazarenko* (Moscow, 1946), 23–24.

5. On *The Triumph of the Powers* (*Torzhestvo derzhav*) at the Mariinskii Theater in October 1914, see the program in GMISP and *Petrogradskii listok*, 9 October 1914, 13. Some costume designs for the show are reproduced in Michael Raeburn, ed., *The Twilight of the Tsars: Russian Art at the Turn of the Century* (London, 1991), 155. On *The Powers of Hell* (*Sily ada*), see *Var'ete i tsirk*, no. 28 (March 1915): 6, and the review by P'er-O [S. V. Zhivotovskii] in *Birzhevye vedomosti*; for an excerpt, see "Tsirk 'Modern,'" 24–25, MTsI.

6. Medvedev, *Leningradskii tsirk*, 44–45.

7. On the dzhigitovka, see E. M. Kuznetsov, comp., *Konnyi tsirk: Vystavka na temu "Konnyi tsirk"* (Leningrad, 1930), 118, and idem, *Tsirk: Proiskhozhdenie,*

razvitie, perspektivy, 2d ed. (Moscow, 1971), 322; Dmitriev, *Tsirk v Rossii*, 346–49. Nikitin's *Velikaia voina 1914 goda na zemle, na vode i v vozdukhe*. *Zatoplenie Bel'gii* of January 1915 and his patriotic fervor are discussed ibid., 267, 281, and in *Organ*, no. 126 (January 1915): n.p.; see also Iu. A. Dmitriev, "Samorodki: K 100-letiiu pervogo russkogo statsionarnogo tsirka," *Sovetskaia estrada i tsirk*, September 1973, 21. On Nikitin's charitable activities, see R. E. Slavskii, *Brat'ia Nikitiny* (Moscow, 1987), 255, 267.

8. Paul Bouissac, *Circus and Culture: A Semiotic Approach* (Lanham, Md., 1985), 7; Firth, *Symbols*, 340–41; Medvedev, *Leningradskii tsirk*, 43.

9. Joel Schechter, *Durov's Pig: Clowns, Politics, and Theatre* (New York, 1985), 4. For anecdotes about the Durov brothers, see Dmitriev, *Tsirk v Rossii*, 214–15, 303–11; A. V. Talanov, *Brat'ia Durovy* (Moscow, 1971), 91, 108–10; and I. S. Radunskii, *Zapiski starogo klouna* (Moscow, 1954), 92–93.

10. See "Sobaka" and "Porosënok" in "Repertuar klouna Eduard Korrado, 1915" (typescript), MTsI. For the censors' attitudes toward crowned heads, see S. S. Danilov, *Ocherki po istorii russkogo dramaticheskogo teatra* (Moscow, 1948), 505.

11. D. S. Al'perov, *Na arene starogo tsirka: Zapiski klouna* (Moscow, 1936), 359. On quick-change artists, see *Tsirk: Malen'kaia entsiklopediia* (Moscow, 1973), 287; Dmitriev, *Tsirk v Rossii*, 287, 297.

12. Much has been written about the Durov brothers and the dynasty of circus artists they founded. For general studies, see Talanov, *Brat'ia Durovy;* Iu. A. Dmitriev, *Brat'ia Durovy* (Moscow, 1945); and V. N. Viren, *Stoletnii iubilei Durovykh* (Moscow, 1963). On the feud between the two, see Kuznetsov, *Tsirk*, 327–28. For Vladimir's Berlin and Wilhelm stories, see V. L. Durov, *V plenu u nemtsev* (Moscow, 1914), 9, 13–14, 19–20, and the book by his daughter A. V. Durova-Sadovskaia,˙ *Po vecheram na staroi bozhedomke* (Moscow, 1977), 105–8. For Anatolii's Wilhelm story, see "Stranichki A.L.D.," in *Anatolii Leonidovich Durov* (n.p., n.d.), 11–18. The feud between the brothers, their mutual stealing of ideas, and the ensuing confusion carried over into later research. Thus the Wilhelm story was attributed to Anatolii by Kuznetsov (*Tsirk*, 324) and to Vladimir by *Tsirk: Malen'kaia entsiklopediia*, 113, and Schechter, *Durov's Pig*, 1–3. The latter version seems closer to the truth. Anatolii's version includes a factual error. He extended the play on words to the loaf of bread, letting a second pig choose the bread. Its words "Will Brot" (I want the bread) allegedly poked fun at the German foreign minister, but no minister's name came even close to this combination of words. Another version of this story has a slightly different twist: Two pigs are led into the arena, one with and one without a helmet. To the question about the difference between the two, the clown replies: "Dieses Schwein hat Helm, das Schwein will Helm." (I thank Hans Rogger for bringing this version to my attention.)

13. Dmitriev, *Tsirk v Rossii*, 303; Radunskii, *Zapiski starogo klouna*, 92. On the film see R. E. Slavskii, *S areny na ekran* (Moscow, 1969), 12, and *Sine-Fono*, no. 4–5 (1914): 58–59.

14. For jokes featuring Germans as pigs see "Korol' shutov, No ne shut korolei," in *Anatolii Leonidovich Durov*, 23, 64. French postcards showing Wilhelm as a pig are reproduced in Zeyons, *Roman-Photo*, 42–44.

15. Radunskii, *Zapiski starogo klouna*, 91; E. M. Kuznetsov, *Arena i liudi sovetskogo tsirka* (Leningrad, 1947), 8; Viren, *Stoletnii iubilei Durovykh*, n.p.; B. Todorskii, "Anatolii Anatol'evich Durov," *Sovetskii tsirk*, July 1958, 9; *Var'ete i tsirk*, no. 7–8 (October 1916): 9–10.

16. Al'perov, *Na arene starogo tsirka*, 384. Kol'petti's lyrics are "Loshadka" in "Sbornik kupletov i monologov, ispolniaemykh artistom Kol'petti, 1916" (typescript), MTsI, and "Son" in "Sbornik kupletov i monologov, ispolniaemykh artistom Kol'petti, 1917" (typescript), MTsI.

17. Al'perov, *Na arene starogo tsirka*, 384; Dmitriev, *Tsirk v Rossii*, 284.

18. L. I. Borisov, *Za kruglym stolom proshlogo: Vospominaniia* (Leningrad, 1971), 144; Al'perov, *Na arene starogo tsirka*, 371. See the announcements for programs presented by Artisty Moskvy–Russkoi Armii i Zhertvam Voiny on the inside cover of *Stsena i arena*, no. 20–21 (1915). A program for Artisty Moskvy na Arene Tsirka on 29 January 1916 is in MTsI; pictures of the evening are in *Rampa i zhizn'*, no. 6 (1916): 6–10. See also N. A. Smirnova, *Vospominaniia* (Moscow, 1947), 282–84.

19. R. E. Slavskii, *Vitalii Lazarenko* (Moscow, 1980), 103–4. See the program of Prozerpi's pantomime *Geroi mirovoi voiny (v 8 kartinakh)* in MTsI; also Dmitriev, *Tsirk v Rossii*, 266–67, 281, 330, 364; A. I. Sosin and M. Lobodin, *Liudi-miachiki: 55 let na arene tsirka* (Leningrad, 1960), 69; Al'perov, *Na arene starogo tsirka*, 383; R. E. Slavskii, comp., *Vstrechi s tsirkovym proshlym* (Moscow, 1990), 84.

20. I. V. Lebedev, *Istoriia professional'noi frantsuzskoi bor'by* (Moscow, 1928), 48; Dmitriev, *Tsirk v Rossii*, 356–68; idem, "Tsirk," in *Russkaia khudozhestvennaia kul'tura kontsa XIX–nachala XX veka*, vol. 3, *Zrelishchnye iskusstva, muzyka* (Moscow, 1977), 236–38; A. Lebedeva, "Blistaiushchii mir: Temy tsirka v tvorchestve Aleksandra Grina," *Sovetskaia estrada i tsirk*, September 1970, 28–29.

21. I. V. Lebedev, "Marina Lurs—sil'neishaia zhenshchina Rossii," *Stsena i arena*, no. 20–21 (1915): 11–12; Roland Barthes, *Mythologies*, trans. Annette Lavers (London, 1972), 21–22. On the concept of *pravda* see Richard Stites, *Revolutionary Dreams: Utopian Vision and Experimental Life in the Russian Revolution* (New York, 1989), 15–17.

22. Eric Hobsbawm, "Mass Producing Traditions: Europe, 1870–1914," in *The Invention of Tradition*, ed. Hobsbawm and Terence Ranger (Cambridge, 1983), 300; O. Langsepp, *Georg Gakkenshmidt: "Russkii Lev"* (Tallinn, 1971); A. Shirai, "Diadia Vania," *Sovetskii tsirk*, December 1960, 19.

23. Mikhail Ialgubtsev, "Pobednaia bor'ba," *Gerkules. Zhurnal sporta*, no. 15 (1914): 16–18.

24. "Da zdravstvuet malen'kaia Bel'giia—velikaia strana geroev!" *Gerkules: Zhurnal sporta*, no. 16 (1914): 19; "Vive la France! Da zdravstvuet

Frantsiia!" ibid., no. 17 (1914): 19; "Moris Meterlink—bokser," ibid., no. 15 (1914): 8–9; see ibid., no. 1 (1915): 3 for a picture of wrestlers and wounded soldiers; M. A. Zisel'son, *Matchi klassicheskoi bor'by* (Leningrad, 1949), 6.

25. Kuznetsov, *Tsirk*, 330; Al'perov, *Na arene starogo tsirka*, 355–56, 380. On the Suhr family, see *Tsirk: Malen'kaia entsiklopediia*, 277, and Dmitriev, *Tsirk v Rossii*, 176–78. Buiakovskii's case is documented in an unnumbered card file at MTsI. See also A. Amasovich, *A. Aleksandrov-Serzh* (Moscow, 1951), 12; P. G. Tarakhno, *Zhizn' otdannaia tsirku* (Moscow, 1977), 70–72; *Organ*, no. 122 (September 1914): n.p.; Slavskii, *Vstrechi s tsirkovym proshlym*, 75–78.

26. *Russkaia sovetskaia estrada: Ocherki istorii, 1917–1929* (Moscow, 1976), 7; E. M. Kuznetsov, *Iz proshlogo russkoi estrady: Istoricheskie ocherki* (Moscow, 1958), 35–100; Nekrylova, *Russkie narodnye gorodskie prazdniki*, 157.

27. S. S. Klitin, *Estrada: Problemy teorii, istorii i metodiki* (Leningrad, 1987), 14–21, 52–53; *Russkaia sovetskaia estrada*, 14–15.

28. *Teatr i iskusstvo* 18 (1914): 628; "Teatral'nyi krizis v Peterburge," ibid., 676; "Moskovskiia vesti," ibid., 693; "Slukhi i vesti," ibid., 771; N. E. Efros, "Moskovskiia pis'ma," ibid., 774, and "Slukhi i vesti," ibid., 787; *Organ*, no. 121 (September 1914): n.p.; Klitin, *Estrada*, 57–59.

29. I. V. Nest'ev, *Zvëzdy russkoi estrady*, 2d ed. (Moscow, 1974), 33–34; Kuznetsov, *Iz proshlogo russkoi estrady*, 309, 339–42.

30. V. M. Sidel'nikov, *Russkoe narodnoe tvorchestvo i estrada* (Moscow, 1950), 21–24; Kuznetsov, *Iz proshlogo russkoi estrady*, 313–14; I. I. Martynov, *Gosudarstvennyi russkii narodnyi khor imeni Piatnitskogo* (Moscow, 1950), 14–17. For the poster, see Baburina, *Russkii plakat*, 73; N. Rechmenskii, "Vstrechi s M. Piatnitskim (Iz vospominanii)," *Sovetskaia muzyka*, no. 3 (1961): 110–12.

31. Sidel'nikov, *Russkoe narodnoe tvorchestvo*, 20–21, 24. See the review of a chorus in boyar costumes presenting "national and patriotic songs" in *Var'ete i tsirk*, no. 28 (1915): 6. The Russko-boiarskii Khor of a certain Mikhailov offered similar fare, according to ibid., no. 7–8 (1916): n.p. Mariia Martynova, the star of the Apollo and Tivoli vaudevilles in Moscow in the fall of 1916, sang patriotic songs in an ornate peasant costume (ibid., no. 7–8 [1916]: 7, and no. 9–10 [1916]: n.p., with picture). On the mental and demographic relationships between village and city, see Reginald E. Zelnik, "The Peasant and the Factory," in *The Peasant in Nineteenth-Century Russia*, ed. Wayne S. Vucinich (Stanford, 1968), 189–90; and Daniel R. Brower, *The Russian City between Tradition and Modernity, 1850–1900* (Berkeley, 1990), 76–91.

32. Nest'ev, *Zvëzdy russkoi estrady*, 69–73, 82–86, 88–92, 100–103, 176–80; Ekaterina Sorokina, "Zapiski tsyganskoi pevitsy," *Nash sovremennik*, no. 3 (1966): 102; Homo novus [A. R. Kugel'], "Zametki," *Teatr i iskusstvo* 19 (1915): 507–10; A. R. Kugel', *Teatral'nye portrety* (Petrograd, 1923), 160–61; "Kontsert N. V. Plevitskoi," *Teatr i iskusstvo* 19 (1915): 790.

33. A. P. Konnov and G. N. Preobrazhenskii, comps., *Orkestr imeni V. V. Andreeva* (Leningrad, 1987), esp. 5, 10, 44–50; Iurii Baranov, *Podvizhnik muzyki narodnoi* (Moscow, 1988), 119–20; P. Obolenskii, "Iz vospominanii o V. Andreeve," *Sovetskaia muzyka*, no. 7 (1959): 133–34; Kuznetsov, *Iz proshlogo russkoi*

estrady, 316–21; bills for concerts on 12 December 1914 and 7 March 1915 in Petrograd's Mikhailovskii Theater and the Narodnyi Dom Imperatora Nikolaia II in GMISP; B. G-r [B. F. Geier], "Kontsert velikorusskago orkestra V. V. Andreeva," *Teatr i iskusstvo* 19 (1915): 924.

34. Kuznetsov, *Iz proshlogo russkoi estrady*, 339–42. For a collection of Krivopolenova's stories, see O. E. Ozarovskaia, *Babushkiny stariny* (Petrograd, 1916); for an evening's program, TsGIA SPb, f. 569, op. 13, d. 1360, ll. 118–118 ob. On audiences' reactions, see Pëtr Iuzhnyi [P. M. Solianyi], "Patrioticheskii repertuar," *Teatr i iskusstvo* 18 (1914): 759.

35. On the bazaar, see TsGIA SPb, f. 569, op. 14, d. 161, ll. 20–21 ob.; on Nelidova, see *Teatr i iskusstvo* 19 (1915): 267.

36. Konstantin Kazamsky, *Cabaret russe* (Paris, 1978), 93.

37. E. P. Gershuni, *Rasskazyvaiu ob estrade* (Leningrad, 1968), 15–16; V. M. Purishkevich, *The Murder of Rasputin: A First-Hand Account from the Diary of One of Rasputin's Murderers*, ed. Michael E. Shaw, trans. Bella Costello (Ann Arbor, 1985), 94–95; Kazamsky, *Cabaret russe*, 75–76, 93; Kusnezow, *Zirkus der Welt*, 193–94; N. P. Okunev, *Dnevnik Moskvicha (1917–1924)* (Paris, 1990), 7–8. About the scandal in the Troitskii Theater, see *Teatr i iskusstvo* 19 (1915): 341, 360.

38. S. Frederick Starr, *Red and Hot: The Fate of Jazz in the Soviet Union, 1917–1980* (New York, 1985), 20–34; Marwick, *Deluge*, 143; Eksteins, *Rites of Spring*, 38–39; Nest'ev, *Zvëzdy russkoi estrady*, 16–19; Gershuni, *Rasskazyvaiu ob estrade*, 20; L. S. Volkov-Lannit, *Iskusstvo zapechatlennogo zvuka* (Moscow, 1964), 79; Boris Groys, Foreword to *Rasputins Ende: Erinnerungen*, by Felix Jussupoff (Munich, 1985), xvi.

39. Babenko, *Artist Aleksandr Vertinskii*, 11–18, 33–37; Kuznetsov, *Iz proshlogo russkoi estrady*, 330–32; Konstantin Rudnitskii, record jacket notes to *Aleksandr Vertinskii*, Melodiia M 60 48689—60 48691, Leningradskii Zavod Gramplastinok, 1989.

40. Babenko, *Artist Aleksandr Vertinskii*, 19, 26–27, 124; Borisov, *Za kruglym stolom proshlogo*, 144–47. Vertinskii's songs, parts of his writings, memories of him, and interviews with him are found in Iu. Tomashevskii, comp., *A. Vertinskii: Za kulisami* (Moscow, 1991).

41. Gershuni, *Rasskazyvaiu ob estrade*, 24; Babenko, *Artist Aleksandr Vertinskii*, 27–28. On Iza Kremer, see M. I. Dneprov, *Polveka v operette* (Moscow, 1961), 108–11; Igor' Severianin, *Stikhotvoreniia* (Moscow, 1988), 95, 100, 259, 262. On Severianin, see Lawton, *Russian Futurism*, 20–25; Johannes Holthusen, *Russische Literatur im 20. Jahrhundert* (Munich, 1978), 93–94; A. E. Parnis and R. D. Timenchik, "Programmy 'Brodiachei sobaki,'" in *Pamiatniki kul'tury. Novye otkrytiia: Pis'mennost', iskusstvo, arkheologiia. Ezhegodnik 1983* (Leningrad, 1985), 236–38; V. V. Maiakovskii, "Poezovecher Igoria Severianina," in *Polnoe sobranie sochinenii v trinadtsati tomakh* (Moscow, 1955–61), 1:338–39. Severianin's piece was obviously written for a special issue of the newspaper *Den'* in October 1914, devoted exclusively to Belgium (see M. S. Berlina, "P'esy Leonida Andreeva na Aleksandrinskoi stsene," in *Russkii teatr i dramaturgiia 1907–1917*

godov: Sbornik nauchnykh trudov [Leningrad, 1988], 80) and first performed at a patriotic matinee organized by Mariia Dolina on 19 October (see the placard in GMISP).

42. Kuznetsov, *Iz proshlogo russkoi estrady*, 293, 298–99; A. M. Konechnyi et al., "Artisticheskoe kabare 'Prival komediantov,' " in *Pamiatniki kul'tury. Novye otkrytiia: Pis'mennost', iskusstvo, arkheologiia. Ezhegodnik 1988* (Moscow, 1989), 96–97, 100; Harold B. Segel, *Turn-of-the-Century Cabaret: Paris, Barcelona, Berlin, Munich, Vienna, Cracow, Moscow, St. Petersburg, Zurich* (New York, 1987), 317–20.

43. Pëtr Solianyi, "Teatry miniatiur," *Teatr i iskusstvo* 18 (1914): 824–26, 839–40; T. M. Rodina, "Russkii teatr predrevoliutsionnogo desiatiletiia," in *Russkaia khudozhestvennaia kul'tura*, 3:11; Babenko, *Artist Aleksandr Vertinskii*, 16–17. Klitin (*Estrada*, 96–97) defines *teatr miniatiur* as it is understood today, without the richness and diversity that characterized it in the early 1900s. See also I. F. Petrovskaia, *Teatr i zritel' rossiiskikh stolits, 1895–1917* (Leningrad, 1990), 133.

44. Parnis and Timenchik, "Programmy 'Brodiachei sobaki,' " 236–40; D. Z. Kogan, *Sergei Iur'evich Sudeikin, 1884–1946* (Moscow, 1974), 78–90; Gershuni, *Rasskazyvaiu ob estrade*, 11. For a sample of wartime poetry, see B. Glinskii, comp., *Sovremennaia voina v russkoi poezii* (Petrograd, 1915); V. Pertsov, *Maiakovskii: Zhizn' i tvorchestvo*, 3d ed. (Moscow, 1976), 1:225–38; V. V. Maiakovskii, "Mama i ubityi nemtsami vecher," in *Polnoe sobranie sochinenii v trinadtsati tomakh*, 1:66–67; Anna Akhmatova, "Iiul' 1914," "Uteshenie," and "Molitva," in *Stikhotvoreniia i poemy* (Leningrad, 1979), 106–9. See also Ben Hellman, "An Aggressive Imperialist? The Controversy over Nikolaj Gumilev's War Poetry," in *Nikolaj Gumilev, 1886–1986: Papers from the Gumilev Centenary Symposium Held at Ross Priory University of Strathclyde, 1986* (Oakland, Calif., 1987), 133–54; Sergei Gorodetskii, "Vozdushnyi vitiaz (Pamiati Nesterova)," *Lukomor'e*, no. 18 (1914): 12–13.

45. Segel, *Turn-of-the-Century Cabaret*, 317–18; Konechnyi et al., "Artisticheskoe kabare 'Prival komediantov,' " 97–100, 108–9; Kelly, "Petrushka and the Pioneers," 82, 93, and *Petrushka: The Russian Carnival Puppet Theatre* (Cambridge, 1990), 77, 140–78; *Petrushka: Ulichnyi teatr* (Moscow, 1915); Nekrylova, *Russkie narodnye gorodskie prazdniki*, 84, 93; Kogan, *Sergei Iur'evich Sudeikin*, 94, 96; "Iz vospominanii L. V. Iakovlevoi-Shaporinoi ob organizatsii i rabote teatra marionetok pri petrogradskom teatre-studii," in *Russkii sovetskii teatr 1917–1921*, ed. A. Z. Iufit (Leningrad, 1968), 287.

46. Kuznetsov, *Iz proshlogo russkoi estrady*, 301–3; *Russkaia sovetskaia estrada*, 306n; *Rampa i zhizn'*, no. 4 (1916): 10 (a *soldatskii* lubok at the Bat); *Teatr i iskusstvo* 19 (1915): 43 (a Wilhelm lubok at the Troitskii Theater).

47. Petrovskaia, *Teatr i zritel' rossiiskikh stolits*, 99–102; Gershuni, *Rasskazyvaiu ob estrade*, 18–19.

48. Petrovskaia, *Teatr i zritel' rossiiskikh stolits*, 102. On Wagner's reception in Russia during the war, see Bernice Glatzer Rosenthal, "Wagner and Wag-

nerian Ideas in Russia," in *Wagnerism in European Culture and Politics*, ed. David C. Large and William Weber (Ithaca, 1984), 212.

49. V. N. Vsevolodskii-Gerngross (*Russkaia ustnaia narodnaia drama* [Moscow, 1959], 133–35) was obviously not aware of Kugel"s revival of *Mal'-bruk*. For the plot of *Tsar' Maksimilian* see *Teatral'naia entsiklopediia* (Moscow, 1961–67), s.v. "Narodnaia drama," by V. N. Vsevolodskii-Gerngross; N. N. Tamarin [Nikolai Okulov], "Krivoe zerkalo," *Teatr i iskusstvo* 18 (1914): 788, 794 (photo of *Mal'bruk*); N. N. [Aleksandr Kugel'], "Predstavlenie o *Tsare Vasil'iane*," *Teatr i iskusstro* 18 (1914): 968, 975–77. The program of *Tsar' Vasil'ian* is in GMB.

50. G. K. Terikov, *Kuplet na estrade* (Moscow, 1987), 64–65, 69–71; N. P. Smirnov-Sokol'skii, *Sorok piat' let na estrade: Fel'etony, stat'i, vystupleniia* (Moscow, 1976), 133; Kio [E. T. Girshfel'd-Renard], *Fokusy i fokusniki* (Moscow, 1958), 21; *Var'ete i tsirk*, no. 9–10 (1916): 9.

51. See "Monolog," in "Sbornik kupletov, razskazov dlia ispolneniia na stsene teatrov, tsirkov, kabare, kinematografov, miniatiurov, var'ete i sadakh, iumorist I. A. Rabchinskii, 1914" (manuscript), MTsI; Kuznetsov, *Iz proshlogo russkoi estrady*, 325.

52. Terikov, *Kuplet na estrade*, 58–63; Kuznetsov, *Iz proshlogo russkoi estrady*, 276–80; Petrovskaia, *Teatr i zritel' rossiiskikh stolits*, 91; *Stsena i arena*, no. 5 (1914): 16; "Obozrenie letnykh var'ete," *Var'ete i tsirk*, no. 6 (1916): 9; review of show by Sokol'skii in Theater Lin by P. Iu. [Pëtr Solianyi] in *Teatr i iskusstvo* 19 (1915): 129, and announcement of new program ibid., 20 (1916): 32; Sergei Sokol'skii, *Pliashushchaia lirika: Stikhotvoreniia i pesni* (Petrograd, 1916).

53. "Pesnia o Kuz'me Kriuchkove. Soldatskaia pesnia," in Sokol'skii, *Pliashushchaia lirika*, 60–61; "Dushu polozhivshii za drugu . . . ," ibid., 7–9; "O Bel'gii prekrasnoi," ibid., 10–12; "Pol'she," ibid., 19–22. The pilot as mythical hero was also popular in Western wartime lore (Mosse, *Fallen Soldiers*, 120–21; John H. Morrow, *The Great War in the Air: Military Aviation from 1909 to 1921* [Washington, D.C., 1993]).

54. "Slovo pro Rossiiu," in Sokol'skii, *Pliashushchaia lirika*, 37–42; V. S. Diakin, *Russkaia burzhuaziia i tsarizm v gody pervoi mirovoi voiny (1914–1917)* (Leningrad, 1967), 53, 68; E. N. Trubetskoi, *Otechestvennaia voina i eia dukhovnyi smysl (Publichnaia lektsiia)* (Moscow, 1915), 20–29.

55. Al'perov, *Na arene starogo tsirka*, 370; "Shakaly," in Sokol'skii, *Pliashushchaia lirika*, 43–46.

56. On the question of the reliability of Jews, government actions against the Jews, and the service of Jews in the Russian army see Heinz-Dietrich Löwe, *Antisemitismus und reaktionäre Utopie. Russischer Konservatismus im Kampf gegen den Wandel von Staat und Gesellschaft, 1890–1917* (Hamburg, 1978), 146–49, 167–69. On sympathy for Jews in Russian liberal circles and the ambiguous image of Jews in popular literature before the war, see Brooks, *When Russia Learned to Read*, 231–33. The movie *Evrei-dobrovolets*, released by Prodalent in early 1915, featured actors of Petrograd's Lin Theater and a Red Cross auto-

mobile unit (*Sine-Fono*, no. 6–7 [1915]: 89). *Voina i evrei* was produced by the Odessa-based company Mizrakh; the film included several battle scenes (*Sine-Fono*, no. 8 [1915]: 47). For a general discussion of the Jewish cinema, see Rashit Iangirov, "Evreiskoe kino Rossii: V poiskakh identichnosti, 1908–1919," *Iskusstvo kino*, no. 5 (1992): 25–35. The journal *Voina i evrei* was published by D. Kumakov in Moscow. The lubok "Boi nashego otriada s germantsami na evreiskom kladbishche" (Mashistov, 1915) is in Gosudarstvennyi muzei V. V. Maiakovskogo, Moscow.

57. Sokol'skii, *Pliashushchaia lirika*, 28–31.

58. "Zakon dikaria," ibid., 50–54. For nightclubs and plush restaurants attacked by Sokol'skii, see Richard Stites, "Prostitute and Society in Pre-Revolutionary Russia," *Jahrbücher für Geschichte Osteuropas* 31 (1983): 353–54; Kuznetsov, *Iz proshlogo russkoi estrady*, 278–80.

59. Ernani, "Sborniki kupletov, stikhotvorenii i razskazov, 1914, 1915, 1916" (collection of typescripts and manuscripts), MTsI; "Otzyvy o spektakliakh V. Ernani, 1906 ff.," MTsI.

60. "V lazarete," in "Sbornik razskazov artista M. I. Filitsanova, 1915" (manuscript), MTsI. The incident in Kiev in 1916 is reported in *Var'ete i tsirk*, no. 9–10 (1916): 8.

61. "Ekstrennoe zasedanie 29-go iiulia v sadu 'Akvarium,'" *Stsena i arena*, no. 5 (1914): 2–3; *Organ*, no. 121 (1914): n.p.; Löwe, "Political Symbols and Rituals," 11–13; about Cherniavskii, see Nest'ev, *Zvëzdy russkoi estrady*, 29.

62. Gershuni, *Rasskazyvaiu ob estrade*, 9–10. On Dolina's early career, see "Mariia Ivanovna Dolina, solistka Ego Velichestva," in *Ezhegodnik Imperatorskikh teatrov. Sezon 1901–1902. Prilozhenie 1*, 12–14. On her estrada activities, see *Vechera i utra "Russkoi pesni" M. I. Dolinoi, 1907–1908* (St. Petersburg, 1907). The most exhaustive treatment of Dolina is A. M. Pruzhanskii, *Otechestvennye pevtsy, 1750–1917: Slovar'* (Moscow, 1991), 1:151–52, 166.

63. Many posters announcing Dolina's concerts are in GMISP. They provide information about admission charges, auditoriums, and so forth. Kuznetsov (*Iz proshlogo russkoi estrady*, 342) gives the unrealistic figure of 500 patriotic concerts between August 1914 and February 1917. When one takes into account the frequency of the programs and the fact that the summer break of 1916 began after the 102d concert, Dolina cannot have given more than 130 performances altogether. On her awards and financial success, see *Rampa i zhizn'*, no. 21 (1916): 8, and *Petrogradskii listok*, 4 March 1916, 4. On the distribution of tickets, see TsGIA SPb, f. 1458, op. 2, d. 1043; f. 1365, op. 1, d. 62, ll. 331–344 ob.; and f. 436, op. 1, d. 14967, l. 35. The proceeds of the 102d patriotic concert on April 24, 1916, went to an army unit bearing Dolina's name.

64. See the program notes in GMISP on benefit concerts in the Mariinskii Theater on 24 January 1915 and 28 November 1915, with the Preobrazhenskii Orchestra playing Bizet, Donizetti, and Glazunov under the composer's direction. On Mozzhukhin and Matveev, see *Rampa i zhizn'*, no. 21 (1916): 8.

65. V. N. Vsevolodskii-Gerngross, *Istoriia russkogo teatra* (Leningrad, 1929), 2:352; Kuznetsov, *Russkie narodnye gulian'ia*, 54, and *Iz proshlogo russkoi estrady*,

343; Löwe, "Political Symbols and Rituals," 16–17. *Teatr i iskusstvo* 18 (1914): 775 shows a photo of a typical tableau vivant. On patriotic tableaux vivants in Germany, see Mosse, *Fallen Soldiers*, 145–46.

66. On Artist—Soldatu, see *Teatr i iskusstvo* 18 (1914): 881, 898, 967–68, and TsGIA SPb, f. 287, op. 1, d. 332, ll. 15–122.

67. Gershuni, *Rasskazyvaiu ob estrade*, 10. For a description of the Narodnyi Dom Imperatora Nikolaia II and its atmosphere, see Kuznetsov, *Russkie narodnye gulian'ia*, 153–60.

68. A. Pavlova, "Al'bom Sergeia Bol'shogo," *Sovetskaia estrada i tsirk*, November 1967, 24. Sergei Bol'shoi appeared as a "flying balalaika player" in 1916. See Borisov, *Za kruglym stolom proshlogo*, 144; Iu. F. Kotliarov and V. I. Garmash, comps., *Letopis' zhizni i tvorchestva F. I. Shaliapina*, 2d ed. (Leningrad, 1989), 2:85–87, 89–91; *Rampa i zhizn'*, no. 4 (1916): 11.

69. On Sektsiia Fabrichnykh i Derevenskikh Teatrov pri Moskovskom Narodnom Universitete, see *Teatr i iskusstvo* 18 (1914): 772; *Organ*, no. 138 (1915): n.p. On Ivanov-Vol'skii see "Kontserty na peredovykh pozitsiiakh," *Rampa i zhizn'*, no. 28 (1916): 9.

70. Iurii Morfessi, *Zhizn', liubov', stsena: Vospominaniia russkago baiana*, 2d ed. (Paris, 1982), 91–97; I. V. Nest'ev, "Muzykal'naia estrada," in *Russkaia khudozhestvennaia kul'tura*, 3:484–85; "Lapotnaia kapella Cherviakova," *Var'ete i tsirk*, no. 3–5 (1917): 6; Sidel'nikov, *Russkoe narodnoe tvorchestvo*, 20–21. "Ta-ra-ra-bum-biia" originated as "A Sweet Tuxedo Girl (Ta-ra-ra boom-de-ay)," music by Theodore A. Metz, lyrics by Henry J. Sayers (New York, 1891), which quickly spread all over Europe and became popular in Russia by 1893. Anton Chekhov saw the refrain as expressing mockery and cynical attack; see Donald Rayfield, "Chekhov and Popular Culture," *Irish Slavonic Studies*, no. 9 (1988): 47–49, 57–59. I thank Stephen Frank for bringing this article to my attention.

71. A. M. Volzhin, "Teatr na peredovykh pozitsiiakh," *Teatr i iskusstvo* 20 (1916): 510, with photos of the audience and the stage.

72. S-oi, "Voina i teatry var'ete," *Var'ete i tsirk*, no. 29–30 (1915): 3–4; *Organ*, no. 128 (1915): n.p.; *Teatr i iskusstvo* 19 (1915): 641, 661–62, 705, and 20 (1916): 658–60, 678–79, 699; *Rampa i zhizn'*, no. 35 (1916): 9. On the requisitioning of buildings under the Bolsheviks see Hubertus F. Jahn, "The Housing Revolution in Petrograd, 1917–1920," *Jahrbücher für Geschichte Osteuropas* 38 (1990): 212–27.

73. Herbert J. Gans, *Popular Culture and High Culture: An Analysis and Evaluation of Taste* (New York, 1974), 67–71.

74. E. A. Znosko-Borovskii, *Russkii teatr nachala XX veka* (Prague, 1925), 397–407; Petrovskaia, *Teatr i zritel' rossiiskikh stolits*, 216–17.

75. *Istoriia russkogo dramaticheskogo teatra*, vol. 7, *1898–1917* (Moscow, 1987), 92–95, 445–560; Rodina, "Russkii teatr predrevoliutsionnogo desiatiletiia," 11; M. N. Stroeva, "Moskovskii khudozhestvennyi teatr," in *Russkaia khudozhestvennaia kul'tura*, 3:56–59. On the "sexual question," see Laura Engelstein, *The Keys to Happiness: Sex and the Search for Modernity in Fin-de Siècle Russia* (Ithaca, 1992), 375–83.

76. N. E. Efros, "Moskovskiia pis'ma," *Teatr i iskusstvo* 18 (1914): 774; Petrovskaia, *Teatr i zritel' rossiiskikh stolits*, 10–11; see also Kugel"s editorial in *Teatr i iskusstvo* 19 (1915): 73–74. For attendance figures, see *Teatr i iskusstvo* 21 (1917): 46. On wartime audiences, see G. G. Dadamian, *Teatr v kul'turnoi zhizni Rossii v gody pervoi mirovoi voiny (1914–1917 gg.)* (Moscow, 1987), 41–44. Changes in the officer corps are discussed in Peter Kenez, "Changes in the Social Composition of the Officer Corps during World War I," *Russian Review* 31 (1972): 369–75. On people's theaters in general, see Lars Kleberg, " 'People's Theater' and the Revolution: On the History of a Concept before and after 1917," in *Art, Society, Revolution: Russia, 1917–1921*, ed. Nils Åke Nilsson (Stockholm, 1979), 179–80; and Gary Thurston, "The Impact of Russian Popular Theater, 1886–1915," *Journal of Modern History* 55, no. 2 (1983): 237–67.

77. For a discussion of similar problems in Munich theaters, see Robert Eben Sackett, *Popular Entertainment, Class, and Politics in Munich, 1900–1923* (Cambridge, Mass., 1982), 70–75.

78. "Dachnye teatry," *Teatr i iskusstvo* 18 (1914): 629; Stroeva, "Moskovskii khudozhestvennyi teatr," 56.

79. "Moskovskiia vesti," *Teatr i iskusstvo* 18 (1914): 677–78, 693; see also the poster in GMB.

80. N. N. Tamarin [Nikolai Okulov], "Dramaticheskie teatry Popechitel'stva o narodnoi trezvosti," *Teatr i iskusstvo* 18 (1914): 728.

81. Petrovskaia, *Teatr i zritel' rossiiskikh stolits*, 183; Stroeva, "Moskovskii khudozhestvennyi teatr," 56–59; Etkind, *A. N. Benua i russkaia khudozhestvennaia kul'tura*, 244–48.

82. A. Ia. Al'tshuller, "Aleksandrinskii teatr," in *Russkaia khudozhestvennaia kul'tura*, 3:102–4; on Andreev's understanding of patriotism, see Ben Hellman, "Leonid Andreev v nachale pervoi mirovoi voiny. Put' ot 'Krasnogo smekha' k p'ese *Korol', zakon i svoboda*," in *Studia Russica Helsingiensia et Tartuensia II. Literaturnyi protsess: Vnutrennie zakony i vneshnie vozdeistviia* (Tartu, 1990), 81–87.

83. Berlina, "P'esy Leonida Andreeva na Aleksandrinskoi stsene," 82.

84. "Moskovskiia vesti," *Teatr i iskusstvo* 18 (1914): 833; Nikolai Efros, "Moskovskiia pis'ma," ibid., 851–52; Hellman, "Leonid Andreev," 85; Berlina, "P'esy Leonida Andreeva na Aleksandrinskoi stsene," 79–82; Al'tshuller, "Aleksandrinskii teatr," 103; Konstantin Derzhavin, *Epokhi Aleksandrinskoi stseny* (Leningrad, 1932), 177–78; *Vestnik kinematografii*, no. 105 (1915): 25, 27–31, 33–35; *Sine-Fono*, no. 8 (1915): 68, 70.

85. T. K. Shakh-Azizova, "Malyi teatr," in *Russkaia khudozhestvennaia kul'tura*, 3:90; Vladimir Filippov, ed., *Aleksandr Ivanovich Iuzhin-Sumbatov: Zapisi, stat'i, pis'ma*, 2d ed. (Moscow, 1951), 164.

86. E. Ia. Dubnova, "Chastnye teatry Moskvy i Peterburga," in *Russkaia khudozhestvennaia kul'tura*, 3:152–54; *Istoriia russkogo dramaticheskogo teatra*, 401, 524–45; Petrovskaia, *Teatr i zritel' rossiiskikh stolits*, 66–73.

87. *Teatral'naia entsiklopediia* (Moscow, 1961–67), s.v. "Dal'skii," by A. P. Klinchin. For a review and photos of *Pozor Germanii (Kul'turnye zveri)*, see

Impr. [B. I. Bentovin], "Malyi teatr," *Teatr i iskusstvo* 18 (1914): 788–89. A poster for the show is in GMISP.

88. Homo novus, "Zametki," *Teatr i iskusstvo* 18 (1914): 959–60; also ibid., 805, 819, 865; 19 (1915): 57; 20 (1916): 640.

89. Impr., "Malyi teatr," *Teatr i iskusstvo* 18 (1914): 951–53; 19 (1915): 128, 133.

90. Ibid., 20 (1916): 7; a poster for *Chudesnye luchi* is in GMB.

91. Petrovskaia, *Teatr i zritel' rossiiskikh stolits*, 77–78.

92. Pëtr Iuzhnyi [Solianyi], "Narodnyi dom," *Teatr i iskusstvo* 18 (1914): 757–58, 761; N. Tamarin [N. N. Okulov], "Narodnyi dom," ibid., 934; and 19 (1915): 302.

93. Pëtr Gnedich, "V nashi dni," *Teatr i iskusstvo* 18 (1914): 649–51; Homo novus, "Zametki," ibid., 731–53; Nikolai Efros, "Moskovskiia pis'ma," ibid., 795; Pëtr Iuzhnyi, "Patrioticheskii repertuar," ibid., 759–61, 807–9. For an overview of the available patriotic pieces, see *1-i [Pervyi] dopolnitel'nyi spisok k katalogu izdanii zhurnala "Teatr i iskusstvo" s 1 ianvaria 1914 g. po 1 maia 1915 g.* (Petrograd, [1915]) and "P'esy dlia nastoiashchago vremeni," *Teatr i iskusstvo* 18 (1914): inside cover.

94. Pëtr Iuzhnyi, "Nemtsy," *Teatr i iskusstvo* 18 (1914): 698; *Istoriia russkogo dramaticheskogo teatra*, 397–98; Kugel''s editorial about the 1914–15 theater season in *Teatr i iskusstvo* 19 (1915): 73–74.

95. "Soiuz dramaticheskikh pisatelei," *Teatr i iskusstvo* 18 (1914): 741; P. Iuzhnyi, "Nemtsy," 666–68, 681–83, 698–701, 712–13, 729–31, 743–44; V. Sh-g, "Pechal'nyi kur'ëz," *Rampa i zhizn'*, no. 40 (1916): 6–7.

96. *Teatr i iskusstvo* 18 (1914): 691 and 19 (1915): 944; E. A. Markov, "Prostaia rech' (Pis'mo v redaktsiiu)," ibid., 20 (1916): 153; *Rampa i zhizn'*, no. 4 (1916): 13 and no. 22 (1916): 3–4; also Dadamian, *Teatr v kul'turnoi zhizni*, 35–38.

97. Vera Kuliabko-Koretskaia, "Dorogovizna," *Teatr i iskusstvo* 19 (1915): 283; "Grimiroval'nyi golod," ibid., 21 (1917): 25.

98. V. Semënova, "Blagorazumnaia roskosh' i pozolochennaia nuzhda," *Zhurnal dlia khoziaek*, no. 12 (1916): 1–2; "Artisty—protiv roskoshi," *Rampa i zhizn'*, no. 8 (1916): 11 and no. 11 (1916): 8; N. A. Smirnova, "O roskoshi i mode," *Rampa i zhizn'*, no. 18 (1916): 3–4; "Demonstratsiia obshchestva bor'by s roskosh'iu v Petrograde," *Rampa i zhizn'*, no. 22 (1916): 11; "Iubka s kolenkorovoiu vstavkoiu (Pis'mo v redaktsiiu)," *Teatr i iskusstvo* 20 (1916): 387–88.

99. For lists of actors drafted, see "Slukhi i vesti," *Teatr i iskusstvo* 18 (1914): 627–28, 677. Stanislavskii and Kugel' were among those caught abroad (ibid., 628, 661); for a lively description of Stanislavskii's journey home via Munich, Marseille, and Odessa, see Vadim Shverubovich, *O starom Khudozhestvennom teatre* (Moscow, 1990), 125–43. L. O. Utësov, *Zapiski aktëra* (Moscow, 1939), 60; Iu. A. Dmitriev, *Leonid Utësov* (Moscow, 1982), 38.

100. Examples of *bivachnye spektakli* are seen in three photographs in GMPIR (f. IX, no. OF 228; f. IX, no. OF 149 [Fig. 49]; f. IX, no. 12584). *Teatr i iskusstvo* 20 (1916): 43; Rybinskii, "Spektakli na fronte," ibid., 663.

101. Z. L'vovskii, "Teatr na pozitsiiakh," *Teatr i iskusstvo* 20 (1916): 223–24;

V. L. Binshtok, "Parizhskiia pis'ma," *Rampa i zhizn'*, no. 7 (1916): 7–9; Hermann Pörzgen, *Theater als Waffengattung: Das deutsche Fronttheater im Weltkrieg, 1914 bis 1920* (Frankfurt, 1935), 24, 36. On the difficulties of front-line theater, see P. P. Gaideburov, *Literaturnoe nasledie. Vospominaniia. Stat'i. Rezhissërskie eksplikatsii. Vystupleniia* (Moscow, 1977), 209–21; on the reception of front-line entertainment see A. A. Bardovskii, *Teatral'nyi zritel' na fronte v kanun Oktiabria* (Leningrad, 1928), 43–44, 51–52, 78, 88, 94. See also Gary Thurston, "Building a Mass Audience for Serious Theater in Russia before October: P. P. Gaideburov at the Ligovsky People's House, in the Provinces and at the Front," paper presented at the Southern Conference on Slavic Studies, Charleston, S.C., 20–23 October 1988; *Teatr i iskusstvo* 20 (1916): 604; Colonel Sapfirskii, "Soiuzu 'Artisty Moskvy russkoi armii i zhertvam voiny,'" *Rampa i zhizn'*, no. 18 (1916): 4–5 (with photos).

102. *Teatr i iskusstvo* 18 (1914): 694, 725; Smirnova, *Vospominaniia*, 281–83 (with photos of collections); "V soiuze 'Artisty—russkoi armii," *Rampa i zhizn'*, no. 11 (1916): 8–9; S. N. Durylin, *Mariia Nikolaevna Ermolova, 1853–1928: Ocherk zhizni i tvorchestva* (Moscow, 1953), 492–93; G. A. Khaichenko, *Russkii narodnyi teatr kontsa XIX–nachala XX veka* (Moscow, 1975), 251, 254. An amateur dacha theater playing for the wounded during World War I figures in Vladimir Nabokov's *Pnin* (New York, 1989), 177–79.

103. Claude Lévi-Strauss, *L'Homme nu* (Paris, 1971), 579. On convention and the nonverbal meaning of music, see Arnold Perris, *Music as Propaganda: Art to Persuade, Art to Control* (Westport, Conn., 1985), 5–6. Conrad L. Donakowski (*A Muse for the Masses: Ritual and Music in an Age of Democratic Revolution, 1770–1870* [Chicago, 1972], 310) has correctly pointed out that music is "the most elusive of the arts in the face of literal analysis." This difficulty has led to the neglect of music by many cultural historians.

104. Carl Dahlhaus, *Between Romanticism and Modernism: Four Studies in the Music of the Later Nineteenth Century*, trans. Mary Whittall (Berkeley, 1980), 87–94.

105. Eero Tarasti, *Myth and Music: A Semiotic Approach to the Aesthetics of Myth in Music, Especially That of Wagner, Sibelius, and Stravinsky* (The Hague, 1979), 30–33, 95–96.

106. Theodor W. Adorno, *Einleitung in die Musiksoziologie* (Frankfurt, 1975), 198–99; Alfred J. Swan, *Russian Music and Its Sources in Chant and Folk Song* (New York, 1973), 65–66; Constant Lambert, *Music Ho! A Study of Music in Decline* (New York, 1967), 140–42.

107. Swan, *Russian Music*, 155–60; [A. N. Rimskii-Korsakov], "Ot redaktora," *Muzykal'nyi sovremennik*, September 1915, 5–15; see also the observations by Musicista in *Stolitsa i usad'ba*, no. 36–37 (1915): 26 and no. 50 (1916): 15.

108. A. D. Kastal'skii, "Iz vospominanii o poslednikh godakh," *Sovetskaia muzyka*, no. 6 (1977): 107–8; S. N. Vasilenko, *Stranitsy vospominanii* (Moscow, 1945), 30. Glazunov's *Parafraza* featured the anthems played one after another and then all together (*Russkaia muzykal'naia gazeta*, no. 11 [1915]: 200).

109. On operetta audiences and their expectations, see Adorno, *Einleitung*, 37–38, 47.

110. On the practical repercussions of the war on the approximately fifty operetta theaters in Russia, see M. O. Iankovskii, *Operetta: Vozniknovenie i razvitie zhanra na zapade i v SSSR* (Leningrad, 1937), 357–59. On attacks on posters and Viennese waltzes, see "Slukhi i vesti," *Teatr i iskusstvo* 18 (1914): 645, and *Organ*, no. 136 (May 1915): n.p.

111. According to G. M. Iaron, *O liubimom zhanre* (Moscow, 1960), 81, approximately fifteen French pieces were available, which were played over and over again. On name changes, see V. Sh-g, "Pechal'nyi kur'ëz," *Rampa i zhizn'*, no. 40 (1916): 6–7, and "Malenkaia khronika," *Teatr i iskusstvo* 20 (1916): 649; the latter issue (540, 610) also has an Italian version of Suppé's name (Francesco Suppe Demelli), put forward by the director of Petrograd's Buff Theater.

112. *Teatr i iskusstvo* 18 (1914): 645, 710. M. O. Iankovskii, "Operetochnyi teatr," in *Russkaia khudozhestvennaia kul'tura*, 3:381–83.

113. *Teatr i iskusstvo* 18 (1914): 694.

114. Posters for these operettas are in GMISP; see also Iaron, *O liubimom zhanre*, 73, and P. Iu., "Luna-Park," *Teatr i iskusstvo* 18 (1914): 790. On Shpachek's prewar activities, see Iankovskii, "Operetochnyi teatr," 383. GMISP has old phonograph recordings of music by Shpachek; e.g., *Sud'ba tsyganki*, Zonofon Rekord, played on the tubaphone by A. Gel'm.

115. N. N. Fatov, "Opernyi sezon 1914–15 g. v Moskve," *Russkaia muzykal'naia gazeta*, no. 21–22 (1915): 379–80.

116. A. A. Gozenpud, *Russkii opernyi teatr mezhdu dvukh revoliutsii, 1905–1917* (Leningrad, 1975), 110–55; Iu. V. Keldysh, "Opernyi teatr," in *Russkaia khudozhestvennaia kul'tura*, 3:321–23; Rosenthal, "Wagner and Wagnerian Ideas," 211–33; "Slukhi i vesti," *Teatr i iskusstvo* 18 (1914): 677. For reactions to Rimski-Korsakov's "Ring" see Musicista, "Itogi muzykal'nago sezona," *Stolitsa i usad'ba*, no. 36–37 (1915): 25, and Nikolai Mileant, "Grekhi ili greshki (Rimskii-Korsakov na Mariinskoi stsene)," *Teatr i iskusstvo* 19 (1915): 222–23; Nikolai Evreinov, "O russkom teatre ne-russkago proiskhozhdeniia i ne-russkago uklada. (V poiskakh samobytnago russkago teatra)," *Teatr i iskusstvo* 19 (1915): 834–37, 858–60, 879–80, 898–901.

117. N. N. Fatov, "Opernyi sezon 1914–15 g. v Moskve," *Russkaia muzykal'naia gazeta*, no. 25–26 (1915): 425–27; idem, "Itogi opernago sezona 1915–16 gg. v Moskve," ibid., no. 26–27 (1916): 519–20.

118. N. N. Fatov, "Itogi opernago sezona 1915–16 gg. v Moskve," *Russkaia muzykal'naia gazeta*, no. 24–25 (1916): 498.

119. Sigmund Freud, hardly an Austrian nationalist, was moved by his country's anthem, according to Theodor Reik, *The Haunting Melody: Psychoanalytic Experiences in Life and Music* (New York, 1953), 59; see also *Materialien zur Geschichte der deutschen Nationalhymne* (Berlin, 1990), 100.

120. Iu. Engel, "Natsional'nye gimny Rossii i derzhav, soiuznykh i

druzhestvennykh ei," *Ezhegodnik Imperatorskikh teatrov,* 1915, 111–50; TsGIA SPb, f. 569, op. 13, d. 1114a, ll. 11–17 and op. 10, d. 154; *Petrogradskii listok,* 9 October 1914, 3; 26 October 1914, 3; 10 March 1915, 3.

121. I. Suvorov, "Zametka o proizvole v ispolnenii narodnago gimna," *Russkaia muzykal'naia gazeta,* no. 1 (1915): 21.

122. Nikolai Popov, "Kumir," *Teatr i iskusstvo* 18 (1914): 648–49; A. V. Bobrishchev-Pushkin, "Khraniteli kul'tury," ibid., 19 (1915): 733–35; S-oi, "Voina i teatry var'ete," *Var'ete i tsirk,* no. 29–30 (1915): 3–4.

3. Violence, Schmaltz, and Chivalry: The War in the Movies

1. B. Kazanskii, "Priroda kino," in *Poetika kino,* ed. Boris Eikhenbaum (Moscow/Leningrad, 1927; Berkeley, 1984), 96; Iurii Lotman, *Semiotika kino i problemy kinoestetiki* (Tallinn, 1973), 50.

2. On the history of the early years of the Russian film, see Leyda, *Kino,* 17–71. L. M. Budiak and V. P. Mikhailov, *Adresa moskovskogo kino* (Moscow, 1987), 46–50; V. R. Gardin, *Vospominaniia,* vol.1, *1912–1921* (Moscow, 1949), 76, 112, 140; R. P. Sobolev, *Liudi i filmy russkogo dorevoliutsionnogo kino* (Moscow, 1961), 49; N. Iezuitov, "Kinoiskusstvo dorevoliutsionnoi Rossii," *Voprosy kinoiskusstva* 2 (1957): 264–65; Marwick, *Deluge,* 142–43; Ann Purser, *Looking Back at Popular Entertainment, 1901–1939* (Wakefield, Yorks., 1978), 34; N. A. Lebedev, *Ocherk istorii kino SSSR: Nemoe kino,* 2d ed. (Moscow, 1965), 49. For an extensive, though incomplete listing of Russian films of the time, see V. E. Vishnevskii, *Khudozhestvennye filmy dorevoliutsionnoi Rossii: Fil'mograficheskoe opisanie* (Moscow, 1945), 35–142.

3. B. S. Likhachëv, "Materialy k istorii kino v Rossii (1914–1916)," *Iz istorii kino: Materialy i dokumenty* 3 (1960): 48–49; Rashit Yangirov, "Pavel Gustavovich Thiemann," in *Silent Witnesses: Russian Films, 1908–1919,* ed. Paolo Cherchi Usai et al. (London, 1989), 588–91; A. A. Levitskii, *Rasskazy o kinematografe* (Moscow, 1964), 60–63; A. A. Khanzhonkov, *Pervye gody russkoi kinematografii: Vospominaniia* (Moscow, 1937), 90; M. S. Arlazorov, *Protazanov* (Moscow, 1973), 52, 58; *Vestnik kinematografii,* no. 99 (1914): 22. On the fate of German theater owners see *Vestnik kinematografii,* no. 100 (1914): 15, and no. 101 (1914): 18. On the "German" riding the bike, see TsGIA SPb, f. 569, op. 10, d. 154, ll. 20–20 ob., and "'Prusskii soldat' v Petrograde," *Vestnik kinematografii,* no. 98 (1914): 18.

4. Khanzhonkov, *Pervye gody,* 82, 90; Gardin, *Vospominaniia,* 1:112; Iezuitov, "Kinoiskusstvo," 265; editorials in *Vestnik kinematografii,* no. 119 (1916): 1–3, and *Proektor,* no. 24 (1916): 1–2; "Sokrashchenie vremeni funktsionirovaniia kinematografov," *Proektor,* no. 2 (1915): 16–17, and no. 4 (1915): 14–15; "Rekvizitsiia Petrogradskikh teatrov," *Proektor,* no. 19 (1916): 14; "Nalog na zrelishcha," *Ekran Rossii,* no. 1 (1916): 2–4.

5. Khanzhonkov, *Pervye gody,* 86–87; "Lazaret kinematograficheskikh deiatelei," *Sine-Fono,* no. 23–24 (1914): 19; "Otdel'nye lazarety kinematograficheskikh predpriiatii," *Sine-Fono,* no. 25–26 (1914): 20; "Osvia-

shchenie lazareta imeni kinematografii," *Sine-Fono*, no. 1–2 (1914): 17–21 (including a photo of the hospital and a list of sponsors); "Stydno!" *Sine-Fono*, no. 13 (1915): 37; "Kinematograf i blagotvoritel'nost'," *Proektor*, no. 2 (1915): 22; "Seansy v lazaretakh," *Sine-Fono*, no. 3 (1914): 31; *Vestnik kinematografii*, no. 100 (1914): 12; "Kinematograf v lazaretakh," *Proektor*, no. 2 (1915): 21.

6. Richard Taylor, "Agitation, Propaganda, and the Cinema: The Search for New Solutions, 1917–21," in *Art, Society, Revolution: Russia, 1917–1921*, ed. Nils Åke Nilsson (Stockholm, 1979), 247–48. Reports about mobile film exhibitors around Orenburg and on the Crimea are in *Vestnik kinematografii*, no. 103 (1914): 14, and no. 110 (1915): 49; see also "Peredvizhnoi kinematograf," *Sine-Fono*, no. 13 (1915): 54; Karl Schlögel, *Jenseits des Großen Oktober: Das Laboratorium der Moderne. Petersburg, 1909–1921* (Berlin, 1988), 186–89; A. V. Zhdankov, "Piterskii proletariat v bor'be protiv kontrrevoliutsionnoi kinopropagandy v 1917 g.," in *Piterskie rabochie v bor'be s kontrrevoliutsiei v 1917–1918 gg.*, ed. G. L. Sobolev (Moscow, 1986), 212; M. Brailovskii, "Pered letnim sezonom," *Sine-Fono*, no. 11–12 (1915): 55–57; Pëtr Solianyi, "Nachala i kontsy (O kinematografe)," *Teatr i iskusstvo* 18 (1914): 900–903; Marwick, *Deluge*, 141.

7. Schlögel, *Jenseits des Großen Oktobers*, 187; N. M. Zorkaia, "Vokrug pervykh russkikh kinoseansov," *Voprosy kinoiskusstva* 15 (1974): 189; idem, "Pervaia russkaia kinozvezda (O Vere Kholodnoi)," *Voprosy kinoiskusstva* 11 (1968): 158–59; Michael T. Isenberg, *War on Film: The American Cinema and World War I, 1914–1941* (London/Toronto, 1981), 47, 52; S. S. Ginzburg, *Kinematografiia dorevoliutsionnoi Rossii* (Moscow, 1963), 215–16. On the attraction of patriotic films to provincial and lower-class audiences, see the letters to the editors in *Sine-Fono*, no. 8 (1915): 51–52, and the report about the Min'on Theater in Kharkov, which could hold on to its *neintelligentnaia publika* only by playing patriotic war films (*Vestnik kinematografii*, no. 118 [1916]: 17). T. Evstigneev (*Sine-Fono*, no. 6–7 [1915]) notes the great popularity of patriotic films in Petrograd's Narvskii and other working-class districts.

8. Iezuitov, "Kinoiskusstvo," 266; N. M. Zorkaia, *Na rubezhe stoletii: U istokov massovogo iskusstva v Rossii 1900–1910 godov* (Moscow, 1976), 276–78, 293–95.

9. Zorkaia, *Na rubezhe stoletii*, 99; Ivan Perestiani, *75 let zhizni v iskusstve* (Moscow, 1962), 267; Vasilii Komardenkov, *Dni minuvshie* (Moscow, 1972), 42–43; Iezuitov, "Kinoiskusstvo," 266–69; Ginzburg, *Kinematografiia dorevoliutsionnoi Rossii*, 211–13; Fritz Göttler, "Schauplätze der Seele: Zur Reihe mit russischen Stummfilmen der Zarenzeit im Münchner Filmmuseum," *Süddeutsche Zeitung* (Munich), 26 November 1990; Yuri Tsivian, "Evgenii Frantsevich Bauer," in *Silent Witnesses*, 546–51.

10. V. R. Gardin, "Pamiati tovarishcha po liubimomu iskusstvu," in *Iakov Protazanov: O tvorcheskom puti rezhissëra*, comp. M. N. Aleinikov, 2d ed. (Moscow, 1957), 315; *Silent Witnesses*, 240–42, 294–96; Zorkaia, *Na rubezhe stoletii*, 201–9; Boris Eikhenbaum, "Problemy kino-stilistiki," in *Poetika kino*, ed. Eikhenbaum (Moscow/Leningrad, 1927; Berkeley, 1984), 24–25.

11. *Var'ete i tsirk,* no. 9–10 (1916): 7; I. Mavich, "Nashi dostizheniia," *Sine-Fono,* no. 6–7 (1915): 45–46. Ginzburg (*Kinematografiia dorevoliutsionnoi Rossii,* 191) notes that the newsreels were not profitable, in direct contradiction to the great interest shown in them. On the manipulations of newsreels, see Isenberg, *War on Film,* 64; Mosse, *Fallen Soldiers,* 148; *Sine-Fono,* no. 3 (1914): 32; *Vestnik kinematografii,* no. 117 (1916): 6 and 22–23; *Ekran Rossii,* no. 1 (1916): 21. "News" was still being staged during World War II, according to Fussell, *Wartime,* 190.

12. Ginzburg, *Kinematografiia dorevoliutsionnoi Rossii,* 181, 185; "Operator—geroi," *Sine-Fono,* no. 8 (1915): 48; M. A-ov, "Operator—geroi," *Sine-Fono,* no. 10 (1915): 48–51, 56 (photo of Ercole in uniform with camera and pistol); V. D., "Mechty i deistvitel'nost'," *Proektor,* no. 22 (1916): 4–5.

13. Budiak, *Adresa moskovskogo kino,* 47–48; Lebedev, *Ocherk istorii kino,* 44; Levitskii, *Rasskazy o kinematografe,* 110–14; Leyda, *Kino,* 97–98; Ginzburg, *Kinematografiia dorevoliutsionnoi Rossii,* 180–82, 187–88; *Vestnik kinematografii,* no. 101 (1914): 16 and no. 116 (1915): 35. On the impact of French newsreels, see "Khronika," *Sine-Fono,* no. 13 (1915): 50; for Khanzhonkov's ersatz *khronika* see *Vestnik kinematografii,* no. 97 (1914): 10, no. 98 (1914): 16, and no. 120 (1916): 5.

14. On the father who recognized his son, see *Vestnik kinematografii,* no. 113 (1915): 42. On the style of German newsreels and the Bild- und Film-Amt, see Pohl, "Der Kaiser im Zeitalter seiner technischen Reproduzierbarkeit," 16. The value of films as sources of information is discussed in "Znachenie kinematografa dlia voennago dela (Beseda s kapitanom Ia. P. Levoshko)," *Ekran Rossii,* no. 1 (1916): 22–23; Veritas [S. D. Makhalov], "Mobilizatsiia ekrana," *Vestnik kinematografii,* no. 115 (1915): 38–39. On films at the front, see "V Skobelevskom komitete," *Proektor,* no. 2 (1915): 20; "V komissii po ustroistvu peredvizhnykh kinematografov na fronte," *Sine-Fono,* no. 11–12 (1916): 64, and editorial in no. 13–14 (1916): 33–34; also "Podvizhnyi kinematograf," *Sine-Fono,* no. 17–18 (1916). Certainly more movies where shown at the Russian front than Jay Leyda (*Kino,* 85n) assumes.

15. Yervant Gianikian and Angela Ricci Lucchi, producers, *Menschen, Jahre, Leben,* television performance, Zweites Deutsches Fernsehen, "Das kleine Fernsehspiel," 22 January 1991; review of *Shturm i vziatie Erzeruma* and "Kak my delali s"ëmku padeniia Erzeruma," *Ekran Rossii,* no. 1 (1916): 20–21, 34, and 24–25. On the scandal surrounding the film's distribution, see *Vestnik kinematografii,* no. 117 (1916): 6; S. L. [S. V. Lur'el], "Po povodu monopolizatsii kartiny *Shturm i vziatie Erzeruma,*" *Sine-Fono,* no. 9–10 (1916): 53–56.

16. Aleksandr Pushkin, "Puteshestvie v Arzrum vo vremia pokhoda 1829 goda," in *Sobranie sochinenii v desiati tomakh* (Moscow, 1959–62), 5:412–62.

17. On musical repertoire and sound effects in patriotic films, see Likhachëv, "Materialy k istorii kino," 45; "Muzyka ekrana," *Sine-Fono,* no. 15–16 (1916): 45; "Kinoobzor," *Kinematograf,* no. 3 (1916): 12–13; Iurii Tsiv'ian, "Tekst i zhest: *Boris Godunov* v ispolnenii provintsial'nykh akterov 1910-kh godov," in *Sbornik statei k 70-letiiu prof. Iu. M. Lotmana* (Tartu, 1992), 210–11.

18. Ginzburg, *Kinematografiia dorevoliutsionnoi Rossii*, 191–92; Iezuitov, "Kinoiskusstvo," 267. For film listings, see *Vestnik kinematografii*, no. 101 (1914): 26–27, and "Programmy," *Sine-Fono*, no. 10 (1915): 80. An overview of the most popular patriotic films is in Likhachëv, "Materialy k istorii kino," 45–46; see also the advertisements in *Sine-Fono*, no. 23 (1914). *Organ*, no. 136 (May 1915): n.p.; V. R. Gardin, *Zhizn' i trud artista* (Moscow, 1960), 130. On the film about Kriuchkov, see Arlazorov, *Protazanov*, 54; Gardin, *Vospominaniia*, 76; "Novye lenty," *Sine-Fono*, no. 25–26 (1914): 20–21.

19. On the relationship between film and lubok, see Zorkaia, *Na rubezhe stoletii*, 95, 230–32. Iezuitov, "Kinoiskusstvo," 267; Ginzburg, *Kinematografiia dorevoliutsionnoi Rossii*, 199–200.

20. I saw *Doloi nemetskoe igo* at the Munich Filmmuseum in December 1990. See also Ginzburg, *Kinematografiia dorevoliutsionnoi Rossii*, 199; Vishnevskii, *Khudozhestvennye filmy*, 38.

21. "Tragediia i poshlost'," *Vestnik kinematografii*, no. 99 (1914): 11–12; "Otkrytoe pis'mo nekotorym gg. deiateliam kinematografii," ibid., no. 100 (1914): 10; *Sine-Fono*, no. 3 (1914): 33.

22. Review of *V luchakh germanskikh prozhektorov*, *Sine-Fono*, no. 6–7 (1915): 118.

23. *Silent Witnesses*, 236; Vishnevskii, *Khudozhestvennye filmy*, 45, 47–48; reviews of *Sestra miloserdiia* and *Slava nam, smert' vragam, Vestnik kinematografii*, no. 101 (1914): 18 and 25, and stills on 7 and 15; "Pod grokhot pushek," *Sine-Fono*, no. 4–5 (1914): 57; Zorkaia, *Na rubezhe stoletii*, 231. On Bebutova, see Brooks, *When Russia Learned to Read*, 160, 224.

24. Review of *Predatel'*, *Proektor*, no. 13–14 (1916): 20–21.

25. Brooks, *When Russia Learned to Read*, 222–26; review of *El'zas, Proektor*, no. 16 (1916): 15–16. A poster for the film with stills is in GMISP.

26. Reviews of *Krovavyi polumesiats, Sine-Fono*, no. 13 (1915): 48, and *Turetskii shpionazh: Voina i zhenshchina*, ibid., no. 6–7 (1915): 92, 97.

27. Vishnevskii, *Khudozhestvennye filmy*, 51; Gardin, "Pamiati tovarishcha," 314, and *Vospominaniia*, 77 (photo), 81; review of *Enver-pasha, predatel' Turtsii, Sine-Fono*, no. 6–7 (1915): 50–51, 80.

28. On the "Orient" as a problem of identity and cultural clash, see Edward W. Said, *Orientalism* (New York, 1978), 3, 40, 55; on Russian attitudes toward the Ottoman Empire, see David M. Goldfrank, *The Origins of the Crimean War* (London/New York, 1994).

29. Isenberg, *War on Film*, 183–84; Ginzburg, *Kinematografiia dorevoliutsionnoi Rossii*, 201–5; Vishnevskii, *Khudozhestvennye filmy*, 79; review of *Taina zavoda Kruppa, Proektor*, no. 2 (1915): 8, 39.

30. Isenberg, *War on Film*, 149, 153; Vishnevskii, *Khudozhestvennye filmy*, 45, 66; review of *Pasynok Marsa, Vestnik kinematografii*, no. 99 (1914): 24; review of *Liliia Bel'gii, Ekran Rossii*, no. 1 (1916): 20; *Silent Witnesses*, 272. *The Belgian Lily* is included in vol. 3 of *Early Russian Cinema*, a video collection released by the British Film Institute in 1992.

31. Review of *Germanskie varvary v Bel'gii, Proektor*, no. 4 (1915): 25.

32. Review of *Uzhasy Reimsa, Sine-Fono*, no. 6–7 (1915): 92.

33. Review of *Dykhanie antikhristovo, Proektor*, no. 3 (1915): 33. A poster for the film with stills is in GMISP.

34. Vishnevskii, *Khudozhestvennye filmy*, 52; reviews of *Antikhrist, Sine-Fono*, no. 13 (1915): 48, 90, and no. 14–15 (1915): 78–79. The harsh criticism of the film is in "Kriticheskie ocherki," *Vestnik kinematografii*, no. 111 (1915): 22–23.

35. For the first "German horrors," see the ad for *Na zashchitu brat'ev slavian* by A. G. Taldykin in *Sine-Fono*, no. 21–22 (1914): 41, issued on 2 August 1914.

36. Vishnevskii, *Khudozhestvennye filmy*, 118; V. I. Simakov, *Soldatskiia pesni. Sbornik voennykh pesen* (Iaroslavl', 1915), 10–13; Nest'ev, *Zvëzdy russkoi estrady*, 100; "Za god," *Vestnik kinematografii*, no. 122 (1916): 1; review of *Umer bedniaga v bol'nitse voennoi, Proektor*, no. 15 (1916): 8–9 (stills), 10; Levitskii, *Rasskazy o kinematografe*, 119; Ginzburg, *Kinematografiia dorevoliutsionnoi Rossii*, 216. For a poster of the film, see Fig. 38.

37. "Kinematograf i voina," *Vestnik kinematografii*, no. 100 (1914): 6.

38. Lotman, *Semiotika kino*, 16–19.

Conclusion: National Identity and Revolution

1. Ernest Gellner, *Culture, Identity, and Politics* (Cambridge, 1987), 15–19. Allan K. Wildman notes that the war made no sense to the simple peasant-soldiers; see his *End of the Russian Imperial Army: The Old Army and the Soldiers' Revolt (March–April 1917)* (Princeton, 1980), 77–80; see also Rogger, "Russia in 1914," 105–6, and P. N. Miliukov, *Vospominaniia* (Moscow, 1991), 390–91.

2. Benedict Anderson, *Imagined Communities: Reflections on the Origin and Spread of Nationalism*, rev. ed. (London/New York, 1991), 5–7. Hobsbawm ("Mass-Producing Traditions," 276) stresses the populistic function of such national symbols as the Deutsche Michel, who supposedly embodied characteristics of the average German.

3. On changes in the popular perception of the tsar, see also Brooks, *When Russia Learned to Read*, 217. On "old" and "new" traditions, see Eric Hobsbawm, "Introduction," in *The Invention of Tradition*, ed. Hobsbawm and Terence Ranger (Cambridge, 1983), 10–11. The relationship between religion and nationalism is discussed in Peter Alter, *Nationalism*, trans. Stuart McKinnon-Evans (London, 1989), 10.

4. For elite adaptation of folk culture to express nationalism, see Gellner, *Nations and Nationalism*, 57–58.

5. For a discussion of cultural and political nations as well as Risorgimento nationalism, see Alter, *Nationalism*, 14–18, 59–91.

6. Ernest Renan, *Qu'est-ce qu'une nation?* (Paris, 1882). For the views of Russian conservatives on the nation, see Edward C. Thaden, *Conservative Nationalism in Nineteenth-Century Russia* (Seattle, 1964), 62–63, 205–6.

Bibliography

Archival Materials

Gosudarstvennyi muzei istorii Sankt-Peterburga, St. Petersburg (GMISP)
    Fond plakatov
    Fond nauki i tekhniki
Gosudarstvennyi muzei V. V. Maiakovskogo, Moscow
Gosudarstvennyi muzei politicheskoi istorii Rossii, St. Petersburg (GMPIR)
    Fond V (posters)
    Fond IX (photographs)
Gosudarstvennyi tsentral'nyi teatral'nyi muzei imeni A. A. Bakhrushina, Moscow (GMB)
Library of Congress, Washington, D.C., Prints and Photographs Division (PPDLC)
    Lot 5452 F (postcards)
    Lot 3502 H (posters)
Muzei tsirkovogo iskusstva, St. Petersburg (MTsI)
Tsentral'nyi gosudarstvennyi istoricheskii arkhiv Sankt-Peterburga, St. Petersburg (TsGIA SPb)
    Fond 287, op. 1, d. 332 (Artist—Soldatu)
    Fond 436, op. 1, d. 14967, l. 35 (Predsedatel'nitsa soveta ob.-va. popecheniia bezpriiutnykh detiakh)
    Fond 569 (Kantseliariia peterburgskogo gradonachal'nika)
    Fond 1365, op. 1, d. 62, ll. 331–344 ob. (O rasprostranenii biletov sredi rabochikh masterskikh na patrioticheskii vecher)

Fond 1458, op. 2, d. 1043 (O priobretenii dlia sluzhashchikh i rabochikh ekspeditsii biletov na patrioticheskie vechera)
University of Helsinki, Slavonic Library
Collections of postcards and posters

Primary Sources

Affiches et imageries russes, 1914–1920. Paris, 1982.

Akhmatova, A. A. *Stikhotvoreniia i poemy.* Leningrad, 1979.

Al'perov, D. S. *Na arene starogo tsirka: Zapiski klouna.* Moscow, 1936.

Arnshtam, A. *Voennyi al'bom no. 1.* N.p., n.d.

Bardovskii, A. A. *Teatral'nyi zritel' na fronte v kanun Oktiabria.* Leningrad, 1928.

Borisov, L. I. *Za kruglym stolom proshlogo: Vospominaniia.* Leningrad, 1971.

Darracott, Joseph. *The First World War in Posters from the Imperial War Museum.* London/New York, 1974.

Darracott, Joseph, and Belinda Loftus. *First World War Posters.* 2d ed. London, 1981.

Denisov, Vladimir. *Voina i lubok.* Petrograd, 1916.

Dneprov, Mitrofan. *Polveka v operette.* Moscow, 1961.

Dovlatov, Sergei. *Zapovednik.* Ann Arbor, Mich., 1983.

Durov, V. L. *V plenu u nemtsev.* Moscow, 1914.

Ershov, P. P. *Konëk-gorbunok. Stikhotvoreniia.* Leningrad, 1976.

Filippov, Vladimir, ed. *Aleksandr Ivanovich Iuzhin-Sumbatov: Zapisi, stat'i, pis'ma.* 2d ed. Moscow, 1951.

Gaideburov, P. P. *Literaturnoe nasledie. Vospominaniia. Stat'i. Rezhissërskie eksplikatsii. Vystupleniia.* Moscow, 1977.

Gardin, V. R. "Pamiati tovarishcha po liubimomu iskusstvu." In *Iakov Protazanov: O tvorcheskom puti rezhissëra,* comp. M. N. Aleinikov, 2d ed., 310–23. Moscow, 1957.

——. *Vospominaniia.* Vol. 1, 1912–1921. Moscow, 1949.

——. *Zhizn' i trud artista.* Moscow, 1960.

Gershuni, E. P. *Rasskazyvaiu ob estrade.* Leningrad, 1968.

Glinskii, B., comp. *Sovremennaia voina v russkoi poezii.* Petrograd, 1915.

Gloria—Viktoria: Der Völkerkrieg in Wort und Bild nach Daten geordnet. Ein Postkartensammelwerk. Munich, n.d.

Goulzadian, Anne. *L'Empire du dernier tsar: 410 cartes postales, 1896–1917.* Argenteuil, 1982.

Iakovleva-Shaporina, L. V. "Iz vospominanii L. V. Iakovlevoi-Shaporinoi ob organizatsii i rabote teatra marionetok pri petrogradskom teatre-studii." In *Russkii sovetskii teatr, 1917–1921,* ed. A. Z. Iufit, 287–89. Leningrad, 1968.

Iaron, G. M. *O liubimom zhanre.* Moscow, 1960.

International Cartoons of the War. Selected and with an Introduction by H. Pearl Adam. London, 1916.

Kalmykova, Aleksandra. "Russkiia lubochnyia kartiny v ikh prosvetitel'nom znachenii dlia naroda za poslednee 75-letie nashei zhizni." In *Polveka dlia* knigi: *Literaturno-khudozhestvennyi sbornik, posviashchennyi piatidesiatiletiiu izdatel'skoi deiatel'nosti I. D. Sytina,* 163–202. Moscow, 1916.

Karikatury "Voina i Pem"—Caricatures "La Guerre et Pême." 2d ed. Petrograd, 1915.

Kartinki: Voina russkikh s nemtsami. Petrograd, [1916?].

Khanzhonkov, A. A. *Pervye gody russkoi kinematografii: Vospominaniia.* Moscow/Leningrad, 1937.

Kio [E. T. Girshfel'd-Renard]. *Fokusy i fokusniki.* Moscow, 1958.

Komardenkov, Vasilii. *Dni minuvshie.* Moscow, 1972.

Konechnyi, A. M. "Peterburgskii 'balagannyi maestro' A. Ia. Alekseev-Iakovlev." Typescript in the author's possession.

"Korol' shutov, No ne shut korolei." In *Anatolii Leonidovich Durov.* N.p., n.d., separate pagination.

Kotliarov, Iurii, and Viktor Garmash, comps. *Letopis' zhizni i tvorchestva F. I. Shaliapina.* 2 vols. 2d ed. Leningrad, 1989.

Kugel', A. R. *Teatral'nye portrety.* Petrograd, Moscow, 1923.

Lekhno, V. B. *Voina. V sharzhakh i karrikaturakh periodicheskikh izdanii.* Moscow, n.d.

Levitskii, A. A. *Rasskazy o kinematografe.* Moscow, 1964.

Lisovskii, M. *Siluety voiny. 1914–1915: Risunki uchastnika.* 2 vols. Petrograd, 1915–16.

Maiakovskii, Vladimir. *Polnoe sobranie sochinenii v trinadtsati tomakh.* Moscow, 1955–61.

"Mariia Ivanovna Dolina, solistka Ego Velichestva." In *Ezhegodnik Imperatorskikh teatrov. Sezon 1901–1902.* Suppl. 1, 12–14.

Merry, W. Mansell. *Two Months in Russia: July–September, 1914.* Oxford, 1916.

Miliukov, P. N. *Vospominaniia.* Moscow, 1991.

Morfessi, Iurii. *Zhizn', liubov', stsena: Vospominaniia russkago baiana.* 2d ed. Paris, 1982.

Nabokov, Vladimir. *Pnin.* New York, 1989.

Nevskii, V. A. *Velikaia evropeiskaia voina. Sistematicheskiia programmy dlia narodnykh chtenii—vecherov po istorii i geografii voiuiushchikh derzhav.* Buzuluk, 1915.

Okunev, N. P. *Dnevnik Moskvicha (1917–1924).* Paris, 1990.

Ozarovskaia, O. E. *Babushkiny stariny.* Petrograd, 1916.

Pasternak, Leonid. *The Memoirs of Leonid Pasternak.* London/New York, 1982.

Perestiani, Ivan. *75 let zhizni v iskusstve.* Moscow, 1962.

1-i [Pervyi] dopolnitel'nyi spisok k katalogu izdanii zhurnala "Teatr i iskusstvo" s 1 ianvaria 1914 g. po 1 maia 1915 g. Petrograd, [1915].

Petrushka: Ulichnyi teatr. Moscow, 1915.

Pushkin, Aleksandr. *Sobranie sochinenii v desiati tomakh.* Moscow, 1959–62.

Radunskii, I. S. *Zapiski starogo klouna.* Moscow, 1954.

Rennikov, A. *Lunnaia doroga: Razskazy.* Petrograd, 1916.

Rickards, Maurice. *Posters of the First World War.* New York, 1968.

Rovinskii, D. A. *Russkiia narodnyia kartinki.* 5 vols. St. Petersburg, 1881–93.

Schmidt, W. *Images of the Great War.* Vol. 2, *An Illustrated Catalogue of Delandre's Non-French Military Vignettes, 1914–1917.* N.p., 1985.

Severianin, Igor'. *Stikhotvoreniia.* Moscow, 1988.

Shverubovich, Vadim. *O starom Khudozhestvennom teatre.* Moscow, 1990.

Shol'te, F. I., comp. *Grimasy voiny, 1914–1915 g.: Plakaty, karikatury, lubki.* 2d ed. Petrograd, 1916.

Simakov, V. I. *Soldatskiia pesni. Sbornik voennykh pesen.* Iaroslavl', 1915.

Smirnova, N. A. *Vospominaniia.* Moscow, 1947.

Smirnov-Sokol'skii, N. P. *Sorok piat' let na estrade: Fel'etony, stat'i, vystupleniia.* Moscow, 1976.

Sokol'skii, Sergei. *Pliashushchaia lirika: Stikhotvoreniia i pesni.* Petrograd, 1916.

"Stranichki A.L.D." In *Anatolii Leonidovich Durov.* N.pl., n.d., separate pagination.

Tarakhno, P. G. *Zhizn' otdannaia tsirku.* Moscow, 1977.

Trubetskoi, E. N. *Otechestvennaia voina i eia dukhovnyi smysl (Publichnaia lektsiia).* Moscow, 1915.

Usai, Paolo Cherchi, Lorenzo Codelli, Carlo Montanaro, and David Robinson, eds. *Silent Witnesses: Russian Films, 1908–1919.* London, 1989.

Utësov, L. O. *Zapiski aktëra.* Moscow, 1939.

Vasilenko, S. N. *Stranitsy vospominanii.* Moscow, 1945.

Vechera i utra "Russkoi pesni" M. I. Dolinoi, 1907–1908. St. Petersburg, 1907.

Wehrhan, Karl. *Gloria Viktoria! Volkspoesie an Militärzügen.* Munich, 1915.

Secondary Sources

Adorno, Theodor W. *Einleitung in die Musiksoziologie.* Frankfurt, 1975.

Aliakritskii, Iu. *Propaganda v armiiakh imperialistov.* Moscow, 1931.

Alter, Peter. *Nationalism.* Trans. Stuart McKinnon-Evans. London, 1989.

Al'tshuller, A. Ia. "Aleksandrinskii teatr." In *Russkaia khudozhestvennaia kul'tura kontsa XIX–nachala XX veka.* Vol. 3, *Zrelishchnye iskusstva, muzyka,* 92–106. Moscow, 1977.

Amasovich, A. A. *Aleksandrov-Serzh.* Moscow, 1951.

Anderson, Benedict. *Imagined Communities: Reflections on the Origin and Spread of Nationalism.* Rev. ed. London/New York, 1991.

Arlazorov, M. S. *Protazanov.* Moscow, 1973.

Babenko, V. G. *Artist Aleksandr Vertinskii: Materialy k biografii. Razmyshleniia.* Sverdlovsk, 1989.

Baburina, N. I. *Russkii plakat: Vtoraia polovina XIX–nachalo XX veka.* Leningrad, 1988.

Bakhtin, V. S., and D. M. Moldavskii. *Russkii lubok XVII–XIX vv..* Moscow, 1962.

Baranov, Iurii. *Podvizhnik muzyki narodnoi.* Moscow, 1988.

Barthes, Roland. *Mythologies.* Trans. Annette Lavers. London, 1972.

Beletskii, Platon. *Georgii Ivanovich Narbut.* Leningrad, 1985.

Benedict, Ruth. *Patterns of Culture.* Cambridge, Mass., 1961.

Berlina, M. S. "P'esy Leonida Andreeva na Aleksandrinskoi stsene." In *Russkii teatr i dramaturgiia, 1907–1917 godov: Sbornik nauchnykh trudov,* 68–93. Leningrad, 1988.

Bogachev, A. *Plakat.* Leningrad, 1926.

Bouissac, Paul. *Circus and Culture: A Semiotic Approach.* Lanham, Md., 1985.

Bowlt, John E. "Nineteenth-Century Russian Caricature." In *Art and Culture in Nineteenth-Century Russia,* ed. Theofanis George Stavrou, 221–36. Bloomington, Ind., 1983.

——. "Russian Painting in the Nineteenth Century." In *Art and Culture in Nineteenth-Century Russia,* ed. Theofanis George Stavrou, 113–39. Bloomington, Ind., 1983.

——. *The Silver Age: Russian Art of the Early Twentieth Century and the "World of Art" Group.* Newtonville, Mass., 1979.

Brooks, Jeffrey. "Competing Modes of Popular Discourse: Individualism and Class Consciousness in the Russian Print Media, 1880–1928." Paper presented at the 19th National Convention of the American Association for the Advancement of Slavic Studies, Boston, 5–8 November 1987.

——. *When Russia Learned to Read: Literacy and Popular Literature, 1861–1917.* Princeton, 1985.

Brower, Daniel R. *The Russian City between Tradition and Modernity, 1850–1900.* Berkeley, 1990.

Budiak, L. M., and V. P. Mikhailov. *Adresa moskovskogo kino.* Moscow, 1987.

Carter, Stephen K. *Russian Nationalism: Yesterday, Today, Tomorrow.* London, 1990.

Dadamian, G. G. *Teatr v kul'turnoi zhizni Rossii v gody pervoi mirovoi voiny (1914–1917 gg.).* Moscow, 1987.

Dahlhaus, Carl. *Between Romanticism and Modernism: Four Studies in the Music of the Later Nineteenth Century.* Trans. Mary Whittall. Berkeley, 1980.

Danilov, S. S. *Ocherki po istorii russkogo dramaticheskogo teatra.* Moscow/Leningrad, 1948.

Derzhavin, Konstantin. *Epokhi Aleksandrinskoi stseny.* Leningrad, 1932.

Deutsch, Karl W. *Interdisciplinary Bibliography on Nationalism.* Cambridge, Mass., 1956.

Diakin, V. S. *Russkaia burzhuaziia i tsarizm v gody pervoi mirovoi voiny (1914–1917).* Leningrad, 1967.

Dinershtein, E. A. *"Fabrikant" chitatelei: A. F. Marks.* Moscow, 1986.

Dmitriev, Iu. A. *Brat'ia Durovy.* Moscow/Leningrad, 1945.

——. *Leonid Utësov.* Moscow, 1982.

——. "Tsirk." In *Russkaia khudozhestvennaia kul'tura kontsa XIX–nachala XX veka.* Vol. 3, *Zrelishchnye iskusstva, muzyka,* 228–39. Moscow, 1977.

——. *Tsirk v Rossii: Ot istokov do 1917 g.* Moscow, 1977.

——. *Vitalii Lazarenko.* Moscow/Leningrad, 1946.

Dmitriev, S. S. *Ocherki istorii russkoi kul'tury nachala XX veka.* Moscow, 1985.

Donakowski, Conrad L. *A Muse for the Masses: Ritual and Music in an Age of Democratic Revolution, 1770–1870.* Chicago, 1972.

Doob, Leonard W. *Patriotism and Nationalism: Their Psychological Foundations.* New Haven, 1964.

Drobizheva, L. M. "Izuchenie natsional'nogo samosoznaniia v SSSR." Paper presented at the symosium "Pre-Modern and Modern National Identity in

Russia/Soviet Union and Eastern Europe," School of Slavonic and East European Studies, University of London, April 1989.

Dubnova, E. Ia. "Chastnye teatry Moskvy i Peterburga." In *Russkaia khudozhestvennaia kul'tura kontsa XIX–nachala XX veka*. Vol. 3, *Zrelishchnye iskusstva, muzyka*, 148–78. Moscow, 1977.

Durova-Sadovskaia, A. V. *Po vecheram na staroi bozhedomke*. Moscow, 1977.

Durylin, S. N. *Mariia Nikolaevna Ermolova, 1853–1928: Ocherk zhizni i tvorchestva*. Moscow, 1953.

Eikhenbaum, Boris. "Problemy kino-stilistiki." In *Poetika kino*, ed. Boris Eikhenbaum, 11–52. Moscow/Leningrad, 1927; Berkeley, 1984.

Eksteins, Modris. *Rites of Spring: The Great War and the Birth of the Modern Age*. New York, 1990.

Engelstein, Laura. *The Keys to Happiness: Sex and the Search for Modernity in Fin-de-Siècle Russia*. Ithaca, 1992.

Etkind, Mark. A. *N. Benua i russkaia khudozhestvennaia kul'tura kontsa XIX–nachala XX veka*. Leningrad, 1989.

Firth, Raymond. *Symbols: Public and Private*. Ithaca, 1973.

Fraenger, Wilhelm. "Deutsche Vorlagen zu russischen Volksbilderbogen des 18. Jahrhunderts." In *Lubok: Der russische Volksbilderbogen*, ed. Wolfgang Till, 35–55. Munich, 1985.

Fussell,Paul. *The Great War and Modern Memory*. London, 1975.

———. *Wartime: Understanding and Behavior in the Second World War*. New York, 1989.

Gans, Herbert J. *Popular Culture and High Culture: An Analysis and Evaluation of Taste*. New York, 1974.

Geertz, Clifford. *The Interpretation of Cultures*. New York, 1973.

Gellner, Ernest. *Culture, Identity, and Politics*. Cambridge, 1987.

———. *Nations and Nationalism*. Ithaca, 1983.

Ginzburg, S. S. *Kinematografiia dorevoliutsionnoi Rossii*. Moscow, 1963.

Glotz, Peter. *Der Irrweg des Nationalstaats: Europäische Reden an ein deutsches Publikum*. Stuttgart, 1990.

Goldfrank, David M. *The Origins of the Crimean War*. London/New York, 1994.

Golynets, G. V., and S. V. Golynets. *Ivan Iakovlevich Bilibin*. Moscow, 1972.

Gozenpud, A. A. *Russkii opernyi teatr mezhdu dvukh revoliutsii, 1905–1917*. Leningrad, 1975.

Gray, Camilla. *Das große Experiment: Die russische Kunst, 1863–1922*. Cologne, 1974.

Groys, Boris. Foreword to *Rasputins Ende: Erinnerungen*, by Felix Jussupoff. Munich, 1985.

Hayes, Carlton J. H. *Essays on Nationalism*. New York, 1937.

Hellman, Ben. "An Aggressive Imperialist? The Controversy over Nikolaj Gumilev's War Poetry." In *Nikolaj Gumilev, 1886–1986: Papers from the Gumilev Centenary Symposium Held at Ross Priory University of Strathclyde, 1986*, 133–54. Oakland, Calif., 1987.

———. "Kogda vremia slavianofil'stvovalo. Russkie filosofy i pervaia mirovaia voina." In *Studia Russica Helsingiensia et Tartuensia. Problemy istorii russkoi literatury nachala XX veka*, ed. Liisa Byckling and Pekka Pesonen, 211–39. Helsinki, 1989.

——. "Leonid Andreev v nachale pervoi mirovoi voiny. Put' ot *Krasnogo smekha* k p'ese *Korol', zakon i svoboda.*" In *Studia Russica Helsingiensia et Tartuensia II. Literaturnyi protsess: vnutrennie zakony i vneshnie vozdeistviia*, 81–101. Tartu, 1990.

Hobsbawm, Eric. "Introduction." In *The Invention of Tradition*, ed. Eric Hobsbawm and Terence Ranger, 1–14. Cambridge, 1983.

——. "Mass Producing Traditions: Europe, 1870–1914." In *The Invention of Tradition*, ed. Eric Hobsbawm and Terence Ranger, 263–307. Cambridge, 1983.

——. *Nations and Nationalism since 1780: Programme, Myth, Reality.* Cambridge, 1990.

Holmes, Richard. *Acts of War: The Behavior of Men in Battle.* New York, 1986.

Holthusen, Johannes. *Russische Literatur im 20. Jahrhundert.* Munich, 1978.

——. *Tiergestalten und metamorphe Erscheinungen in der Literatur der russischen Avantgarde (1909–1923).* Bayerische Akademie der Wissenschaften, Philosophisch-Historische Klasse, Sitzungsberichte 1974, no. 12. Munich, 1974.

Hubbs, Joanna. *Mother Russia: The Feminine Myth in Russian Culture.* Bloomington, Ind., 1988.

Hundhausen, Carl. "Über das politische Plakat." In *Politische Kommunikation durch das Plakat*, 11–44. Bonn, 1975.

Hunter, Earl L. *A Sociological Analysis of Certain Types of Patriotism.* New York, 1932.

Huss, Marie-Monique. "Pronatalism and the Popular Ideology of the Child in Wartime France: The Evidence of the Picture Postcard." In *The Upheaval of War: Family, Work and Welfare in Europe, 1914–1918*, ed. Richard Wall and Jay Winter, 329–67. Cambridge, 1988.

Iankovskii, M. O. "Operetochnyi teatr." In *Russkaia khudozhestvennaia kul'tura kontsa XIX–nachala XX veka.* Vol. 3, *Zrelishchnye iskusstva, muzyka*, 381–91. Moscow, 1977.

——. *Operetta: Vozniknovenie i razvitie zhanra na zapade i v SSSR.* Leningrad/Moscow, 1937.

Isenberg, Michael T. *War on Film: The American Cinema and World War I, 1914–1941.* London/Toronto, 1981.

Istoriia russkogo dramaticheskogo teatra. Vol. 7, *1898–1917.* Moscow, 1987.

Itkina, E. G. "Der russische Volksbilderbogen." In *Lubok: Der russische Volksbilderbogen*, ed. Wolfgang Till, 9–19. Munich, 1985.

Ivanov, E. P. *Russkii narodnyi lubok.* Moscow, 1937.

Janecek, Gerald. *The Look of Russian Literature: Avant-Garde Visual Experiments, 1900–1930.* Princeton, 1984.

Kaduck, John M. *Patriotic Postcards.* Des Moines, 1974.

Kämpfer, Frank. *"Der rote Keil." Das politische Plakat. Theorie und Geschichte.* Berlin, 1985.

Kazamsky, Konstantin. *Cabaret russe.* Paris, 1978.

Kazanskii, B. "Priroda kino." In *Poetika kino,* ed. Boris Eikhenbaum, 87–135. Moscow/Leningrad, 1927; Berkeley, 1984.

Keldysh, Iu. V. "Opernyi teatr." In *Russkaia khudozhestvennaia kul'tura kontsa XIX–nachala XX veka.* Vol. 3, *Zrelishchnye iskusstva, muzyka,* 310–40. Moscow, 1977.

Kelly, Catriona. *Petrushka: The Russian Carnival Puppet Theatre.* Cambridge, 1990.

———."Petrushka and the Pioneers: The Russian Carnival Puppet Theatre after the Revolution." In *Discontinuous Discourses in Modern Russian Literature,* ed. Catriona Kelly, Michael Makin, and David Shepherd, 73–111. London, 1989.

Kenez, Peter. *The Birth of the Propaganda State: Soviet Methods of Mass Mobilization, 1917–1929.* Cambridge, 1985.

Khaichenko, G. A. *Russkii narodnyi teatr kontsa XIX–nachala XX veka.* Moscow, 1975.

Khmelevskii, G. *Mirovaia imperialisticheskaia voina, 1914–1918: Sistematicheskii ukazatel' knizhnoi i stateinoi voenno-istoricheskoi literatury za 1914–1935 gg.* Moscow, 1936.

Kleberg, Lars. "'People's Theater' and the Revolution: On the History of a Concept before and after 1917." In *Art, Society, Revolution: Russia, 1917–1921,* ed. Nils Åke Nilsson, 179–97. Stockholm, 1979.

Klitin, S. S. *Estrada: Problemy teorii, istorii i metodiki.* Leningrad, 1987.

Kogan, D. Z. *Sergei Iur'evich Sudeikin, 1884–1946.* Moscow, 1974.

Konechnyi, A. M. "Peterburgskie narodnye gulian'ia na maslenoi i paskhal'noi nedeliakh." In *Peterburg i guberniia: Istoriko-etnograficheskie issledovaniia,* ed. N. V. Iukhnëva, 21–52. Leningrad, 1989.

———. "Shows for the People: Public Amusement Parks in Nineteenth-Century St. Petersburg." In *Cultures in Flux: Lower-Class Values, Practices, and Resistance in Late Imperial Russia,* ed. Stephen Frank and Mark Steinberg, 121–30. Princeton, 1994.

Konechnyi, A. M., V. Ia. Morderer, A. E. Parnis, and R. D. Timenchik. "Artisticheskoe kabare 'Prival komediantov.'" In *Pamiatniki kul'tury. Novye otkrytiia: Pis'mennost', iskusstvo, arkheologiia. Ezhegodnik, 1988,* 96–154. Moscow, 1989.

Konnov, A. P., and G. N. Preobrazhenskii, comps. *Orkestr imeni V. V. Andreeva.* Leningrad, 1987.

Koschmal, Walter. *Der russische Volksbilderbogen (Von der Religion zum Theater).* Slavistische Beiträge, vol. 251. Munich, 1989.

———, ed. *Russkija narodnyja kartinki.* Specimina Philologiae Slavicae, vol. 84. Munich, 1989.

Kovtun, E. F. *Russkaia futuristicheskaia kniga.* Moscow, 1989.

Kowtun, J. F. [E. F. Kovtun]. *Die Wiedergeburt der künstlerischen Druckgraphik: Aus der Geschichte der russischen Kunst zu Beginn des zwanzigsten Jahrhunderts.* Dresden, 1984.

"Krasnyi perets" i drugie. Stranitsy istorii sovetskoi satiricheskoi grafiki. Moscow, 1990.

Kusnezow, Je. [E. M. Kuznetsov]. *Der Zirkus der Welt.* Berlin, 1970.

Kuznetsov, E. M. *Arena i liudi sovetskogo tsirka*. Leningrad/Moscow, 1947.
———. *Iz proshlogo russkoi estrady: Istoricheskie ocherki*. Moscow, 1958.
———. *Tsirk: Proiskhozhdenie, razvitie, perspektivy*. 2d ed. Moscow, 1971.
———, comp. *Konnyi tsirk: Vystavka na temu "Konnyi tsirk."* Leningrad, 1930.
———, comp. *Russkie narodnye gulian'ia po rasskazam A. Ia. Alekseeva-Iakovleva*. Leningrad/Moscow, 1948.
Lambert, Constant. *Music Ho! A Study of Music in Decline*. New York, 1967.
Langsepp, O. *Georg Gakkenshmidt: "Russkii Lev."* Tallinn, 1971.
Lapshin, V. I. *Khudozhestvennaia zhizn' Moskvy i Petrograda v 1917 godu*. Moscow, 1983.
Laqueur, Walter. *Russia and Germany: A Century of Conflict*. Boston/Toronto, 1965.
Lasswell, Harold Dwight. *Propaganda Technique in the World War*. London, 1938.
Lawton, Anna, ed. *Russian Futurism through Its Manifestoes, 1912–1928*. Ithaca, 1988.
Lebeck, Robert, and Manfred Schütte, eds. *Propagandapostkarten*. Dortmund, 1980.
Lebedev, I. V. *Istoriia professional'noi frantsuzskoi bor'by*. Moscow, 1928.
Lebedev, N. A. *Ocherk istorii kino SSSR: Nemoe kino*. 2d ed. Moscow, 1965.
Lemberg, Hans. "Der 'Drang nach Osten.' Schlagwort und Wirklichkeit." In *Deutsche im europäischen Osten. Verständnis und Mißverständnis*, ed. Friedhelm B. Kaiser and Bernhard Stasiewski, 1–17. Cologne/Vienna, 1976.
Lévi-Strauss, Claude. *L'Homme nu*. Paris, 1971.
Leyda, Jay. *Kino: A History of the Russian and Soviet Film*. 3d ed. Princeton, 1983.
Lotman, Iu. M. "Khudozhestvennaia priroda russkikh narodnykh kartinok." In *Narodnaia graviura i fol'klor v Rossii XVII–XIX vv. K 150-letiiu so dnia rozhdeniia D. A. Rovinskogo*, 247–67. Moscow, 1976.
———. *Semiotika kino i problemy kinoestetiki*. Tallinn, 1973.
Löwe, Heinz-Dietrich. *Antisemitismus und reaktionäre Utopie. Russischer Konservatismus im Kampf gegen den Wandel von Staat und Gesellschaft, 1890–1917*. Hamburg, 1978.
———. "Political Symbols and Rituals of the Russian Radical Right, 1900–1917." Unpublished paper.
Lukomskii, G. K. *Egor Narbut: Khudozhnik-Grafik*. Berlin, 1923.
MacKenzie, John M. "Introduction." In *Imperialism and Popular Culture*, ed. John M. MacKenzie, 1–16. Manchester, 1986.
Martynov, I. I. *Gosudarstvennyi russkii narodnyi khor imeni Piatnitskogo*. Moscow, 1950.
Marwick, Arthur. *The Deluge: British Society and the First World War*. New York, 1965.
Masanov, I. F. *Slovar' psevdonimov russkikh pisatelei, uchënykh i obshchestvennykh deiatelei*. 4 vols. Moscow, 1956–60.
Materialien zur Geschichte der deutschen Nationalhymne. Berlin, 1990.
McReynolds, Louise. *The News under Russia's Old Regime: The Development of a Mass-Circulation Press*. Princeton, 1991.
Medvedev, M. N. *Leningradskii tsirk*. Leningrad, 1975.

Miasoedov, G. "Russkii lubok kontsa XIX–nachala XX veka." In *Illiustratsiia*, comp. G. V. El'shevskaia, 236–50. Moscow, 1988.

Monahan, Barbara. *A Dictionary of Russian Gesture*. Tenafly, N.J., 1983.

Morrow, John H. *The Great War in the Air: Military Aviation from 1909–1921*. Washington, D.C., 1993.

Mosse, George L. *Fallen Soldiers: Reshaping the Memory of the World Wars*. New York, 1990.

Nekrylova, A. F. *Russkie narodnye gorodskie prazdniki, uveseleniia i zrelishcha: Konets XVIII–nachalo XX veka*. 2d ed. Leningrad, 1988.

Nest'ev, I. V. "Muzykal'naia estrada." In *Russkaia khudozhestvennaia kul'tura kontsa XIX–nachala XX veka*. Vol. 3, *Zrelishchnye iskusstva, muzyka*, 483–89. Moscow, 1977.

——. *Zvëzdy russkoi estrady*. 2d ed. Moscow, 1974.

Nye, David E. *Image Worlds: Corporate Identities at General Electric, 1890–1930*. Cambridge, Mass., 1985.

Okhochinskii, V. *Plakat*. Leningrad, n.d.

Ovsiannikov, Iu. M. *Russkii lubok*. Moscow, 1962.

Parnis, A. E., and R. D. Timenchik. "Programmy 'Brodiachei sobaki.'" In *Pamiatniki kul'tury. Novye otkrytiia: Pis'mennost', iskusstvo, arkheologiia. Ezhegodnik, 1983*, 160–257. Leningrad, 1985.

Perris, Arnold. *Music as Propaganda: Art to Persuade, Art to Control*. Westport, Conn., 1985.

Pertsov, V. *Maiakovskii: Zhizn' i tvorchestvo*. 3d ed. Vol. 1. Moscow, 1976.

Petrovskaia, I. F. *Teatr i zritel' rossiiskikh stolits, 1895–1917*. Leningrad, 1990.

Piltz, Georg. *Geschichte der europäischen Karikatur*. Berlin, 1976.

Poety "Satirikona." Moscow/Leningrad, 1966.

Pohl, Klaus-D. "Der Kaiser im Zeitalter seiner technischen Reproduzierbarkeit: Wilhelm II. in Fotografie und Film." In *Der letzte Kaiser: Wilhelm II. im Exil*, ed. Hans Wilderotter and Klaus-D. Pohl, 9–18. Berlin, 1991.

Pörzgen, Hermann. *Theater als Waffengattung: Das deutsche Fronttheater im Weltkrieg, 1914 bis 1920*. Frankfurt, 1935.

Pruzhanskii, A. M. *Otechestvennye pevtsy, 1750–1917: Slovar'*. Moscow, 1991.

Purishkevich, V. M. *The Murder of Rasputin: A First-Hand Account from the Diary of One of Rasputin's Murderers*. Ed. Michael E. Shaw. Trans. Bella Costello. Ann Arbor, Mich., 1985.

Purser, Ann. *Looking Back at Popular Entertainment, 1901–1939*. Wakefield, Yorks., 1978.

A. Radakov, A. Iunger. Moscow, 1989.

Raeburn, Michael, ed. *The Twilight of the Tsars: Russian Art at the Turn of the Century*. London, 1991.

Reik, Theodor. *The Haunting Melody: Psychoanalytic Experiences in Life and Music*. New York, 1953.

Renan, Ernest. *Qu'est-ce qu'une nation?* Paris, 1882.

Rodina, T. M. "Russkii teatr predrevoliutsionnogo desiatiletiia." In *Russkaia khudozhestvennaia kul'tura kontsa XIX–nachala XX veka*. Vol. 3, *Zrelishchnye iskusstva, muzyka*, 11–21. Moscow, 1977.

Rogger, Hans. *Russia in the Age of Modernisation and Revolution, 1881–1917.* London/New York, 1983.

Rosenthal, Bernice Glatzer. "Wagner and Wagnerian Ideas in Russia." In *Wagnerism in European Culture and Politics,* ed. David C. Large and William Weber, 198–245. Ithaca, 1984.

Rudnitskii, Konstantin. Record jacket notes to *Aleksandr Vertinskii.* Melodiia M 60 48689—60 48691. Leningradskii zavod gramplastinok, 1989.

Russkaia sovetskaia estrada: Ocherki istorii, 1917–1929. Moscow, 1976.

Sackett, Robert Eben. *Popular Entertainment, Class, and Politics in Munich, 1900– 1923.* Cambridge, Mass., 1982.

Said, Edward W. *Orientalism.* New York, 1978.

Savushkina, N. I. *Russkii narodnyi teatr.* Moscow, 1976.

Schechter, Joel. *Durov's Pig: Clowns, Politics, and Theatre.* New York, 1985.

Schlögel, Karl. *Jenseits des Großen Oktober: Das Laboratorium der Moderne. Petersburg, 1909–1921.* Berlin, 1988.

Segel, Harold B. *Turn-of-the-Century Cabaret: Paris, Barcelona, Berlin, Munich, Vienna, Cracow, Moscow, St. Petersburg, Zurich.* New York, 1987.

Shakh-Azizova, T. K. "Malyi teatr." In *Russkaia khudozhestvennaia kul'tura kontsa XIX–nachala XX veka.* Vol. 3, *Zrelishchnye iskusstva, muzyka,* 65–91. Moscow, 1977.

Sidel'nikov, V. M. *Russkoe narodnoe tvorchestvo i estrada.* Moscow, 1950.

Sidorov, A. L. *Finansovoe polozhenie Rossii v gody pervoi mirovoi voiny (1914– 1917).* Moscow, 1960.

Slavskii, R. E. *Brat'ia Nikitiny.* Moscow, 1987.

———. *S areny na ekran.* Moscow, 1969.

———. *Vitalii Lazarenko.* Moscow, 1980.

———, comp. *Vstrechi s tsirkovym proshlym.* Moscow, 1990.

Smith, Anthony D. *Theories of Nationalism.* 2d ed. London, 1983.

Sobolev, R. P. *Liudi i filmy russkogo dorevoliutsionnogo kino.* Moscow, 1961.

Sosin, A. I., and M. Lobodin. *Liudi-miachiki: 55 let na arene tsirka.* Leningrad/ Moscow, 1960.

Starn, Randolph. "Seeing Culture in a Room for a Renaissance Prince." In *The New Cultural History,* ed. Lynn Hunt, 205–32. Berkeley, 1989.

Starr, S. Frederick. *Red and Hot: The Fate of Jazz in the Soviet Union, 1917–1980.* New York, 1985.

Stites, Richard. *Revolutionary Dreams: Utopian Vision and Experimental Life in the Russian Revolution.* New York, 1989.

———. *Russian Popular Culture: Entertainment and Society since 1900.* Cambridge, 1992.

Stökl, Günther. "Die historischen Grundlagen des russischen Deutschlandbildes." In *Deutsche im europäischen Osten. Verständnis und Mißverständnis,* ed. Friedhelm B. Kaiser and Bernhard Stasiewski, 18–34. Cologne/ Vienna, 1976.

Stroeva, M. N. "Moskovskii khudozhestvennyi teatr." In *Russkaia khudozhestvennaia kul'tura kontsa XIX–nachala XX veka.* Vol. 3, *Zrelishchnye iskusstva, muzyka,* 22–64. Moscow, 1977.

Swan, Alfred J. *Russian Music and Its Sources in Chant and Folk Song*. New York, 1973.

Tagrin, N. S. *Mir v otkrytke*. Moscow, 1978.

Talanov, A. V. *Brat'ia Durovy*. Moscow, 1971.

Tarasti, Eero. *Myth and Music: A Semiotic Approach to the Aesthetics of Myth in Music, Especially That of Wagner, Sibelius, and Stravinsky*. The Hague/Paris/New York, 1979.

Taylor, Richard. "Agitation, Propaganda, and the Cinema: The Search for New Solutions, 1917–21." In *Art, Society, Revolution: Russia, 1917–1921*, ed. Nils Åke Nilsson, 237–63. Stockholm, 1979.

Teppe, Julien. *L'Idole patrie . . .* Paris, 1967.

Terikov, G. K. *Kuplet na estrade*. Moscow, 1987.

Thaden, Edward C. *Conservative Nationalism in Nineteenth-Century Russia*. Seattle, 1964.

Thurston, Gary. "Building a Mass Audience for Serious Theater in Russia before October: P. P. Gaideburov at the Ligovsky People's House, in the Provinces, and at the Front." Paper presented at the Southern Conference on Slavic Studies, Charleston, S.C., 20–23 October 1988.

Tomashevskii, Iu., comp. *A. Vertinskii: Za kulisami*. Moscow, 1991.

Tsekhnovitser, O. V. *Literatura i mirovaia voina, 1914–1918*. Moscow, 1938.

Tsirk: Malen'kaia entsiklopediia. Moscow, 1973.

Tsiv'ian, Iurii. "Tekst i zhest: *Boris Godunov* v ispolnenii provintsial'nykh akterov, 1910-kh godov." In *Sbornik statei k 70-letiiu prof. Iu. M. Lotmana*, 208–25. Tartu, 1992.

Turner, Victor. *Dramas, Fields, and Metaphors: Symbolic Action in Human Society*. Ithaca, 1974.

Viren, V. N. *Stoletnii iubilei Durovykh*. Moscow, 1963.

Vishnevskii, V. E. *Khudozhestvennye filmy dorevoliutsionnoi Rossii: Fil'mograficheskoe opisanie*. Moscow, 1945.

Volkov-Lannit, L. S. *Iskusstvo zapechatlennogo zvuka*. Moscow, 1964.

Vsevolodskii-Gerngross, V. N. *Istoriia russkogo teatra*. Vol. 2. Leningrad, Moscow, 1929.

———. *Russkaia ustnaia narodnaia drama*. Moscow, 1959.

Wall, Richard, and Jay Winter, eds. *The Upheaval of War: Family, Work and Welfare in Europe, 1914–1918*. Cambridge, 1988.

Waschik, Klaus. *Seht her, Genossen! Plakate aus der Sowjetunion*. Dortmund, 1982.

White, Stephen. *The Bolshevik Poster*. New Haven, 1988.

———. "The Political Poster in Bolshevik Russia." In *Sbornik No. 8: Papers of the Eighth International Conference of the Study Group on the Russian Revolution held at Hertford College, Oxford, January 1982*, 24–37. Leeds, 1982.

Wildman, Allan K. *The End of the Russian Imperial Army: The Old Army and the Soldiers' Revolt (March–April 1917)*. Princeton, 1980.

Zelnik, Reginald E. "The Peasant and the Factory." In *The Peasant in Nineteenth-Century Russia*, ed. Wayne S. Vucinich, 158–90. Stanford, 1968.

Zeyons, Serge. *Le Roman-photo de la Grande Guerre: Les Cartes-postales "Bleu-Horizon."* Paris, 1976.
——. *Les Cartes postales.* Paris, 1979.
Zhdankov, A. V. "Piterskii proletariat v bor'be protiv kontrrevoliutsionnoi kinopropagandy v 1917 g." In *Piterskie rabochie v bor'be s kontrrevoliutsiei v 1917–1918 gg.*, ed. G. L. Sobolev, 212–17. Moscow, 1986.
Zisel'son, M. A. *Matchi klassicheskoi bor'by.* Leningrad, 1949.
Znosko-Borovskii, E. A. *Russkii teatr nachala XX veka.* Prague, 1925.
Zorkaia, N. M. *Na rubezhe stoletii: U istokov massovogo iskusstva v Rossii, 1900–1910 godov.* Moscow, 1976.

Contemporary Periodicals

Ekran Rosii
Ezhegodnik Imperatorskikh teatrov
Gerkules: Zhurnal sporta
Il'ia Muromets
Kinematograf
Lukomor'e
Muzykal'nyi sovremennik
Niva
Novyi Satirikon
Organ
Petrogradskii listok
Proektor
Rampa i zhizn'
Russkaia muzykal'naia gazeta
Sine-Fono
Stolitsa i usad'ba: Zhurnal krasivoi zhizni
Stsena i arena
Teatr i iskusstvo
Var'ete i tsirk
Vestnik kinematografii
Voin i pakhar'
Voina
Voina i Evrei
Zhurnal dlia khoziaek i zhenskaia zhizn'

Index

Page numbers in italics refer to illustrations.